Castilla y León

Andy Symington

Credits

Footprint credits

Editor: Felicity Laughton
Production and layout: Emma Bryers
Maps: Kevin Feeney
Cover: Pepi Bluck

Publisher: Patrick Dawson
Advertising: Elizabeth Taylor
Sales and marketing: Kirsty Holmes

Photography credits

Front cover: Gannet77/iStockphoto
Back cover: PHB.cz (Richard Semik)/
Shutterstock.com

Printed in Great Britain by CPI Antony Rowe,
Chippenham, Wiltshire

Publishing information

Footprint *Focus Castilla y León*
1st edition
© Footprint Handbooks Ltd
March 2013

ISBN: 978 1 909268 05 0
CIP DATA: A catalogue record for this book
is available from the British Library

® Footprint Handbooks and the Footprint
mark are a registered trademark of
Footprint Handbooks Ltd

Published by Footprint
6 Riverside Court
Lower Bristol Road
Bath BA2 3DZ, UK
T +44 (0)1225 469141
F +44 (0)1225 469461
footprinttravelguides.com

Distributed in the USA by Globe Pequot
Press, Guilford, Connecticut

The content of Footprint *Focus Castilla y León*
has been taken directly from Footprint's
Northern Spain Handbook which was
researched and written by Andy Symington
and Footprint *Spain Handbook* by Andy
Symington and Mary-Ann Gallagher.

Contents

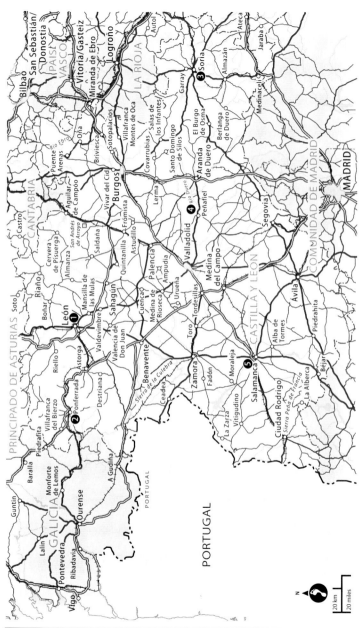

For many people, Castilla is the image of Spain: a dry, harsh land of pious Inquisition-ravaged cities, ham, wine and bullfighting. Visitors tend to love or hate the dusty *meseta* with its extremes of summer and winter temperatures; it's a bleak, almost desert landscape in parts.

The main route to Santiago crosses the heart of the region and is dignified by numerous churches and monasteries in noble Romanesque or Gothic. Burgos itself is much visited for its elegant cathedral and is a courteous, genteel city. Palencia doesn't attract many tourists, but it deserves more. Quiet and friendly, it's got a definite charm and boasts a province full of treasures. Despite being amicably joined with Castilla, the province of León is culturally, geographically and socially somewhat distinct. The city of León is vibrant, rich in architectural heritage and draws the crowds to its sublime Gothic cathedral. Similarly, the south of the region's major attraction is its architecture. Castilla is named for its huge number of castles, many of them found in the Duero Valley. But it has much more to offer than faded reminders of past glories. The cities of southern Castilla are all interesting: Romanesque Soria glows in the evening light, busy Valladolid preserves an imperial air, Segovia's fabulous aqueduct and Ávila's stunning walls are world-famous, Zamora is a model for sensitive urban blending of the old and the new, and Salamanca is a stunningly beautiful ensemble of Renaissance architecture, topped off by Spain's most beautiful main square. Throughout the region, small villages harbour architectural treasures, rustic accommodation, and places to fill up on heart-warming traditional food.

Planning your trip

Best time to visit Castilla y León

Castilla y León is set on the high meseta plateau, with a continental climate that makes for baking hot summers and cold, dry winters. If you can handle the heat, July and August is a fun time to visit, with lots of fiestas and plenty of street life - though this is focused on the cool of the evening. June is a good time too, with slightly cooler temperatures and far fewer crowds, as Spanish holidays haven't started. Spring (apart from Easter week) and autumn are the best times for mild weather. In winter, it's cold, temperatures well below zero are common right across Castilla. Accommodation is much cheaper, but less attractions are open.

Getting to Castilla y León

Air

With budget airlines having opened up several regional airports to international flights, it's easier than ever to get to Spain's north. **Ryanair** service Valladolid from London Stansted among other destinations, and fly to Santander – not far from Castilla – from many European destinations. Asturias airport is handy for León province, and sees **Easyjet** flights from London and elsewhere.

There are far more flight options via Madrid: Spain's capital is less than an hour away from various cities in Castilla y León by fast train. Bilbao is another possible destination.

Before booking, it's worth doing a bit of online research. Two of the best search engines for flight comparisons are **www.kelkoo.com** and **www.kayak.com**, which compare prices from travel agencies and websites. To keep yourself up to date with the ever-changing routes of the bewildering number of budget airlines **www.whichbudget.com** is recommended. **Flightchecker** (http://flightchecker.moneysavingexpert.com) is handy for checking multiple dates for budget airline deals.

Rail

Travelling from the UK to Northern Spain by train is unlikely to save either time or money; the only advantages lie in the pleasure of the journey itself, the chance to stop along the way, and the environmental impact of flying versus rail travel. Using **Eurostar** ① *T0870 160 6600, www.eurostar.com*, changing stations in Paris and boarding a TGV to Hendaye can have you in Castilla y León 15 hours after leaving Waterloo if the connections are kind. Once across the Channel, the trains are reasonably priced, but factor in £100-200 return on **Eurostar** and things don't look so rosy, unless you can take advantage of a special offer. Using the train/ Channel ferry combination will more or less halve the cost and double the time.

The main rail gateway from the rest of Europe is Paris (Austerlitz). There's a Paris–Madrid sleeper daily, which stops at Burgos and Valladolid. Check www.elipsos.com for specials. The cheaper option is to take a **TGV** from Paris to Hendaye, from where you can catch a Spanish train to San Sebastián and beyond.

For students, the **InterRail** pass is an attractive and cheap possibility, which can be obtained from travel agents, but note that the pass is not valid on the high-speed **AVE** or **EuroMed** trains. If you are planning the train journey, **Rail Europe** ① *T0844 484 064, www.*

Don't miss...

raileurope.co.uk, is a useful company. **RENFE**, Spain's rail network, has online timetables at www.renfe.es. Also see the extremely useful www.seat61.com.

Road

Bus Eurolines (www.eurolines.com) run several buses from major European cities to a variety of destinations in Northern Spain. From London, there's a bus that leaves London Victoria at 0800 on Monday and Saturday, and arrives in Bilbao at 0430 the next morning. The return leaves Bilbao at 0030 on Thursday and Saturday night, getting to London at 1945 the next evening. There's an extra bus in summer. A return fare costs about £100; it's marginally cheaper for pensioners and students, but overall isn't great value unless you're not a fan of flying. Book on T01582 404 511 or www.gobycoach.com.

Car The main route into Northern Spain is the E05/E70 tolled motorway that runs down the southwest coast of France, crossing into Spain at Irún, near San Sebastián. Most other motorways are free and in good condition.

Cars must be insured for third party and practically any driving licence is acceptable (but if you're from a country that a Guardia Civil would struggle to locate on a map, take an International Driving Licence). Unleaded petrol costs about €1.50 per litre in Spain.

Sea

Bear in mind that from the UK it's usually cheaper to fly and hire a car in Northern Spain than bring the motor across on the ferry. For competitive fares by sea to France and Spain, check with **Ferrysavers** ① *T0844 576 8835, www.ferrysavers.com* and **www.ferrycheap. com**, which list special offers from various operators. The website **www.seat61.com** is good for investigating train/ferry combinations.

Now that P&O no longer run a Bilbao service, the only UK-Spain ferry is the service run by **Brittany Ferries** ① *T0871 244 0744, www.brittany-ferries.co.uk*, from Plymouth and Portsmouth to Santander. There's one weekly sailing on each route, taking around 24 hours from Portsmouth and 20 hours from Plymouth. Prices are variable but can usually be found for about £70-90 each way in a reclining seat. A car adds about £150 each way, and cabins start from about £80.

There's also a ferry service (you must have a vehicle) between Gijón and St Nazaire in France, potentially saving a good deal of driving.

Transport in Castilla y León

Public transport between the larger towns in Northern Spain is good; you can expect several buses a day between adjacent provincial capitals; these services are quick and efficient. The new network of high-speed **AVE** trains link major cities in double-quick time, but are significantly more expensive than the bus. Other train services are slow. If you want to explore much of rural Castilla, however, you'll probably want to hire a car, or take a bike.

Rail

The Spanish national rail network **RENFE** ⓘ *T902 240 202 (English-speaking operators)*, *www.renfe.es*, is useful for getting around Northern Spain. AVE trains run from Madrid to Valladolid, via Segovia, with routes under construction to all of Castilla y León's provincial capitals. These trains cover these large distances impressively quickly and reliably. It is an expensive but excellent service that refunds part or all of the ticket price if it arrives late. Elsewhere though, you'll find the bus is often quicker and cheaper than the train.

Prices vary significantly according to the type of service you are using. The standard fast-ish intercity service is called *Talgo*, while other intercity services are labelled *Altaria*, *Intercity*, *Diurno* and *Estrella* (overnight). Slower local trains are called *regionales*.

It's always worth buying a ticket in advance for long-distance travel, as trains are often full. The best option is to buy them via the website, which sometimes offers advance-purchase discounts. You can also book by phone, but they only accept Spanish cards. In either case, you get a reservation code, then print off your ticket at the terminals at the station. If buying your ticket at the station, allow plenty of time for queuing. Ticket windows are labelled *venta anticipada* (in advance) and *venta inmediata* (six hours or less before the journey).

All Spanish trains are non-smoking. The faster trains will have first-class (*preferente*) and second-class sections as well as a *cafetería*. First class costs about 30% more than standard and can be a worthwhile deal on a crowded long journey. Buying a return ticket is 10-20% cheaper than two singles, but you qualify for this discount even if you buy the return leg later (but not on every service).

An **ISIC student card** or **under-26 card** grants a discount of between 20% to 30% on train services. If you're using a European railpass, be aware that you'll still have to make a reservation on Spanish trains and pay the small reservation fee (which covers your insurance).

Road

Bus Buses are the staple of Spanish public transport. Services between major cities are fast, frequent, reliable and fairly cheap; the three-hour trip from Salamanca to León, for example, costs €15. When buying a ticket, always check how long the journey will take, as the odd bus will be an 'all stations to' job, calling in at villages that seem surprised to even see it. *Directo* is the term for a bus that doesn't stop; it won't usually cost any more either. Various premium services (called *Supra*, *Ejecutivo* or similar) add comfort, with onboard drinks service, lounge area in the bus station and more space, but cost around 60% more.

Most cities have a single terminal, the *estación de autobuses*, which is where all short- and long-haul services leave from. Buy your tickets at the relevant window; if there isn't one, buy it from the driver. Many companies don't allow baggage in the cabin of the bus, but security is pretty good. Most tickets will have a seat number (*asiento*) on them; ask when buying the ticket if you prefer a window (*ventana*) or aisle (*pasillo*) seat. The platform that the bus leaves from is called a *dársena* or *andén*. If you're travelling at busy times (particularly a fiesta or national holiday) always book the bus ticket in advance.

Rural bus services are slower, less frequent and more difficult to coordinate. They typically run early in the morning and late in the evening; they're designed for villagers who visit the big city once a week or so to shop.

All bus services are reduced on Sundays and, to a lesser extent, on Saturdays; some services don't run at all at weekends. Local newspapers publish a comprehensive list of departures; expect few during siesta hours. While most large villages will have at least some bus service to their provincial capital, don't expect there to be buses running to tourist attractions like monasteries or castles; it's assumed that all tourists have cars.

Most Spanish cities have their sights closely packed into the centre, so you won't find local buses particularly necessary. There's a fairly comprehensive network in most towns, though; the Getting around and Transport sections in this guide indicate where they come in handy. In most cities, you just board and pay the driver.

Car The roads in Northern Spain are good, excellent in many parts. While driving isn't as sedate as in parts of Northern Europe, it's generally of a very high standard, and you'll have few problems. To drive in Spain, you'll need a full driving licence from your home country. This applies to virtually all foreign nationals, but in practice, if you're from an 'unusual' country, consider an International Driving Licence or official translation of your licence into Spanish.

There are two types of motorway in Spain, *autovías* and *autopistas*; the quality of both is generally excellent, with a speed limit of 120 kph. They are signposted in blue and may have tolls payable, in which case there'll be a red warning circle on the blue sign when you're entering the motorway. An 'A' prefix to the road number indicates a motorway; an 'AP' prefix indicates a toll motorway. Tolls are generally reasonable, but likely to rise, and will possibly be applied to the whole motorway network. You can pay by cash or card. Most motorways in Northern Spain, however, are free.

Rutas Nacionales form the backbone of Spain's road network. Centrally administered, they vary wildly in quality. Typically, they are choked with traffic backed up behind trucks, and there are few stretches of dual carriageway. Driving at siesta time is a good idea if you're going to be on a busy stretch. *Rutas Nacionales* are marked with a red 'N' number. The speed limit is 100 kph outside built-up areas, as it is for secondary roads, which are numbered with a provincial prefix (eg BU-552 in Burgos province), although some are demarcated 'B' and 'C' instead.

In urban areas, the speed limit is 50 kph. Many towns and villages have sensors that will turn traffic lights red if you're over the limit on approach. City driving can be confusing, with signposting generally poor and traffic heavy; it's worth taking a GPS or printing off the directions that your hotel may send you with a reservation. In some towns and cities, many of the hotels are officially signposted, making things easier. Larger cities may have their historic quarter blocked off by barriers: if your hotel lies within these, ring the buzzer and say the name of the hotel, and the barriers will open.

Police are increasingly enforcing speed limits in Spain, and foreign drivers are liable to a large on-the-spot fine. Drivers can also be punished for not carrying two red warning triangles to place on the road in case of breakdown, a bulb-replacement kit and a fluorescent green waistcoat to wear if you break down by the side of the road. Drink driving is being cracked down on more than was once the case; the limit is 0.5 g/l of blood, slightly lower than the equivalent in the UK, for example.

Parking is a problem in nearly every town and city. Red or yellow lines on the side of the street mean no parking. Blue lines indicate a metered zone, while white lines mean that some restriction is in place; a sign will give details. Parking meters can usually only be dosed up for a maximum of two hours, but they take a siesta at lunchtime too. Print the ticket off and display it in the car. Once the day's period has expired, you can charge it up for the next morning to avoid an early start. If you get a ticket, you can pay a minimal fine at the machine within the first half hour or hour instead of the full whack (though it must be said that parking fines are rarely even pursued outside the city they are issued in, let alone in another country). Underground car parks are common and well signposted, but fairly pricey; €12-20 a day is normal. However, this is the safest option if you are going to leave any valuables in your car.

Liability insurance is required for every car driven in Spain and you must carry proof of it. If bringing your own car, check carefully with your insurers that you're covered, and get a certificate (green card). If your insurer doesn't cover you for breakdowns, consider joining the **RACE** ① *T902 120 441, www.race.es*, Spain's automobile association, which provides good breakdown cover.

Hiring a car in Spain is easy but not especially cheap. The major multinationals have offices at all large towns and airports; the company with the broadest network is **National/ATESA** ① *www.atesa.es*. Brokers, such as **Holiday Autos** ① *www.holidayautos.co.uk*, are usually cheaper than booking direct with the rental companies. Prices start at around €150 per week for a small car with unlimited mileage. You'll need a credit card and most agencies will either not accept under 25s or demand a surcharge. Rates from the airports tend to be cheaper than from towns. Before booking, use a price-comparison website like www.kelkoo.com to find the best deals.

Cycling Cycling presents a curious contrast; Spaniards are mad for the competitive sport, but comparatively uninterested in cycling as a means of transport. Thus there are plenty of cycling shops but very few bike lanes, though these are appearing in most cities in the region. Contact the **Real Federación de Ciclismo en España** ① *www.rfec.com*, for more links and assistance.

Motorcycling Motorcycling is a good way to enjoy Spain and there are few difficulties to trouble the biker; bike shops and mechanics are relatively common. Hiring a motorbike, however, is difficult; there are few outlets in Northern Spain. The **Real Federación Motociclista Española** ① *www.rfme.net*, can help with links and advice.

Taxis Taxis are a good option; flagfall is €2-3 in most places (it increases slightly at night and on Sundays) and it gets you a good distance. A taxi is available if its green light is lit; hail one on the street or ask for the nearest rank (*parada de taxis*). In smaller towns or at quiet times, you'll have to ring for one. All towns have their own taxi company; phone numbers are given in the text.

Maps

The Michelin road maps are reliable for general navigation, although if you're getting off the beaten track you'll often find a local map handy. Tourist offices provide these, which vary in quality. The best topographical maps are published by the **Instituto Geográfico Nacional (IGN)**. These are not necessarily more accurate than those obtainable in Britain or North America. A useful website for route planning is www.guiarepsol.com. Car hire companies have navigation systems available, though they cost a hefty supplement: you're better bringing your own if you've got one.

Where to stay in Castilla y León

There are a reasonable number of well-equipped but characterless places on the edges or in the newer parts of towns in Spain. Similarly, chains such as NH, AC, and Hesperia have stocked Northern Spain's cities with reasonably comfortable but frequently featureless four-star business hotels. This guide has expressly minimized these in the listings, preferring to concentrate on more atmospheric options, but they are easily accessible via their websites or hotel booking brokers. These things change, but at time of writing, by far the best booking website for accommodation in Spain was www.booking.com. If booking accommodation without this guide, always be sure to check the location if that's important to you – it's easy to find yourself a 15-minute cab ride from the town you want to be in. Having said this, the standard of accommodation in Northern Spain is very high; even the most modest of *pensiones* are usually very clean and respectable. Places to stay (*alojamientos*) are divided into three main categories; the distinctions between them follow an arcane series of regulations devised by the government.

All registered accommodations charge a 10% value-added tax (IVA); this is often included in the price at cheaper places and may be waived if you pay cash. If you have any problems, a last resort is to ask for the *libro de reclamaciones* (complaints book), an official document that, like stepping on cracks in the pavement, means uncertain but definitely horrible consequences for the hotel if anything is written in it. If you do write something in it, you have to go to the police within 24 hours and report the fact.

Hoteles, hostales and pensiones
Hoteles (marked H or HR) are graded from one to five stars and usually occupy their own building. *Hostales* (marked Hs or HsR) are cheaper guesthouse-style places that go from one to three stars. *Pensiones* (P) are the standard budget option, and are usually family-run flats in an apartment block. Although it's worth looking at a room before taking it, the majority are very acceptable. Spanish traditions of hospitality are alive and well; even the simplest of hostales and *pensiones* will generally provide a towel and soap, and check-out time is almost uniformly a very civilized midday. Most *pensiones* will give you keys to the exterior door; if they don't, be sure to mention the fact if you plan to stay out late.

Casas rurales
An excellent option if you've got transport are the networks of rural homes, called *casas rurales*. Although these are under a different classification system, the standard is often as high as any country hotel. The best of them are traditional farmhouses or old village cottages. Some are available only to rent out whole, while others operate more or less as hotels. Rates tend to be excellent compared to hotels, and many offer kitchen facilities and home-cooked meals. The Castilla y León government publishes a list of them in a booklet, which is available at any tourist office in the area; the regional tourism website www.turismocastillayleon.com also lists them. The website www.toprural.com is another good place to find them.

Albergues
There are a few youth hostels (*albergues*) around, but the accessible price of *pensiones* rarely makes it worth the trouble except for solo travellers. Spanish youth hostels are frequently populated by noisy schoolkids and have curfews and check-out times unsuitable for the late hours the locals keep.

Price codes

Where to stay

€€€€ over €170   €€€ €110-170

€€ €55-110   € under €55

Price codes refer to a standard double/twin room, inclusive of the 8% IVA (value-added tax). The rates are for high season (usually June-August).

Restaurants

€€€ over €20   €€ €10-20   € under €10

Price codes refer to the cost of a main course for one person, without a drink.

Campsites

Most campsites are set up as well-equipped holiday villages for families; many are open only in summer. While the facilities are good, they get extremely busy in peak season; the social scene is good, but sleep can be tough. They've often got playground facilities and a swimming pool; an increasing number now offer cabin or bungalow accommodation, normally a good-value option for groups or families. In other areas, camping, unless specifically prohibited, is a matter of common sense.

Food and drink in Castilla y León

Nothing in Spain illustrates its differences from the rest of Europe more than its eating and drinking culture. Whether you're halfway through Sunday lunch at 1800, ordering a plate of octopus some time after midnight, snacking on *pinchos* in the street, or watching a businessman down a hefty brandy with his morning coffee, it hits you at some point that the whole of Spanish society more or less revolves around food and drink.

Eating hours are the first point of difference. Spaniards eat little for breakfast, usually just a coffee and maybe a croissant or pastry. The mid-morning coffee and piece of tortilla is a ritual, especially for office workers, and then there might be a quick bite and a drink in a bar before lunch, which is usually started between 1400 and 1530. This is the main meal of the day and the cheapest time to eat, as most restaurants offer a good-value set menu. Lunch (and dinner) is extended at weekends, particularly on Sundays, when the *sobremesa* (chatting over the remains of the meal) can go on for hours. Most folk head home for the meal during the working week and get back to work about 1700; some people have a nap (the famous siesta), some don't. It's common to have an evening drink or *tapa* in a bar after a stroll, or *paseo*, if this is extended into a food crawl it's called a *tapeo*. Dinner (*cena*) is normally eaten from about 2200 onwards; sitting down to dinner at midnight at weekends isn't unusual. In smaller towns, however, and midweek you might not get fed after 2200. Be aware that any restaurant open for dinner before 2030 could well be a tourist trap. After eating, *la marcha* (the nightlife) hits drinking bars (*bares de copas*) and then nightclubs (*discotecas*; a *club* is a brothel). Many of these places only open at weekends and are usually busiest from 0100 onwards.

Food

While Castilian cooking has its own specialities, it remains a classically Spanish cuisine. Spanish cooking relies on meat, fish/seafood, beans and potatoes given character by the chef's holy trinity: garlic, peppers and, of course, olive oil. The influence of the colonization of the Americas is evident, and the result is a hearty, filling style of meal ideally washed down with some of the nation's excellent red wines. The following is an overview of the most common dishes.

Even in areas far from the coast, the availability of good **fish and seafood** can be taken for granted. *Merluza* (hake) is the staple fish, but is pushed hard by *bacalao* (salt cod) on the north coast. A variety of farmed white fish are also increasingly popular. *Gambas* (prawns) are another common and excellent choice, backed up by a bewildering array of molluscs and crustaceans as well as numerous tasty fish. Calamari, squid and cuttlefish are common; if you can cope with the slightly slimy texture, *pulpo* (octopus) is particularly good, especially when simply boiled *a la gallega* (Galician style) and flavoured with paprika and olive oil. Supreme among the seafood are *rodaballo* (turbot) and *rape* (monkfish/anglerfish).

Wherever you go, you'll find cured ham (*jamón serrano*), which is always excellent, but particularly so if it's the pricey *ibérico*, taken from acorn-eating porkers in Salamanca, Extremadura and Huelva. Other cold **meats** to look out for are *cecina*, made from beef and, of course, *embutidos* (sausages), including the versatile *chorizo*. Pork is also popular as a cooked meat; its most common form is sliced loin (*lomo*). Beef is common throughout; cheaper cuts predominate, but the better steaks (*solomillo, entrecot, chuletón*) are usually superbly tender. Spaniards tend to eat them rare (*poco hecho*; ask for *al punto* for medium-rare or *bien hecho* for well done). The *chuletón* is worth a mention in its own right; a massive T-bone best taken from an ox (*de buey*) and sold by weight, which often approaches a kilogram. It's an imposing slab of meat, best shared between two or three unless you're especially peckish. *Pollo* (chicken) is common, but usually unremarkable (unless its free-range – *pollo de corral* – in which case it's superb); game birds such as *codorniz* (quail) and *perdiz* (partridge) as well as *pato* (duck) are also widely eaten. The innards of animals are popular; *callos* (tripe), *mollejas* (sweetbreads) and *morcilla* (black pudding in solid or semi-liquid form) are all excellent, if acquired, tastes. Fans of the unusual will be keen to try *jabalí* (wild boar), *potro* (foal), *morros* (pig cheeks) and *oreja* (ear, usually from a pig or sheep).

Main dishes often come without any **accompaniments**, or chips at best. The consolation, however, is the *ensalada mixta*, whose simple name (mixed salad) often conceals a meal in itself. The ingredients vary, but it's typically a plentiful combination of lettuce, tomato, onion, olive oil, boiled eggs, asparagus, olives and tuna. The *tortilla* (a substantial potato omelette) is ever-present and often excellent. *Revueltos* (scrambled eggs), are usually tastily combined with prawns, asparagus or other goodies. Most **vegetable** dishes are based around that New World trio: the bean, the pepper and the potato. There are numerous varieties of bean in Northern Spain; they are normally served as some sort of hearty stew, often with bits of meat or seafood. *Fabada* is the Asturian classic of this variety, while *alubias con chorizo* are a standard across the region. A *cocido* is a typical mountain dish, a massive stew of chickpeas or beans with meat and vegetables; the liquid is drained off and eaten first (*sopa de cocido*). Peppers (*pimientos*), too, come in a number of forms. As well as being used to flavour dishes, they are often eaten in their own right; *pimientos rellenos* come stuffed with meat or seafood. Potatoes come as chips, *bravas* (with a garlic or spicy tomato sauce) or *a la riojana*, with chorizo and paprika. Other common vegetable dishes include *menestra* (delicious blend of cooked vegetables), which usually has some ham in it, and *ensaladilla rusa*, a tasty blend of potato, peas, peppers, carrots and mayonnaise. *Setas* (wild mushrooms) are a delight, particularly in autumn.

Desserts focus on the sweet and milky. *Flan* (a sort of crème caramel) is ubiquitous; great when *casero* (home-made), but often out of a plastic tub. *Natillas* are a similar but more liquid version, and *arroz con leche* is a cold, sweet, rice pudding typical of Northern Spain. **Cheeses** tend to be bland or salty. Though the standard Manchego-style cheese is still the staple of its kind (it comes *semi-curado*, semi-cured, or *curado* – much stronger and tastier), there are a number of interesting regional cheeses that are well worth trying.

Regional cuisine

Castilian cuisine typically involves dishes more suited to the harsh winters than the baking summers. Roast meats, particularly young lamb or piglet, are a speciality, particularly in the south of the region around Segovia, Soria, and Aranda del Duero.

Stews based on legumes are common, whether the classic pork, cabbage and chickpeas cocido, or the Burgos favourite *olla podrida*, made with red beans, chorizo and the local black pudding. Garlic soups and *sopa castellana* are other winter warmers, as are *callos* (tripe), *mollejas guisadas* (stewed sweetbreads), *manitas de cerdo* (pigs' trotters), *rabo de toro* (stewed bull tail) and some of Spain's best beef.

Salamanca is famous for its ham, while *cecina* (Leonese cured beef) has a delicious dark flavour.

Castilla y León go for filling roast meat and bean dishes more suited to the harsh winters than the baking summers.

Eating out

One of the great pleasures of travelling in Northern Spain is eating out, but it's no fun sitting in an empty restaurant so adapt to the local hours as much as you can; it may feel strange leaving dinner until 2200, but you'll miss out on a lot of atmosphere if you don't.

The standard distinctions of bar, café and restaurant don't apply in Spain. Many places combine all three functions, and it's not always evident; the dining room (*comedor*) is often tucked away behind the bar or upstairs. *Restaurantes* are restaurants, and will usually have a dedicated dining area with set menus and à la carte options. Bars and cafés will often display food on the counter, or have a list of tapas; bars tend to be known for particular dishes they do well. Many bars, cafés and restaurants don't open on Sunday nights, and most are closed one other night a week, most commonly Monday or Tuesday.

Cafés will usually provide some kind of **breakfast** fare in the mornings; croissants and sweet pastries are the norm; freshly squeezed orange juice is also common. About 1100 they start putting out savoury fare; maybe a *tortilla*, some *ensaladilla rusa* or little ham rolls in preparation for pre-lunch snacking. It's a workers' tradition – from labourers to executives – to drop down to the local bar around 1130 for a *pincho de tortilla* (slice of potato omelette) to get them through until two.

Lunch is the biggest meal of the day for most people in Spain, and it's also the cheapest time to eat. Just about all restaurants offer a *menú del día*, which is usually a set three-course meal that includes wine or soft drink. In unglamorous workers' locals this is often as little as €8; paying anything more than €13 indicates the restaurant takes itself quite seriously. Most places open for lunch at about 1300, and stop serving at 1500 or 1530, although at weekends this can extend; it's not uncommon to see people still lunching at 1800 on a Sunday. The quality of à la carte is usually higher than the *menú*, and quantities are larger.

Simpler restaurants won't offer this option except in the evenings. **Tapas** has changed in meaning over the years, and now basically refers to all bar food. This range includes free snacks given with drinks (now only standard in León and a few other places), *pinchos*, small saucer-sized plates of food (this is the true meaning of *tapa*) and more substantial dishes, usually ordered in *raciones* and designed to be shared. A *ración* in Northern Spain is no mean affair; it can often comfortably fill one person, so if you want to sample a range of things, you're better to ask for a half (*media*) or a *tapa* (smaller portion, when available).

Most restaurants open for dinner at 2030 or later. Although some places do offer a cheap set *menú*, you'll usually have to order à la carte. In quiet areas, places stop serving at 2200 on week nights, but in cities and at weekends people sit down at 2230 or later. A cheap option at all times is a *plato combinado*, most commonly offered in cafés. They're usually a greasy spoon-style mix of eggs, steak, bacon and chips or similar and are filling but rarely inspiring.

Vegetarians in Spain won't be spoiled for choice, but at least what there is tends to be good. There's a small but rapidly increasing number of dedicated vegetarian restaurants, but most other places won't have a vegetarian main course on offer, although the existence of *raciones* and salads makes this less of a burden than it might be. *Ensalada mixta* nearly always has tuna in it, but it's usually made fresh, so places will happily leave it out. *Ensaladilla rusa* is normally a good bet, but ask about the tuna too, just in case. Tortilla is simple but delicious and ubiquitous. Simple potato or pepper dishes are tasty options (although beware of peppers stuffed with meat), and many *revueltos* (scrambled eggs) are just mixed with asparagus. Annoyingly, most vegetable *menestras* are seeded with ham before cooking, and bean dishes usually contain at least some meat or animal fat. You'll have to specify *soy vegetariano/a* (I am a vegetarian), but ask what dishes contain, as ham, fish and chicken are often considered suitable vegetarian fare. Vegans will have a tougher time. What doesn't have meat nearly always contains cheese or egg.

Drink

In good Catholic fashion, **wine** is the lifeblood of Spain. It's the standard accompaniment to most meals, but also features very prominently in bars, where a glass of cheap *tinto* or *blanco* can cost as little as €0.80, although it's more normally €1.20-1.60. A bottle of house wine in a cheap restaurant is often no more than €5 or €6. *Tinto* is red (although if you just order *vino* it's assumed that's what you want); *blanco* is white, and rosé is either *clarete* or *rosado*. A well-regulated system of *denominaciones de origen* (DO), similar to the French *appelation contrôlée* has lifted the reputation of Spanish wines high above the party plonk status they once enjoyed. Much of Spain's wine is produced in Castilla y León, and recent years have seen regions such as the Ribera del Duero, Rueda, Toro, Bierzo, and Arribes achieve worldwide recognition. But the daddy, of course, is still Rioja, whose area encompasses La Rioja province, a substantial swathe of the Basque country and a tiny bit of Navarra and Castilla y León.

The overall standard of Riojas has improved markedly since the granting of the higher DOC status in 1991, with some fairly stringent testing in place. Red predominates; these are mostly medium-bodied bottles from the Tempranillo grape (with three other permitted red grapes often used to add depth or character). Whites from Viura and Malvasia are also produced: the majority of these are young, fresh and dry, unlike the traditional powerful oaky Rioja whites now on the decline. Rosés are also produced. The quality of individual Riojas varies widely according to both producer and the amount of time the wines have been aged in oak barrels and in the bottle. The words *crianza*, *reserva* and *gran reserva* refer to the length of the ageing process, while the vintage date is also given. Rioja producers store their wines at the bodega until deemed ready for drinking, so it's common to see wines dating back a decade or more on shelves and wine lists.

A growing number of people feel, however, that Spain's best reds come from the Castilian heartland, the Ribera del Duero region east of Valladolid. The king's favourite tipple, Vega Sicilia, has long been Spain's most prestigious wine, but other producers from the area have also gained stellar reviews.

Visiting the area in the baking summer heat, it's hard to believe that nearby Rueda can produce quality whites, but it certainly does. Most come from the Verdejo grape and have an attractive, dry, lemony taste; Sauvignon Blanc has also been planted with some success.

The intense summer heat of nearby Toro makes for traditional, full-bodied reds, but some more subtle wines of striking quality have emerged from there recently, including Vega Sicilia-owned Pintia.

The Bierzo, in western León province, also produces interesting wines, some of exceptional quality, from the red Prieto Picudo and Mencía grapes.

One of the joys of Spain, though, is the rest of the wine. Order a *menú del día* at a cheap restaurant and you'll be unceremoniously served a cheap bottle of local red (sometimes without even asking for it). Wine snobbery can leave by the back door at this point: it may be cold, but you'll find it refreshing; it may be acidic, but once the olive-oil laden food arrives, you'll be glad of it. It's not there to be judged, it's a staple like bread and, like bread, it's sometimes excellent, it's sometimes bad, but mostly it fulfils its purpose perfectly. Wine is not a luxury item in Spain, so people add water to it if they feel like it, or lemonade (*gaseosa*), or *cola* (to make the party drink called *calimocho*). Tinto de verano is a summer slurper similar to sangría, a mixture of red wine, gaseosa, ice, and optional fruit.

Spanish **beer** is mostly lager, usually reasonably strong, fairly gassy, cold and good. A *caña* is a regular draught beer, usually about 200 ml. Order a *cerveza* and you'll get a bottled beer. Many people order their beer *con gas* (half beer and half fizzy sweet water) or *con limón* (half lemonade, also called a *clara*). In some pubs, particularly those specializing in different beers (*cervecerías*), you can order pints (*pintas*).

Spirits are cheap in Spain. Vermouth (*vermut*) is a popular pre-lunch *aperitif*, as is *patxarán*. Many bars make their own vermouth by adding various herbs and fruits and letting it sit in barrels; this can be excellent, particularly if its from a *solera*. This is a system where liquid is drawn from the oldest of a series of barrels, which is then topped up with the next oldest, resulting in a very mellow characterful drink. After dinner or lunch it's time for a *copa*: people relax over a whisky or a brandy, or hit the mixed drinks (*cubatas*): *gin tonic* is obvious, as is *vodka con cola*. Spirits are free-poured and large; don't be surprised at a 100 ml measure. A mixed drink costs €4-7. Whisky is popular, and most bars have a good range. Spanish brandy is good, although its oaky vanilla flavours don't appeal to everyone. There are numerous varieties of rum and flavoured liqueurs. When ordering a spirit, you'll be expected to choose which brand you want; the local varieties (eg *Larios* gin, *DYC* whisky) are marginally cheaper than their imported brethren but lower in quality. *Chupitos* are shots; restaurants will often throw in a free one at the end of a meal, or give you a bottle of *orujo* (grape spirit) to pep up your black coffee.

Juice is normally bottled and expensive; *mosto* (grape juice; really pre-fermented wine) is a cheaper and popular soft drink in bars. There's the usual range of **fizzy drinks** (*gaseosas*) available. Horchata is a summer drink, a sort of milkshake made from tiger nuts. **Water** (*agua*) comes *con* (with) or *sin* (without) *gas*. The tap water is totally safe to drink, but it's not always the nicest; many Spaniards drink bottled water at home.

Coffee (*café*) is usually excellent and strong. *Solo* is black, mostly served espresso style. Order *americano* if you want a long black, *cortado* if you want a dash of milk, or *con leche* for about half milk. A *carajillo* is a coffee with brandy. **Tea** (*té*) is served without milk unless you ask; herbal teas (*infusiones*) are common, especially chamomile (*manzanilla*) and mint (*menta poleo*). **Chocolate** is a reasonably popular drink at breakfast time or in the afternoon (*merienda*), served with *churros*, fried doughsticks that seduce about a quarter of visitors and repel the rest.

Festivals in Castilla y León

Even the smallest village in Spain has a fiesta, and some have several. Although mostly nominally religious in nature, they usually include the works; a mass and procession or two to be sure, but also live music, bullfights, competitions, fireworks, a funfair, concerts and copious drinking of *calimocho*, a mix of red wine and cola (not as bad as it sounds). A feature of many are the *gigantes y cabezudos*, huge-headed papier-mâché figures based on historical personages who parade the streets. Adding to the sense of fun are *peñas*, boisterous social clubs who patrol the streets making music, get rowdy at the bullfights and drink wine all night and day. Most fiestas are in summer, and if you're spending much time in Spain in that period you're bound to run into one; expect some trouble finding accommodation. Details of the major town fiestas can be found in the travel text. National holidays and long weekends (*puentes*) can be difficult times to travel; it's important to reserve tickets in advance. If the holiday falls mid-week, it's usual form to take an extra day off, forming a long weekend known as a *puente* (bridge).

Public holidays

The holidays listed here are national or Castilian; local fiestas and holidays are detailed in the main text. These can be difficult times to travel; it's important to reserve travel in advance to avoid queues and lack of seats.

1 Jan Año Nuevo, New Year's Day.
6 Jan Reyes Magos/Epifanía, Epiphany; when Christmas presents are given.
Easter Jueves Santo, Viernes Santo, Día de Pascua (Maundy Thu, Good Fri, Easter Sun).
23 Apr Fiesta de la Comunidad de Castilla y León.

1 May Fiesta de Trabajo, Labour Day.
15 Aug Asunción, Feast of the Assumption.
12 Oct Día de la Hispanidad, Spanish National Day (Columbus Day, Feast of the Virgin of the Pillar).
1 Nov Todos los Santos, All Saints' Day.
6 Dec Día de la Constitución Española, Constitution Day.
8 Dec Inmaculada Concepción, Feast of the Immaculate Conception.
25 Dec Navidad, Christmas Day.

Essentials A-Z

Accident and emergency
There are various emergency numbers, but the general one across the nation is now T112. This will get you the police, ambulance, or fire brigade. T091 gets just the police.

Electricity
Spain uses the standard European 220V plug, with 2 round pins.

Embassies and consulates
For embassies and consulates of Spain, see www.maec.es.

Health
Health for travellers in Spain is rarely a problem. Medical facilities are good, and the worst most travellers experience is an upset stomach, usually merely a result of the different diet rather than any bug.

The water is safe to drink, but isn't always that pleasant, so many travellers (and locals) stick to bottled water. The sun in Spain can be harsh, so take adequate precautions to prevent heat exhaustion/sunburn. Many medications that require a prescription in other countries are available over the counter at pharmacies in Spain. Pharmacists are highly trained but don't necessarily speak English. In all medium-sized towns and cities, at least one pharmacy is open 24 hrs; this is organized on a rota system; details are posted in the window of all pharmacies and in local newspapers.

Language
For travelling purposes, everyone in Northern Spain speaks Spanish, known either as *castellano* or *español*, and it's a huge help to know some. Most young people know some English, and standards are rapidly rising, but don't assume that people aged 40 or over know any at all. Spaniards are often shy to attempt to speak English. While many visitor attractions have some sort of information available in English (and to a lesser extent French and German), many don't, or have English tours only in times of high demand. Most tourist office staff will speak at least some English, and there's a good range of translated information available in most places.

While efforts to speak the language are appreciated, it's more or less expected, to the same degree as English is expected in Britain or the USA. Nobody will be rude if you don't speak any Spanish, but nobody will think to slow their rapidfire stream of the language for your benefit either, or pat you on the back for producing a few phrases in their tongue.

Money
Check www.xe.com for exchange rates.

Currency
In 2002, Spain switched to the euro, bidding farewell to the peseta. The euro (€) is divided into 100 *céntimos*. Euro notes are standard across the whole zone, and come in denominations of 5, 10, 20, 50, 100, and the rarely seen 200 and 500. Coins have one standard face and one national face; all coins are, however, acceptable in all countries. The coins are slightly difficult to tell apart when you're not used to them. The coppers are 1, 2 and 5 cent pieces, the golds are 10, 20 and 50, and the silver/gold combinations are €1 and €2. People still tend to think in pesetas when talking about large amounts like house prices.

ATMs and banks
The best way to get money in Spain is by plastic. ATMs are plentiful, and just about all of them accept all the major international debit and credit cards. The Spanish bank won't charge for the transaction, though they will charge a mark-up on the exchange

rate, but beware of your own bank hitting you for a hefty fee: check with them before leaving home. Even if they do, it's likely to be a better deal than exchanging cash. The website www.moneysavingexpert.com has a good rundown on the most economical ways of accessing cash while travelling.

Banks are usually open Mon-Fri 0830-1400 (and Sat in winter) and many change foreign money (sometimes only the central branch in a town will do it). Commission rates vary widely; it's usually best to change large amounts, as there's often a minimum commission of €6 or so. Nevertheless, banks nearly always give better rates than change offices (*casas de cambio*), which are fewer by the day. If you're stuck outside banking hours, some large department stores such as the *Corte Inglés* change money at knavish rates. Traveller's cheques are accepted in many shops, although they are far less common than they were.

Tax

Nearly all goods and services in Spain are subject to a value-added tax (IVA). This is only 10% for most things the traveller will encounter, including food and hotels, but is as high as 21% on some things. IVA is normally included in the stated prices. You're technically entitled to claim it back if you're a non-EU citizen, for purchases over €90. If you're buying something pricey, make sure you get a stamped receipt clearly showing the IVA component, as well as your name and passport number; you can claim the amount back at major airports on departure. Some shops will have a form to smooth the process.

Cost of living and travelling

Prices have soared since the euro was introduced; some basics rose by 50-80% in 3 years, and hotel and restaurant prices can even seem dear by Western European standards these days.

Spain can still be a reasonably cheap place to travel if you're prepared to forgo a few luxuries. If you're travelling as a pair, staying in cheap *pensiones*, eating a set meal at lunchtime, travelling short distances daily, and snacking on tapas in the evenings, €65 per person per day is reasonable. If you camp and grab picnic lunches from shops, you could reduce this considerably. In a cheap hotel or good *hostal* and using a car, €130 each a day and you'll not be counting pennies; €250 per day and you'll be very comfy indeed unless you're staying in 4- or 5-star accommodation.

Accommodation is more expensive in summer than in winter. The news isn't great for the solo traveller; single rooms tend not to be particularly good value, and they are in short supply. Prices range from 60% to 80% of the double/twin price; some establishments even charge the full rate. If you're going to be staying in 3- to 5-star hotels, booking them ahead on internet discount sites can save a lot of money.

Public transport is generally cheap; intercity bus services are quick and low-priced and trains are reasonable, though the fast AVE trains cost substantially more.

Standard unleaded petrol is around €1.50 per litre and diesel around €1.40. In some places, particularly in tourist areas, you may be charged up to 20% more to sit outside a restaurant. It's also worth checking if the 10% IVA (sales tax) is included in meal prices, especially in the more expensive restaurants; it should say on the menu whether this is the case.

Opening hours

Business hours Mon-Fri 1000-1400, 1700-2000; Sat 1000-1400. **Banks** Mon-Fri 0830-1400; Sat (not in Aug) 0900-1300. **Government offices** Mornings only.

Safety

Northern Spain is generally a very safe place. Tourist crime is very low in this region, and you're more likely to have something returned (that you left on that train) than something stolen. That said, don't invite crime by leaving luggage or cash in cars. If parking in a city or, particularly, a popular hiking zone, try to make it clear there's nothing to nick inside by opening the glovebox, etc.

There are several types of police, helpful enough in normal circumstances. The paramilitary **Guardia Civil** dress in green and are responsible for the roads (including speed traps and the like), borders and law enforcement away from towns. They're not a bunch to get the wrong side of but are polite to tourists and have thankfully lost the bizarre winged hats they used to sport. The **Policía Nacional** are responsible for most urban crimefighting. These are the ones to go to if you need to report anything stolen, etc. **Policía Local/Municipal** are present in large towns and cities and are responsible for some urban crime, as well as traffic control and parking.

Time

Spain operates on western European time, ie GMT +1, and changes its clocks in line with the rest of the EU.

'Spanish time' isn't as elastic as it used to be, but if you're told something will happen *'enseguida'* ('straight away') it may take 10 mins, if you're told *'cinco minutos'* (5 mins), grab a seat and a book. Transport leaves promptly.

Tipping

Tipping in Spain is far from compulsory, but much practised. Around 10% is considered extremely generous in a restaurant; 3-5% is more usual. It's rare for a service charge to be added to a bill. Waiters do not normally expect tips but in bars and cafés people will often leave small change, especially for table service. Taxi drivers don't expect a tip, but will be pleased to receive one. In rural areas, churches will often have a local keyholder who will open it up for you; if there's no admission charge, a tip or donation is appropriate (say €1 per head; more if they've given a detailed tour).

Tourist information

The tourist information infrastructure in Castilla y León is organized by the regional governments and is generally excellent, with a wide range of information, often in English, German and French as well as Spanish. Offices within the region can provide maps of the area and towns, and lists of registered accommodation, with 1 booklet for hotels, *hostales*, and *pensiones*; another for campsites, and another, especially worth picking up, listing farmstay and rural accommodation, which has taken off in a big way in the last decade or so. Opening hours are longer in major cities; many rural offices are only open in summer. Average opening hours are Mon-Sat 1000-1400, 1600-1900, Sun 1000-1400. Offices are often closed on Sun or Mon. Staff often speak English and other European languages and are well trained. The offices (*oficinas de turismo*) are often signposted to some degree within the town or city. Staff may ask where you are from; this is not nosiness but for statistical purposes.

The regional tourist board has a useful website, with extensive accommodation, restaurant, and sights listings: www.turismocastillayleon.com

Other useful websites

http://maps.google.es Street maps of most Spanish towns and cities.

www.alsa.es Northern Spain's major bus operator. Book online.

www.dgt.es The transport department website has up-to-date information in Spanish on road conditions throughout the country. Useful for snowy winters.

www.elpais.es Online edition of Spain's biggest-selling non-sports daily paper. English edition available.

www.guiarepsol.com Excellent online route planner for Spanish roads, also available in English.

www.inm.es Site of the national metereological institute, with the day's weather and next-day forecasts.

www.movelia.es Online timetables and ticketing for several bus companies.

www.paginasamarillas.es Yellow Pages.

www.paginasblancas.es White Pages.

www.parador.es Parador information, including locations, prices and photos.

www.renfe.com Online timetables and tickets for RENFE train network.

www.spain.info The official website of the Spanish tourist board.

www.ticketmaster.es Spain's biggest ticketing agency for concerts, etc, with online purchase.

www.todoturismorural.com and **www.toprural.com** 2 excellent sites for *casas rurales*.

www.tourspain.es A useful website run by the Spanish tourist board.

www.typicallyspanish.com News and links on all things Spanish.

Visas

Entry requirements are subject to change, so always check with the Spanish tourist board or an embassy/consulate if you're not an EU citizen. EU citizens and those from countries within the Schengen agreement can enter Spain freely. UK/Irish citizens will need to carry a passport, while an identity card suffices for other EU/Schengen nationals. Citizens of Australia, the USA, Canada, New Zealand and Israel can enter without a visa for up to 90 days. Other citizens will require a visa, obtainable from Spanish consulates or embassies. These are usually issued very quickly and valid for all Schengen countries. The basic visa is valid for 90 days, and you'll need 2 passport photos, proof of funds covering your stay and possibly evidence of medical cover (ie insurance). For extensions of visas, apply to an *oficina de extranjeros* in a major city.

Weights and measures

Metric.

Contents

Footprint features

At a glance

⊖ **Getting around** Easy train and bus services between cities. International flights to Valladolid. Driving's easy, but with long distances to cover.

◉ **Time required** 3-4 weeks.

☀ **Weather** Dry and hot in summer, dry and cold in winter, which can be chilly into May.

✖ **When not to go** Aug, when temperatures exceed 40°. Jan-Feb if chill winds and snow are a turn-off.

Castilla y León

Burgos

"They have very good houses and live very comfortably, and they are the most courteous people I have come across in Spain."
Andrés Navagero, 1526.

This Venetian traveller's comment on 16th-century Burgos could equally apply today to the city where courtesy and courtliness still rule the roost. Formerly an important and prosperous trading town, Burgos achieved infamy as the seat of Franco's Civil War junta and is still a sober and reactionary town, the heartland of Castilian conservatism. But Burgos is far from being stuck in the past; the fantastic new Museum of Human Evolution sits on the Arlanzón river, a committed programme of inserting cycleways along every major road that is way ahead of its time in Castilla, and the S-4 urbanization project has turned heads in the architecture world.

Burgos's collection of superb Gothic buildings and sculpture, as well as its position on the Camino de Santiago, make it a popular destination, but the city copes well with the summer influx. Just don't come for gentle spring sunshine; Burgos is known throughout Spain as a chilly city, the epitome of the saying *'nueve meses de invierno, tres meses de infierno'* (nine months of winter, three months of hell). The chills can be banished with the traditionally hearty local cuisine and Ribera reds from the south of the province.

Arriving in Burgos → *Phone code: 947. Population: 178,966. Altitude: 860 m.*

Getting there Burgos is roughly in the centre of Northern Spain and easily accessed from most parts of the country by bus or train. There are regular services from Madrid and the Basque country as well as Santander and all Castilian towns. ⏵⏵ *See Transport, page 35.*

Getting around As usual, the old centre is fairly compact, but you may want to use the local bus service to access a couple of the outlying monasteries, the new train station and the campsite.

Best time to visit Burgos has a fairly unpleasant climate with short, hot summers and long, cold winters (it often snows) punctuated by the biting wind that 'won't blow out a candle but will kill a man'. The most moderate weather is found in May, June and September.

Tourist information There is a **municipal office** ① *Plaza del Rey San Fernando 2, T947 288 874, www.turismoburgos.org, summer daily 1000-2000,* across from the cathedral; and also a **regional office** ① *Plaza Alonso Martínez 7, T947 203 125, oficinadeturismodeburgos@ jcyl.es, mid-Sep-Jun Mon-Sat 0930-1400, 1600-1900, Sun 0930-1700, summer daily 0900-2000.* There are **city tours** and a rather tacky **tourist train** ① *daily in summer and at weekends Oct-Jun, €4,* which rolls around the sights, leaving from outside the cathedral square tourist office.

Background

Burgos is comfortably the oldest city in Europe, if you count the nearby cave-dwellers from Atapuerca, who were around over a million years ago. That aside, the city's effective foundation was in the late ninth century, when it was resettled during the Reconquista. Further honours soon followed; it was named capital of Castilla y León as early as the 11th century.

The city's position at the northern centre of the Castilian plain, near the coastal mountain passes, made it a crucial point for the export of goods. Burgos flourished, becoming a wealthy city of merchants and beasts of burden; in the 16th century its mule population often exceeded the human one, as bigger and bigger convoys of wool made their way over the mountains and by ship to Flanders.

The Consulado de Burgos, a powerful guild-like body, was created to administer trade, and succeeded in establishing a virtual monopoly; Burgos became one of three great 16th-century Spanish trading cities, along with Sevilla and Medina del Campo. The strife in Flanders hit the city hard, though, and other towns broke into the market. Burgos' population declined by 75% in the first half of the 17th century, and the city lapsed into the role of genteel provincial capital, apart from a brief and bloody interlude:during the Civil War the Nationalist junta was established here; the city had shown its credentials with a series of atrocities committed on Republicans after the rising.

Places in Burgos → *For listings, see pages 32-35.*

Cathedral

① *Cathedral and museum, www.catedraldeburgos.es, are open mid-Mar to Oct daily 0930-1930, Nov to mid-Mar 1000-1900, last entry an hour before, €7, €3.50 for pilgrims. Some of the chapels are only accessible on guided tours; the guides are independent and prices vary. Before entering the cathedral, you must buy a ticket in the reception office on the square below.*

Burgos's famed cathedral is a remarkable Gothic edifice whose high hollow spires rise over the city. Its beauty is an austere and solemn one, and the technical excellence of its stonework has to be admired. It also houses a collection of significant artwork.

The current structure was begun in 1221 over an earlier church by Fernando III and his Germanic wife, Beatrice of Swabia, with the bishop Maurice overseeing things. Beatrice

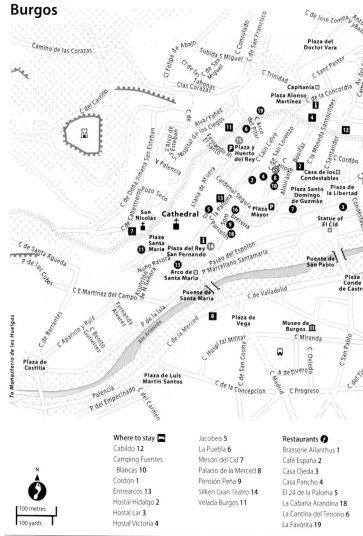

Burgos

Where to stay 🛏		Jacobeo 5	Restaurants 🍴
Cabildo 12		La Puebla 6	Brasserie Ailanthus 1
Camping Fuentes		Mesón del Cid 7	Café España 2
Blancas 10		Palacio de la Merced 8	Casa Ojeda 3
Cordón 1		Pensión Peña 9	Casa Pancho 4
Entrearcos 13		Silken Gran Teatro 14	El 24 de la Paloma 5
Hostal Hidalgo 2		Velada Burgos 11	La Cabaña Arandina 18
Hostal Lar 3			La Cantina del Tenorio 6
Hostal Victoria 4			La Favorita 19

brought him with her from Swabia, and the northern influence didn't stop there; Gil and Diego de Siloé, the top sculptors who are responsible for many masterpieces inside and throughout the province, originated from those parts, while the towers were designed by master builder Hans of Cologne.

Entering through the western door, under the spires (only completed in the 19th century), one of the strangest sights is in the chapel to the right. It's reserved for private prayer, but the figure you see through the glass is the **Christ of Burgos**. Made from buffalo hide and sporting a head of real hair, the crucified Jesus wears a green skirt and looks a little the worse for wear. The limbs are movable, no doubt to impress the 14th-century faithful with a few tricks; apparently the Christ was once so lifelike that folk thought the fingernails had to be clipped weekly. Opposite, high on the wall, the strange figure of Papamoscas strikes the hours, the closest thing to levity in this serious building.

Like those of many Spanish cathedrals, the **choir** is closed off, which spoils any long perspective views. Once inside, admire the Renaissance main *retablo* depicting scenes from the life of the Virgin. Underfoot at the crossing are the bones of El Cid and his wife Doña Jimena, underwhelmingly marked by a simple slab. The remains were only transferred here in 1927 after being reclaimed from the French, who had taken them from the monastery of San Pedro de Cardeña during the Peninsular War. They lie under the large octagonal tower, an elaborate 16th-century add-on. The choir itself is incredibly elegant and intricate – you could spend hours examining the carved wooden images; Bishop Maurice's tomb is in the centre of it.

There's a wealth of side chapels, many unfortunately shielded by *rejas* (grilles), although if an attendant is around they are happy to open them up. The chapels date from different architectural periods; some of the Renaissance ones feature stunningly fine stonework around the doorways. The **Capilla de Santa Teresa** sports a riotous Churrigueresque ceiling, while the soaring late Gothic *retablo* in the **Capilla de Santa Ana** and the painted Romanesque tombs in the **Capilla de San Nicolás** are also striking.

The grandest, however, is at the very far end of the apse, the **Capilla de los Condestables**. The Velasco family, hereditary Constables of Castilla, were immensely influential in their time, and one of the most powerful, Don Pedro Fernández, is entombed here with his wife. Few kings have lain in a more elaborate setting, with a high vaulted roof, fabulous stonework and three *retablos*, the most ornate of which, the central one, depicts the purification of Mary. The alabaster figures on the sepulchre itself are by another German, Simon of Cologne, and his son. The room, oddly asymmetrical, is a memorable shrine to earthly power and heraldry. Just outside, around the ambulatory, a series of sensitive alabaster panels depicts Biblical scenes.

The **museum**, set around the top of the two-tiered tomb-lined cloister, is reasonably interesting. After passing through the baroque sacristy, the first stop is the chapterhouse, where, high on the wall, hangs a coffer that belonged to the Cid; possibly the one that was involved in a grubby little deed of his, where he sneakily repaid some Jews with a coffer of sand, rather than the gold that he owed them. In the adjacent chamber is a pretty red *mudéjar* ceiling. A 10th-century Visigothic Bible is the highlight of the next room, as well as the Cid's marriage contract, the so-called *Letter of Arras*. Finally, the museum has an excellent collection of well-restored 15th-century Flemish paintings. They are full of life and action – the mob mentality of the Crucifixion is well portrayed. There are several reliquaries holding various bits of saints (including Thomas Becket) and nothing less than a spine from the crown of thorns. A *retablo* depicts Santiago in Moor-slaying mode.

Iglesia de San Nicolás

ⓘ *Jun-Sep Mon-Sat 1000-1400, 1700-1900, rest of year Mon-Sat 1200-1330, 1700-1900, €1.50; free Mon.*

This small church above the cathedral has a superb *retablo*, a virtuoso sculptural work, probably by Simon and Francis of Cologne. It's a bit like looking at a portrait of a city, or a theatre audience, so many figures seem to be depicted in different sections. The main scene at the top is Mary surrounded by a 360° choir of angels. The stonework is superb throughout; have a look for the ship's rigging, a handy piece of chiselling to say the least. There's also a good painting of the Last Judgement in the church, an early 16th-century Flemish work, only recently rediscovered. The demons are the most colourful aspect; one is trying to tip the scales despite being stood on by Saint Michael.

The old town is entered across one of two main bridges over the pretty Río Arlanzón, linked by a leafy *paseo*. The eastern of the two, the **Puente de San Pablo**, is guarded by an imposing mounted statue of El Cid, looming Batman-like above the traffic, heavy beard flying. The inscription risibly dubs him "a miracle from among the great miracles of the creator". The other, **Puente de Santa María**, approaches the arch of the same name, an impressively pompous gateway with a statue of a very snooty Carlos V. East of here is the **Plaza Mayor**, which is normally fairly lifeless. The **Casa Consistorial** has marks and dates from two of Burgos's biggest floods; it's hard to believe that the friendly little river could ever make it that high.

Other interesting buildings in the old centre include the **Casa de los Condestables**, with a massive corded façade. Felipe I (Philip the Fair) died here prematurely in 1506; it was also here that the Catholic Monarchs received Columbus after he returned from his second voyage. The ornate neo-Gothic **Capitanía** was the headquarters for the Nationalist *junta* in the Civil War.

El Cid

Although portrayed as something of a national hero in the 12th-century epic *El Cantar de Mío Cid* (Song of the Cid), the recorded deeds of Rodrigo Díaz de Vivar certainly give the devil's advocate a few sharp darts in the fight for places in the pantheon of Spanish heroes. Born just outside Burgos in AD 1043, El Cid (the Boss) was in fact a mercenary who fought with the Moors if the price was right.

His ability to protect his own interests was recognized even by those who sought to idolize him. The Song of the Cid recounts that, on being expelled, from Burgos the great man wrapped up his beard to protect it from being pulled by irate citizens angry at his nefarious dealings.

Operating along the border between Christian and Muslim Spain, the Cid was a man of military guile who was able to combine a zeal for the Reconquista with a desire to further his own fortune. The tawdry moment when he swindled two innocent Jewish merchants by delivering a chest filled with sand instead of gold is celebrated with gusto in Burgos cathedral where his mortal remains now lie.

Banished by Alfonso VI for double dealing, his military skills proved indispensable and he was re-hired in the fight against the Almoravids. The capture of Valencia in 1094 marked the height of his powers and was an undoubted blow to the Moors. If having his own city wasn't reward enough, the Cid was given the formidable Gormaz castle as a sort of fortified weekend retreat.

By the standards of his own time where the boundaries, both physical and cultural, between Christian and Moorish Spain were flexible, the Cid's actions make perfect sense. It is only later ages (preferring their heroes without ambiguity) that felt the need to gloss over the actual facts. By the time of his death in 1099 the Cid was well on his way to national hero status.

The Cid's horse, Babieca, has her own marked grave in the monastery of San Pedro de Cardeña. The Cid himself was buried here for 600 years until Napoleon's forces, perhaps fearing a re-appearance by the man himself, removed the body to France. He was reburied in Burgos in the 1930s.

Museo de la Evolución Humana and around

① *T902 024 246, www.museoevolucionhumana.com, Tue-Fri 1000-1430, 1630-2000, Sat 1000-2000, Sun 1000-1500, €6 (€4 for pilgrims). You can combine your visit with a trip to the excavation site at Atapuerca by prior reservation. This includes transport from the museum and costs €18, including entry to this museum, the interpretation centre at Atapuerca, and a visit to the excavations themselves.*

The excavations in the caves and galleries of the Atapuerca site near Burgos in recent years have completely changed ideas about the presence of prehistoric hominids in western Europe, and this excellent new museum brings together the information gleaned from here and other sites around the globe about our ancestors and distant cousins. Set on the riverbank in a striking building with limitless space and light, the display gives an overview of finds at Atapuerca and a comprehensive picture of our current knowledge of the numerous members of the 'homo' genus, as well as background on evolutionary theory and the voyage of the Beagle.

While Neanderthal man and homo sapiens both used the Atapuerca area, it is two earlier occupations that are most of interest here. Cosmogenic nuclide dating has put the oldest (so far) remains here at 1.3 million years old; they are sufficiently different to have been named as a new species, homo antecessor. There is evidence of their presence at Atapuerca until about 800,000 years ago. Later, Homo heidelbergensis, likely ancestors of the Neanderthals, lived here from around 600,000 years ago. The Atapuerca site is responsible for some 83% of excavated hominid material from this period, the middle-Pleistocene.

All panels are translated – perfectly – into English, as are the audiovisual features. While there are a few interactive exhibits, it's mostly a fairly serious archaeological and palaentological display, so the kids might get restless.

Not far away, and attractively set around the patioed **Casa Miranda** sections of the **Museo de Burgos** ① *Tue-Sat 1000-1400, 1600-1900 (1700-2000 summer), Sun 1000-1400; €1.20, free at weekends*, are prehistoric finds from Atapuerca (see page 31), Roman finds from Clunia, religious painting and sculpture, and some more modern works by Burgalese artists.

Above the town, a park covers the hilltop, which is crowned by the **Castillo de Burgos** ① *T947 288 874, Oct-Mar phone for weekday visits, Sat-Sun 1100-1400, Apr-Jun phone for weekday visits, Sat-Sun 1100-1400, 1600-1900, Jul-Sep daily 1100-1400, 1700-2030, €3.70, €2.60 without tunnels*. Heavily damaged by being blown up by the French in the Napoleonic Wars, it's recently been renovated and can be visited. A new museum summarizes some of the town and fortress's history, and the visit includes the sturdy ramparts and a claustrophobic trip into a system of tunnels dug deep into the hillside. It's a nice place to come on a sunny day, with excellent views down over the cathedral and plenty of woods to stroll in, and there are a couple of bars up here to enjoy a coffee or a drink at night.

Monasterio de las Huelgas
① *Tue-Sat 1000-1300, 1600-1730, Sun 1030-1400, €7, €4 pilgrims, free Wed and Thu afternoons; bus Nos 5, 7 and 39 run here from Av Valladolid across the river from the old town*. A 20-minute walk through an upmarket suburb of Burgos, the Monasterio de las Huelgas still harbours some 40 cloistered nuns, heiresses to a long tradition of power. In its day, the convent wielded enormous influence. The monastery was founded by Eleanor of England, daughter of Henry II and Eleanor of Aquitaine, who came to Burgos to marry Alfonso VIII in 1170. The Hammer of the Scots, Edward I, came here to get hitched as well; he married Eleanor, Princess of Castilla, in the monastery in 1254. Las Huelgas originally meant 'the reposes', as the complex was a favourite retreat for the Castilian monarchs. Here they could regain strength, ponder matters of state – and perhaps have a bit on the side; several abbesses of Las Huelgas bore illegitimate children behind the closed doors.

To keep the nuns separate from the public, the church was partitioned in the 16th century, and the naves separated by walls. The public were just left with a small aisle, where the visit starts. In here are a couple of curios: a moving pulpit that enabled the priest to address both the congregation and the separated nuns; and a strange statue of Santiago, sword in hand. Part of the coronation ceremony of the kings of Castilla used to involve them being knighted; as they judged no-one else in the land fit to perform the task, a statue of the saint with moveable arms used to perform the deed; this is probably one of those. There's also a retablo by the tireless Diego de Siloé in here.

The real attractions are on the nuns' side of the barricade. The church contains many ornate tombs of princes and other Castilian royals. These were robbed of much of their contents by Napoleon's soldiers. All were opened in 1942 and, to great surprise, an array of superb royal garments remained well preserved 700 years on, as well as some jewellery from the one tomb the French had overlooked. In the central nave are the tombs of Eleanor and Alfonso, who died in the same year. The arms of England and Castilla adorn the exquisite tombs. They lie beneath an ornate Plateresque *retablo*, which is topped by a 13th-century crucifixion scene and contains various relics.

Around a large cloister are more treasures; a *mudéjar* door with intricate wooden carving, a Moorish standard captured from the famous battle at Navas de Tolosa in 1212, and a postcard-pretty smaller cloister with amazing carved plasterwork, no doubt Moorish-influenced. For many, the highlight is the display of the clothing found in the tombs: strange, ornate, silken garments embroidered with gold thread. The colours have faded over the centuries, but they remain in top condition, a seldom-seen link with the past that seems to bring the dusty royal names alive.

Cartuja de Miraflores
① *Mon-Tue and Thu-Fri (closed Wed) 1015-1500, 1600-1800 (1900 summer), Sat-Sun 1100-1500, 1600-1800 (1900 summer), free. Catch bus No 26 or 27 from Plaza de España and get off at the Fuente del Prior stop; the monastery is a 5-min walk up a marked side road. Otherwise, it's a 50-min walk through pleasant parkland from the centre of town.*

This former hunting lodge is another important Burgos monastery, also still functioning and populated by silent Carthusians. Juan II de Castilla, father of Isabel (the Catholic monarch), started the conversion and his daughter finished it. Like so much in Burgos, it was the work of a German, Hans of Cologne. Inside, the late-Gothic design is elegant, with elaborate vaulting, and stained glass from Flanders depicting the life of Christ. The wooden choir stalls are carved with incredible delicacy, but attention is soon drawn by the superb alabaster work of the *retablo* and the tombs that lie before it. These are all designed by Gil de Siloé, the Gothic master and they are the triumphant expression of genius. The central tomb is star-shaped, and was commissioned by Isabel for her parents; at the side of the chamber rests her brother Alonso, heir to the Castilian throne until his death at the age of 14. The *retablo* centres on the crucifixion, with many saints in attendance. The sculptural treatment is beautiful, expressing emotion and sentiment through stone. Equally striking is the sheer level of detail in the works; a casual visitor could spend weeks trying to decode the symbols and layers of meaning.

Monasterio de San Pedro de Cardeña
① *Tue-Sat 1000-1300, 1600-1800, Sun 1215-1300, 1615-1800; wait in the church for a monk to appear; €2; accommodation available at the monastery.*

Close to the city, at a distance of 10 km, the Monasterio de San Pedro de Cardeña is worth a visit, especially for those with an interest in the Cid. The first point of interest is to one side, in front of the monastery, where a gravestone marks the supposed burial site of the Cid's legendary mare, Babieca. The monastery has a community of 24 Cistercians; a monk will show you around the church, most of which dates from the 15th century. In a side chapel is an ornate tomb raised (much later) over the spot where the man and his wife were buried until Napoleon's troops nicked the bones in the 19th century; they were reclaimed and buried in Burgos cathedral. The *mudéjar* cloister dates from the 10th century and is the most impressive feature of the building, along with a late Gothic doorway in the *sala capitular*.

Atapuerca
① *You can enter the area via Ibeas, 13 km east of Burgos on the N120, or the village of Atapuerca – take the N1 towards Vitoria, turn off at Olmos de Atapuerca and follow the signs. The camino francés passes through the village of Atapuerca. There's a visitor centre at both Ibeas and Atapuerca. Shuttle buses run from these visitor centres into the park, and also run*

from the Museo de Evolución Humana in Burgos. Check the museum's website for details and times of tours, as they vary greatly throughout the year. T902 024 246, www.visitasatapuerca. com, €6 for the excavation areas, €5 for the thematic park, ring to book at all times.

Some 13 km east of Burgos, an unremarkable series of rocky hills have been the site of incredibly significant palaeontological and archaeological finds. Prehistoric human remains dated to over a million years were found here in 2008; the oldest known physical evidence of humans in Europe. Several fossilized remnants of Homo heidelbergensis have also been discovered here; dating has placed the bones from 500,000 to 200,000 years old. It's a crucial link in the study of hominid evolution; Neanderthals seemed to evolve directly from these Heidelbergers. A tour takes you round some of the most important excavation sites, and also to the thematic park, where there are some reconstructions and demonstrations of elements of the prehistoric hominid skillset, such as fire-making and bowmanship.

Burgos listings

For hotel and restaurant price codes and other relevant information, see pages 11-17.

🛏 Where to stay

Burgos *p24, map p26*

€€€ Hotel Cabildo, Av del Cid 2, T947 257 840, www.hotelcabildo.com. Well located, modern, and comfortable, this makes a reliable, if not spectacular, central base. Good facilities are allied with the suave contemporary decor, and helpful staff round out the experience.

€€€ Hotel La Puebla, C La Puebla 20, T947 200 011, www.hotellapuebla.com. An intimate hotel in the centre of Burgos with classy modern design, good facilities, and comfortable furnishings. Rooms are compact but comfortable, but the price seems a little elevated in high season. Parking available.

€€€ Hotel Mesón del Cid, Plaza Santa María 8, T947 208 715, www.mesondelcid.es. Superbly located opposite the cathedral, this hotel and restaurant is an excellent place to stay, with spacious, quiet and modern rooms and helpful staff. There are larger rooms and apartments available for families.

€€€ Hotel Velada Burgos, C Fernán González 6, T947 257 680, www.velada hoteles.com. Set in a beautifully converted old *palacio* in the heart of town, this stylish spot features sweet rooms with small bathrooms; most are duplex, with the sleeping area accessed via a staircase. Rooms are mostly quiet despite the noisy streets around here at weekends. You can get some good prices on their website.

€€€ Palacio de la Merced, C La Merced 13, T947 479 900, www.nh-hoteles.com. Attractively set in a 16th-century *palacio*, this hotel successfully blends minimalist, modern design into the old building, whose most charming feature is its cloister in Isabelline Gothic style. The rooms are comfortable and attractively decked out in wood. Extras like breakfast and parking are overpriced. Recommended.

€€€ Silken Gran Teatro, Av Arlanzón 8, T947 253 900, www.hoteles-silken.com. Although primarily aimed at business visitors, this hotel makes a sound choice a short walk from the historic centre and right across a pedestrian bridge from the evolution museum. Rooms are quiet and comfortable, and, as is often the case with this chain, staff are excellent. There are good rates to be found online.

€€ Hotel Cordón, C La Puebla 6, T947 265 000, www.hotelcordon.com. A central, reasonable option, geared up for business travellers. Nothing stunning about the rooms, but there are very reasonable weekend rates if you book ahead. Free internet; Wi-Fi in some rooms.

€€ Hotel Entrearcos, C Paloma 4, T947 252 911, www.hotelentrearcos.com. Under the arcades on the main pedestrian street very near the cathedral, this makes a fine modern base in the heart of town. Rooms are compact but shiny and new, with free Wi-Fi that actually works, and helpful service to back it up. Prices are more than fair, especially off-season.

€ Hostal Lar, C Cardenal Benlloch 1, T947 209 655, www.hostallar.es. This quiet and decent place has well-priced en suite rooms with TV. The management is friendly; and despite pocket-sized bathrooms it's a good all-round budget option.

€ Hostal Victoria, C San Juan 3, T947 201 542. A good choice with friendly management, this *hostal* is central and relatively quiet, and the rooms with shared bath are comfortable and fairly spacious.

€ Hotel Jacobeo, C San Juan 24, T947 260 102, www.hoteljacobeo.com. This smallish central hotel is well managed and features good en suite rooms with comfortable new beds in a pretty old building. Recently renovated, it features free Wi-Fi and DVD players in the rooms. It's pretty good value, particularly outside of the summer months.

€ Pensión Peña, C Puebla 18, T947 206 323. An excellent cheapie, well located and maintained on a pedestrian street. The rooms are heated and have good shared bathrooms. It's often full, however, so don't hold your breath.

Camping

Camping Fuentes Blancas, Ctra Burgos–Cartuja s/n, T947 486 016, www.campingburgos.com. A well-situated campsite in woody riverside parkland about 4 km from the centre, with a pool and bungalows on site. Take bus No 26 or 27 from Plaza de España (not terribly frequent).

Burgos *p24, map p26*

Burgos is famous for its *morcilla*, a tasty black pudding filled with rice. Roast lamb is also a speciality here.

A popular new zone for tapas and late-night bars, known as Las Bernardillas, can be found around Plaza de Roma, in the spread-out Gamonal district northeast of the centre off the road to Vitoria. Bus No 1 will get you there from near the Puente de San Pablo.

€€€ Casa Ojeda, C Vitoria 5, T947 209 052, www.restauranteojeda.com. One of Burgos' better-known restaurants, backing on to Plaza de la Libertad. Traditional cuisine a bit on the heavy side, but good. Oven-roasted meats are the pride of the house, and the homemade foie is excellent. There's cheaper food available in the bar-café.

€€€ El 24 de la Paloma, C Paloma 24, T947 208 608, www.restauranteel24dela paloma.com. A smart restaurant near the cathedral with a range of succulent dishes like *cigalas* in tempura with cherry ketchup, or de-boned suckling pig. There's a degustation menu for €48, or a lunchtime one for €27 that includes roast lamb. They run regular themed Spanish wine tastings.

€€€ Puerta Real, Plaza Rey San Fernando s/n, T947 265 200, www.puertareal.es. On the cathedral square, this smart *asador* specializes in succulent roast meats, with lamb foremost among them. There's a set menu for €30, which includes that, as well as the other Burgos speciality *morcilla* and a decent Ribera wine. They also show a confident touch with fish dishes. Service here is excellent.

€€ La Favorita, C Avellanos 8, T947 205 949, www.lafavoritaburgos.com. This large barn-like spot is modern but feels traditional with its hanging hams, rows of wine bottles and wooden fittings. There's plenty of space to enjoy tasty *pinchos* – try the grilled foie gras or chopped ham with garlic mayonnaise for a rich treat – or *raciones* of traditional products. There's an attractive dining room out the back for sit-down meals. Recommended.

€€ La Posada, Plaza Santo Domingo de Guzmán 18, T947 204 578, www.restaurantelaposada.net. This central spot is a likeable restaurant with a cheery downstairs bar that spills onto the street, and comforting and delicious home-style cooking in the upstairs *comedor*. Dishes, including soups and stews, are prepared to perfection.

€€ Mesón Burgos, C Sombrerería 8, T947 206 150. One of Burgos' better tapas bars downstairs, famous for its *patatas bravas*, is complemented by a friendly upstairs restaurant with good, if unexceptional fare. The service is good and the decor traditional and comfortable.

€€ Mesón La Cueva, Plaza de Santa María 7, T947 205 946, www.restaurante-lacueva.es. A small dark Castilian restaurant with good service and a traditional feel. The *menestra de verduras* is tasty and generous, and the roast meats are good.

€ Casa Pancho, C San Lorenzo 13, T947 203 405. One of several good options on this street, Casa Pancho is large, warm, light and stylish, with an array of excellent *pinchos* adorning the bar, and cheerful service. Anything involving prawns or mushrooms is a good bet.

€ La Cabaña Arandina, C Sombrerería 12, T947 261 932, www.lacabanaarandina.com. This spot near the cathedral is a Burgos favourite. It's cheery and light and there's plenty of competition to sit at the wooden tables and enjoy *raciones* of cheeses, *revueltos* or *morcilla*; or stand at the bar and sample the delicious tapas. Recommended.

€ La Cantina del Tenorio, C Arco del Pilar 10, T947 269 781, www.lacantinadeltenorio.es. This delicatessen and bar is a buzzy and cosy retreat from the Burgos wind. A range of delicious fishy bites and small rolls is strangely complemented by baked potatoes, given a Spanish touch with lashings of paprika. Characterful and friendly.

€ Los Herreros, C San Lorenzo 20, T947 202 448, www.mesonlosherreros.es.

This old favourite is an excellent tapas bar with a big range of hot and cold platelets for very little; its popularity with Burgos folk speaks volumes.

€ Mesón La Amarilla, C San Lorenzo 26, T947 205 936. A good sunken bar serving some decent *tapas*, some seeming to use a whole jar of mayonnaise. There's a good cheap restaurant upstairs too, with a €12 *menú del día*.

€ Mesón San Lesmes, C Puebla 37, T947 205 956. This likeable little corner place offers cheerful cheap eats in a gregarious downmarket bar. Simple *raciones* of things like *callos* (tripe), calamari and mixed salad cost €5-10 and are filling and satisfying. Or you could weigh down the checked tablecloth with a monster *chuletón* steak.

€ Taberna Pecaditos, C Sombrerería 3, T947 278 573. The Burgos answer to the credit crunch: this upbeat little bar uses good-quality produce from its deli opposite and offers a range of tasty snacks and drinks, all at €1. Fill in your order using the forms at the bar.

Cafés

Café España, C Laín Calvo 12, T947 205 337. There's a sepia tinge to this venerable old-style café in the heart of Burgos. Warm in winter and with a terrace in summer, it's friendly and specializes in liqueur coffees.

🕐 Bars and clubs

Burgos *p24, map p26*
During the week, nightlife is poor, but it picks up at weekends, when on C Huerta del Rey the bars spill out onto the street.

Fox Tavern, Paseo del Espolón 4, T947 273 311. Impossible to miss, this is a decent pub that doesn't push the Irish theme too far. Comfy seats including a terrace looking up at the cathedral; the food is nothing special.

La Negra Candela, C Huerta del Rey 18, T947 202 844. One of the best options in this busy weekend drinking zone, warm and dark.

Ram Jam Club, C San Juan 29, T607 7 84 339. A popular basement bar with a good vinyl collection, mostly playing British music from the 1970s and 1980s. It's always filled with interesting people. The decor changes regularly; there's live music fairly often here too.

⊕ Entertainment

Burgos *p24, map p26*
Teatro Principal, Paseo del Espolón s/n, T947 288 873, on the riverbank.

⊕ Festivals

Burgos *p24, map p26*
Jan 30 Fiesta de San Lesmes, Burgos' patron saint.
Mar/Apr Semana Santa (Easter week) processions are important in Burgos, with a fairly serious religious character.
End Jun Fiesta de San Pedro, Burgos' main festival of the year.

⊙ Shopping

Burgos *p24, map p26*
Burgos is a fairly upmarket place to shop, focused on the old town streets.

Books
Luz y Vida, C Laín Calvo 38, T947 265 783. A decent bookseller's spread over 2 shops.

Food
La Vieja Castilla, C Paloma 21, T947 207 367. A tiny but excellent shop to buy ham, Burgos *morcilla* (black pudding) and other Castilian produce, with friendly management.

⊖ Transport

Burgos *p24, map p26*
Burgos is a transport hub, with plenty of trains and buses for all parts of the country.

Bus
The bus station is handily close to town, on C Miranda just across the Puente de Santa María. All buses run less often on Sun.

Within the province buses run to **Aranda de Duero** 6-7 a day (1 hr 15 mins), **Miranda** 3 a day, 0645, 1315, 2030, **Santo Domingo de Silos** 1 a day, 1730 Mon-Thu, 1830 Fri, 1400 Sat, none on Sun, **Roa** 1 a day Mon-Fri, 1800 (1 hr 30 mins), **Sasamón** 1 a day, 1830, none on Sun, **Castrojeriz** 2 a day, 1445, 1830, **Oña** 3 a day, 0645, 1300, 1830.

Further afield, there are services to **Madrid** hourly (2 hrs 45 mins), **Bilbao** 9 a day (2 hrs), **León** 4 a day (2hrs), **Santander** 3-5 a day (2 hrs 45 mins), **Logroño** 7 a day (2 hrs), **Valladolid** 5 a day (2 hrs), and **Zaragoza** 4 a day (4 hrs, via **Logroño**).

Trains
The swish new Burgos train station is a long way from the centre in the northeast of town, and is connected by buses to the centre. There are several trains daily to **Madrid** (2½-4½ hrs, €33-43) via **Aranda**, 4 west to **León** via **Palencia** (2 hrs), and services east to **Vitoria**, **Logroño**, **San Sebastián** and **Zaragoza**. You can also buy tickets at a central booking office at C de la Moneda 19.

Burgos Province

While the barren stretches to the east and west of the city of Burgos are relatively dull and relentless, there are some very worthwhile trips to be made to the north and south, where the country is greener and hillier. To the south, the cloister of the monastery of Santo Domingo de Silos is worth a journey in its own right, but there's more to see in that region too. To the north are quiet hidden valleys and one of Northern Spain's most lovable Romanesque churches, the Iglesia de San Pedro de la Tejera.

South of Burgos → *For listings, see pages 40-42.*

Covarrubias

This attractive village south of Burgos gets a few tour coaches but hasn't remotely been spoiled. Its attractive wooden buildings and cobbled squares make a picturesque setting by the side of a babbling brook. An impressive 10th-century **tower** stands over the big town wall on the riverbank; it's a Mozarabic work that's said to be haunted by the ghost of a noble lady who was walled up alive there. Behind it is the **Colegiata** ① *Wed-Mon 1030-1400, 1600-1900; €2 guided tour*, a Gothic affair containing a number of tombs of fat-lipped men and thin-lipped ladies, including that of Fernán González, a count of these lands who united disparate Christian communities into an efficient force to drive the Moors southwards, thereby setting the foundations of Castilla. Opposite the church is a statue of the Norwegian princess Kristina, who married the king's brother and former archbishop of Sevilla here in 1257; her tomb is in the 16th-century cloister. The village has several places to stay and makes a relaxing stop.

Santo Domingo de Silos

① *T947 390 049, www.abadiadesilos.es, Tue-Sat 1000-1300, 1630-1800, Sun 1200-1300, 1600-1800, €3.50, also includes admission to a small museum of musical instruments in the village.*

The **cloister** of the monastery of Santo Domingo de Silos, the equal of any in the peninsula, should not be missed. It was started in the 11th century and the finished result is superb: two levels of double-columned harmony decorated with a fine series of sculptured capitals. It's not known who the artist was, but the expertise is unquestionable. Most of the capitals have vegetable and animal motifs, while at each corner are reliefs with Biblical scenes. Curiously, the central column of the western gallery breaks the pattern, with a flamboyant twist around itself, a humorous touch. The ceiling around the cloister is also memorable; a colourful *mudéjar* work. A cenotaph of Santo Domingo, who was born just south of here, stands on three lions in the northern gallery.

In the 1990s the monks of Santo Domingo de Silos went platinum with a CD of Gregorian chanting.

Another interesting aspect is the old pharmacy, in a couple of rooms off the cloister. It's full of phials and bottles in which the monks used to prepare all manner of remedies;

even more fascinating are some of the amazing old books of pharmacy and science that fill the shelves. Other rooms off the cloister hold temporary exhibitions. Next door, visitors are welcome to attend offices in the **monastery church** ① *Mon-Sat 0600, 0730, 0900, 1345, 1900, 2140; Sun 0600, 0800, 0915, 1100, 1345, 1900, 2140*, where the monks use Gregorian chant. The church itself is bare and uninteresting, but an office is well worth attending, especially in the evening; wrap up well.

Some 3 km away is a small natural chasm, the **Desfiladero de La Yecla**. Follow the road towards Caleruega; a snaking path leads down into the gorge just before a long tunnel. The path follows the tortuous twists of rock with vultures circling above; it's only a five- or 10-minute walk, but it's atmospheric, although the path is in need of repair.

Lerma

Although Lerma was once a reasonably important local town, what we see today is a product of the early 17th century, when the local duke effectively ruled Spain as the favourite of Felipe III. He wasn't above a bit of pork-barrelling, and used his power to inflict a massive building programme on his hometown. Six **monasteries** were built for different orders between 1605 and 1617, but the **Palacio Ducal** tops it all; a massive structure out of all proportion to the size of the town. It bears a passing resemblance to Colditz castle; there's certainly a martial aspect to both it and the parade-ground-style square that fronts it. Inside, however, it's a more sympathetic space, and has recently been converted into a parador. Nearby, the **tourist office** ① *C Audiencia 6, T947 177 002, www.citlerma.com, Tue-Sun 1000-1400, 1600-1900 (2000 in summer)*, itself located in a former monastery, will point out the other monasteries (three of which are still functioning) on the town map for you. Their guided tour (€4, phone to book) is the only way to visit some of Lerma's notable buildings. **San Blas** is the most interesting, with a fine 17th-century *retablo* in the church.

North of Burgos → *For listings, see pages 40-42.*

The land to the north rises into the Cordillera Cantábrica, where the beautiful valleys are excellent, little-visited places to explore. Avoid coming in winter, when temperatures can drop well below zero.

El Gran Cañón del Ebro

From Sotopalacios, the N623 continues through increasingly mountainous terrain, finally descending to the coast and Santander on the other side of the range. The Ebro, near its source here, has carved a picturesque canyon into the rock; it's a lovely cool valley full of trees and vultures. A marked trail, **El Gran Cañón del Ebro**, can be walked, starting from the spa village of **Valdelateja**; the whole trail is a six-hour round trip.

Valdivielso Valley

East of here, accessible via a winding road through the village of **Pesquera de Ebro**, the Valdivielso Valley (which runs northwest to southeast) is a quiet little gem also carved by the Ebro. Green (or white in winter), pretty and reasonably isolated, the valley is perfect for walking, climbing or even canoeing, but it also has several buildings of interest. As an important north-south conduit it was fortified with a series of towers; one of the better examples is at the valley's northern end, in the village of **Valdenoceda**. To get here direct from Burgos, take the CL-629 north from **Sotopalacios** on the main road north to Santander. It's a strange road that crosses a sort of Alpine plateau. A series of large stone waymarkers irregularly dot the route marking the road that Carlos V used on entering Spain to claim the throne.

Near here, above the pretty hamlet of Puente Arenas, is one of the finest Romanesque churches you could hope to see. **Iglesia de San Pedro de la Tejada** ① *Jul-Aug 1130-1400, 1630-1930, Jun and Sep weekends only, T947 303 200 or T636 264 447 to arrange a visit at other times, €1.20*, is a beautiful little structure overlooking the valley. It's in superb condition, built in the 11th and 12th centuries. The façade is fantastic, exquisitely carved with various allegorical scenes, including a lion eating a man. Around the outside are a series of animal heads in relief. The sunken interior features more carvings of animals, musicians and acrobats as well as an impressively painted *mudéjar* gallery, installed in the 15th century. The simple apse is harmonious; it's the beautiful Romanesque proportions as much as the carvings that make this building such a delight.

Oña, a small town at the southeastern end of the Valdivielso Valley, is worth a visit for its monuments. The massive **Monasterio de San Salvador** ① *admission by guided visit only, Tue-Sun 1030, 1130, 1230, 1600, 1700, plus 1815 in summer, €2.50*, is an attractive fortified former monastery that seems bigger than the rest of the town put together. It's now a psychiatric hospital but its quite remarkable church can still be visited.

The royals of the Middle Ages always favoured burial in a monastery; they shrewdly figured that the ongoing monkish prayers for their souls (after a sizeable cash injection, of course) lessened the chance of being blackballed at the Pearly Gates. A number of notable figures are buried here in an attractive pantheon; foremost among them is the Navarran king Sancho the Great, who managed to unite almost the whole of Northern Spain under his rule in the 11th century. The main pantheon is in Gothic style, with *mudéjar* influences, and sits at the back of the church. There are lesser notables buried in the harmonious cloister, a work of Simon of Cologne.

There's a small **tourist office** ① *Easter-Oct Tue-Fri 1030-1330, 1600-1900, Sat and Sun 1030-1400, 1600-1900; Nov-Easter Tue-Sun 1000-1400, 1600-1800, Sat and Sun 1000-1400, 1530-1800*, in the square outside the church.

There's a traditional little *botería*, one of the few left of a formerly widespread craft, on the main road through town. Have a look even if you don't want to buy one; the process hasn't changed much over the years. *Botas*, goatskin winebags, once essential for every farmer and shepherd who couldn't return to their village at lunchtime, are still used to drink from at fiestas and bullfights. Drinking from them is something of an art; it's easy to spray yourself with a jet of cheap red that was meant for the mouth.

Medina de Pomar

Northeast of Valdivielso, the town of Medina de Pomar was the stamping ground of the Velascos, a powerful Castilian family. Their legacy includes a sturdy castle and the 14th-century **Monastery of Santa Clara**, which they basically founded to be buried in; it features an attractive *retablo* by Diego de Siloé and a small museum. It's a more popular holiday base than the Valdivielso and as a result there are more facilities for tourism.

East of Burgos → *For listings, see pages 40-42.*

The N120 crosses wooded hills on its way to Logroño, while the N1 makes its way to Miranda de Ebro and the Basque hills. This is one of the most unpleasant roads in Spain, a conga-line of trucks enlivened by the suicidal overtaking manoeuvres of impatient drivers. It's worth paying the motorway toll to avoid it.

Some 4 km north of the N120, peaceful **San Juan de Ortega** is the last stop before Burgos for many pilgrims on the way to Santiago. In the green foothills, it's nothing more than a church and *albergue*, and has been a fixture of the Camino ever since Juan, inspired by the good works of Santo Domingo de la Calzada in the Rioja, decided to do the same and dedicate his life to easing the pilgrims' journey. He started the church in the 12th century; the Romanesque apse survives, although the rest is in later style. It's a likeable if unremarkable place. San Juan is buried here in an ornate Gothic tomb. Pilgrims stay at the hospital that he founded.

Further along towards La Rioja, **Villafranca Montes de Oca** is an unremarkable pilgrim stop with a small *ermita* in a green valley. North again from here, just off the N1, is an unlikely picnic spot. The hamlet of **Alcocero de Mola**, 2 km from the main road on the BU703, bears the name of the general who masterminded the Nationalist rising. He was killed before the end of the Civil War in a plane crash, probably to Franco's relief. Some 3 km up a neglected side road from Alcocero is a massive concrete monument to him, on the wooded hilltop where the plane hit, with good views across the plains. All of 20 m high and completely forgotten, it's in characteristically pompous Fascist style; an intriguing reminder of a not too distant past. The concrete's in decline now, and weeds carpet the monumental staircase; take a torch if you want to climb the stairs inside.

Further east, **Briviesca** is a sizeable service town, which seems to have beaten the decline that afflicts so many towns of Castilla. The tree-lined plaza is pleasant and shady; on it stands the nicest of the three big churches, with a damaged Renaissance façade. The **tourist office** is on the square too. The town is famous for its almond biscuits but beyond its churches, there's little to see here.

Beyond here, the main road passes through a dramatic craggy pass at **Pancorbo**, which would be a nice hiking base were it not for the trucks thundering through. This is geographically where Castilla ends; the *meseta* more or less gives way here to the Basque foothills. From here, too, it's a short drive across country to Haro, heart of the Rioja Alta wine region.

Castilla officially ends at **Miranda de Ebro**, a hardbitten town which, while attractive in parts, is mostly dusty and vaguely depressing; and is full of big boulevards where nothing much happens. The main reason to come here is to change bus or train; by all means take a stroll down the pretty riverside, but don't miss your connection.

Southwest from Burgos: the Pilgrim Route → *For listings, see pages 40-42.*

Castrojeriz

West of Burgos, the principal branch of the Camino de Santiago tracks southwest to the town of Castrojeriz, a somewhat bleak place that's unlikely, despite its attractive paved main street, to cheer the heart after a long trudge across treeless Castilian terrain. It was formerly a Celtic settlement, and the *castro* hilltop structure has been preserved. There are three churches, linked by Calle Real. The **Church of San Juan** is the village's main attraction; it's a clean, if over-restored Gothic building influenced by the Burgos German tradition and features a nice double-columned cloister. As well as the bare ruin of a castle on the hill, there are a couple of other impressive buildings in the town, most notably the **Casa de Gutiérrez Barona**, a large knightly residence. This predates Castrojeriz's only moment in the spotlight. During the *comunero* revolt this town was deemed unlikely enough to rebel that the Council of Castilla took up residence here, and the place briefly buzzed with noblemen.

Sasamón

A more interesting, if longer route would take the pilgrim through Sasamón, 2-3 km north of the main Burgos–León road. The **Iglesia de Santa María la Real** ① *daily 1100-1400, 1600-1900 (ask in the bar opposite if shut), €1.25 includes a helpful explanation by the knowledgeable and justly proud caretaker*, is its very lovely church in light honey-coloured stone. It was originally a massive five-naved space, but was partitioned after a fire destroyed half of it in the 19th century. The exterior highlight is an excellent 13th-century Gothic portal featuring Christ and the Apostles, while the museum has some well-displayed Roman finds as well as a couple of top-notch pieces; a couple of Flemish tapestries featuring the life of Alexander the Great, and a Diego de Siloe polychrome of San Miguel, the pretty-boy bully. It's fairly plain, a reflection of the Inquisition passing into irrelevance. In the church itself, two works of the German school stand out; the ornate pulpit, from around 1500, and a large baptismal font. A 16th-century Plateresque *retablo* of Santiago is one of many that adorn the building, so monumental for such a small town.

A statue of **Octavian** stands in a square nearby. The town of Segisama was used as a base in 26 BC for his campaigns against the Cantabrians and Asturians. The inscription reads *Ipse venit Segisamam, castro posuit* (then he came to Segisama and set up camp).

Don't leave town without checking out the **Ermita de San Isidro**, dominated by a massive 6-m carved crucifix that once would have stood at a crossroads to comfort weary travelling souls. Under Christ is the Tree of Knowledge, Adam, Eve, Cain and Abel. It dates from the 16th century and is a lovely work. Atop it is a nesting pelican; it was formerly believed that a pelican short of fish to feed the kids would wound itself in the breast to let them feed on its own blood. This became a metaphor for Christ's sacrifice, and pelicans are a common motif in Castilian religious sculpture.

Burgos Province listings

For hotel and restaurant price codes and other relevant information, see pages 11-17.

🛏 Where to stay

Covarrubias *p36*
€€ Hotel Doña Sancha, Av Barbadillo 31, T947 406 400, www.hoteldonasancha.com. On the road to Hortiguela, but close to the centre, this charming rural hotel is just about the best place to stay in town. Offering a genuine Castilian welcome and great home-style breakfasts (extra), it makes a good base for exploring the region. Recommended.
€€ Hotel Nuevo Arlanza, Plaza Mayor 11, T947 400 511, www.hotelnuevoarlanza.com. This is a good option set in a stately old house. The rooms are beautiful, particularly those on the top floor with sloping attic roof. There's an atmospheric restaurant too which has riotous medieval dinners

on Sat nights in spring and autumn. Prices include breakfast and are at the bottom end of this category.
€€ La Posada del Conde, C Fernán González 8, T609 406 698, www.laposadadel conde.es. This is a very cosy *casa rural* with original and comfortable decor backed up by welcoming owners. Breakfast is included.
€ Pensión Galin, Plaza Doña Urraca 4, T947 406 552, www.casagalin.com. This *pensión* above a bar has plenty of charm. The best of the renovated en suite rooms look over the square. A bargain.

Santo Domingo de Silos *p36*
€€ Hotel Santo Domingo de Silos, C Santo Domingo 10, T947 390 053, www.hotelsantodomingodesilos.com. Set in 2 adjacent buildings on the main road, this offers excellent quality for the price. There's a variety of rooms available, but all have

plenty of space, and comfortable furnishings. The newer ones have excellent bathrooms. The hotel restaurant does an excellent *cochinillo* (suckling pig). Recommended.

€€ Tres Coronas de Silos, Plaza Mayor 6, T947 390 047, www.hoteltrescoronasde silos.com. Attractive and comfortable, set in a solid stone mansion just across from the monastery. The rooms are rustic and charming. They run an annexe on the same square, with slightly cheaper rooms.

€ Arco de San Juan, Pradera de San Juan 1, T947 390 074, arcosanjuan@wanadoo.es. This is a hotel and restaurant peacefully set by a stream just past the monastery. The rooms are quiet and clean, and there are some nice terraces to relax on.

Lerma *p37*
€€€ Parador de Lerma, Plaza Mayor 1, T947 177 110, www.parador.es. Set in the massive ducal palace, this recently inaugurated parador has a sumptuous interior and makes a fine place to stay. Built around a high-arched covered patio, it oozes class, and the cool tiled-floor rooms have excellent facilities and bathrooms; many have great views.

€€ El Zaguán, C Barquillo 6, T947 172 165, www.elzaguanlerma.com. This makes another very comfortable base. It's a 17th-century *casa rural* with attractive stone walls and interesting furniture. The rooms are great and equipped to hotel standard; a couple have lovely wooden sloping ceilings.

El Gran Cañón del Ebro *p37*
€€ Casa de Lolo y Vicent, C Callejón 18, T947 150 267, www.casadeloloyvicent.es. Colourful, and with a wonderful welcome, this *casa rural* is in the village of Escalada further up the road. It's set in a sensitively restored 15th-century house, and offers a good welcome and pretty views.

Valdivielso Valley *p37*
€ Camino Condal, Plaza Padre Cereceda 6, Oña, T615 144 167, www.caminocondal. com. Excellent value is to be had at this great *casa rural* in the pretty heart of Oña. Rooms are compact, but most cosy, with individual colour schemes making for a soothing sleep. Recommended.

€ Hostal Once Brutos, C del Pan 6, Oña, T947-300 010, www.hostaloncebrutos. com. A simple but clean place just off the square that also provides simple meals. Some rooms have a lot more natural light than others.

Castrojeriz *p39*
€€ Hotel Cachava, C Real 93, T947 378 547, www.lacachava.com. On the paved main street that winds through town, this is a welcoming choice for pilgrims to put their deserving feet up for a night. Rooms are simply decorated and comfortable, and meals and bikes are available for guests. There's a patio/garden to relax in on sunny days.

€€ La Posada, C Landelino Tardajos 5, T947 378 610, www.laposadadecastrojeriz.es. A *casa rural* with some charm, set in a historic old mansion built around a pleasing interior patio. There's also a very good restaurant.

Sasamón *p40*
There are various *casas rurales* for complete let; check www.toprural.com for details.
€ Casa Gloria, C Arco 1, T947 370 059. The village's main accommodation option, this is right opposite the church. It's cordial, clean and well presented; the simple rooms have spick and span white-sheeted beds and small bathrooms. They're heated, the owner will lend you a bike, and you can eat downstairs.

❷ Restaurants

Lerma *p37*
€€ Casa Antón, C Luis Cervera 5, T947 170 362. Something of a local classic, this homely place specializes in the local lamb. Truth is, they serve almost nothing else – you'll get a lettuce salad and some local wine to accompany it. It's excellent. Leave room for the scrumptious home-made desserts though. Recommended.

Castrojeriz *p39*

€ La Taberna, C General Mola 43, T947 377 120. One of a handful of cheap restaurants catering to locals and pilgrims. It's decent and also has internet access and simple rooms.

⊖ Transport

Covarrubias *p36*
Bus There are 3 buses a day to Covarrubias from **Burgos** (none on Sun).

Santo Domingo de Silos *p36*
Bus There is a daily bus Mon-Thu and Sat from **Burgos** in the afternoon (2 hrs), returning in the morning.

Lerma *p37*
Bus There are several daily buses and the odd train that make their way to Lerma from **Burgos** and to a lesser extent **Madrid**.

Valdivielso Valley *p37*
Bus There are daily buses from **Burgos** to Oña via Briviesca.

East of Burgos *p38*
Bus and train Briviesca is visited by 7 daily buses from **Burgos** and also several trains.

Miranda de Ebro is well connected to major cities in Northern Spain, particularly **Bilbao**, **Vitoria**, **Burgos**, **Logroño** and **Madrid**. It's a major transport hub between the Basque regions and the rest of the nation.

Castrojeriz *p39*
Bus Buses run from from **Burgos** to Castrojeriz twice a day (none on Sun).

Sasamón *p40*
Bus There are 2 buses a day to Sasamón from **Burgos** (none on Sun).

Palencia

Though it's not that small, never a sentence seems to be written about Palencia without the word 'little'. And it's understandable; on some approaches to the provincial capital, it seems that you're in the centre of town before even noticing there was a town. It is a quiet and friendly place, bypassed by pilgrims, tourists and public awareness of its presence. This is partly an accident of geography – the town is situated in the middle of a triangle of the more important places of Valladolid, Burgos and León – but also one of history.

Palencia sits on the Carrión, so murky and green it surely merits mangroves and crocodiles. The old town stretches along its eastern bank in elongated fashion. It is studded with churches, headed up by the superb cathedral. Ernest Hemingway summed up Palencia as a "nice Castilian town with good beer".

Arriving in Palencia → *Phone code: 979. Population: 82,651. Altitude: 740 m.*
Getting there and around The train and bus stations are just beyond the northern end of Calle Mayor, a pedestrian street stretching the length of the old town. The main sights are all within easy walking distance of each other, concentrated in the old town. ➤ *See Transport, page 51.*

Tourist information The regional **tourist office** ⓘ *C Mayor 105, T979 740 068, oficinadeturismodepalencia@jcyl.es, mid-Sep to Jun Mon-Sat 0930-1400, 1600-1900, Sun 0930-1700, summer daily 0900-2000,* is at the southern end of Calle Mayor and has a wide range of information on the city, the province and the rest of Castilla y León. The **provincial office** ⓘ *C Mayor 31, T979 706 523, www.palenciaturismo.es, Mon-Fri 0900-1400, 1700-2000, Sat 1030-1400, 1700-2000, Sun 1030-1430,* is more centrally located and also helpful. It opens shorter hours in winter.

Background
Palencia has a proud past. The region was inhabited in prehistoric times, then the local villages resisted the Romans for nearly a century before Pompey swept them aside in 72 BC and set up camp here. Pliny the Elder cited Palencia as one of the important Roman settlements of the 1st century AD. It wasn't until the 12th century that the city reached its zenith, however; *fueros* (legal privileges) were granted by Alfonso VIII, and Spain's first university was established. In 1378 the city became legendary for resisting a siege by the Duke of Lancaster, fighting for Pedro I. The defences were mounted by the Palentine women, as the men were off fighting at another battleground. But things turned sour in the *comunero* revolt, a Castilian revolution against the 'foreign' regime of Carlos V, which

became an anti-aristocratic movement in general. The *comuneros* were heavily defeated in 1521 and Palencia suffered thereafter, as Castilian towns were stripped of some of their privileges and influence.

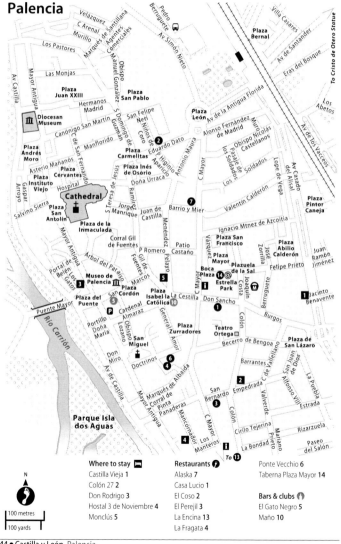

Palencia

Where to stay 🛏
Castilla Vieja **1**
Colón 27 **2**
Don Rodrigo **3**
Hostal 3 de Noviembre **4**
Monclús **5**

Restaurants 🍴
Alaska **7**
Casa Lucio **1**
El Coso **2**
El Perejil **3**
La Encina **13**
La Fragata **4**

Ponte Vecchio **6**
Taberna Plaza Mayor **14**

Bars & clubs 🍸
El Gato Negro **5**
Maño **10**

Places in Palencia → *For listings, see pages 49-51.*

Palencia's scenic highlight is its superb **cathedral** ① *T979 701 347, Mon-Fri 1000-1330, 1630-1930, Sat 1000-1400, 1600-1930, Sun 1600-2000, closes half an hour earlier in winter; €2,* known as 'La Bella Desconocida' (the unknown beauty). Built in the 14th century on Visigothic and Romanesque foundations, it's a massive structure, although it hardly dominates the town, tucked away somewhat on a quiet square. The magnificent main portal depicts the Virgin flanked by apostles. Inside, the massive *retablo* paints the story of Christ's life; it's a work of the Flemish master Jan of Flanders, who also painted an attractive triptych on one side of the choir. The city's patron, the Virgen de la Calle, sits on a silver coffer in the ambulatory, while there's an amusing sculpture of lions eating a martyr at the back end of the *coro*. The Visigothic/Romanesque crypt is also worth a look. There's a painting by El Greco just off the cloister, but this is only accessible on a guided tour (€3, regular departures) of the whole building. Similarly annoying is the lighting system; to properly see the impressive works of art around the building will cost you a small fortune in euro coins.

A couple of blocks away is the **Diocesan museum** ① *mid-Sep to Jun open by tour only Mon-Sat 1030 and 1130, Jul to mid-Sep Mon 1030-1330, Tue-Sun 1030-1330, 1630-1930, €4,* set around a cloister, with a collection of paintings and *retablos* from around the province.

Further south, the Romanesque **Iglesia de San Miguel** ① *daily 0930-1330, 1830-1930, free,* is a knobbly affair with a hollow tower. It's fairly unadorned inside, with elegant vaulting. There's a small gilt *retablo* of the saint, and some fragmentary wall paintings. El Cid is reputed to have been married in a previous church on this site.

Nearby, the **Museo de Palencia** ① *T979 752 328, Tue-Sat 1000-1400, 1600-1900 (Jul-Sep 1700-2000), Sun 1000-1400, €1.20, free at weekends,* is housed in an attractive building on Plaza del Cordón, named for the sculpted cord that is tied around the doorway. It's a good display with plenty of artefacts from the province's Roman and pre-Roman past. The museum is situated in what was once Palencia's Jewish quarter.

Palencia's **Plaza Mayor** sits secluded just to the east of the long Calle Mayor. It's a lovely space with trees, *soportales,* and a monument to Renaissance sculptor Alonso Berruguete.

Just out of town, the looming Lego-like **Cristo de Otero** claims to be the second tallest statue of Jesus in the world (after Cochabamba, Bolivia). There are good views from the 850-m elevation. The sculptor, Victorio Macho's, last wish was to be buried at the statue's feet; his body is in the small chapel. There's a little exhibition here too.

Around Palencia → *For listings, see pages 49-51.*

Basílica de San Juan de Baños
① *T979 770 338, winter Tue-Sun 1100-1400, 1600-1800; summer Tue-Sun 1030-1400, 1650-2000, €2.*
South of Palencia and around 2 km east of Venta de Baños, a mainline train hub with frequent connections to Palencia and Valladolid, is a church that's well worth visiting, the Basílica de San Juan de Baños. At least some of the pretty little building is awesomely old; an inscription above the altar states that it was founded by the Visigothic King Recesvinth in AD 661. To be sure, it's been altered substantially over the years, but it still preserves much of its original character, principally in the central aisle. Its architectural value is high, as clear links are evident with late Roman building traditions, but apart from all that, it's an enchanting simple structure, a relic from a time when Christianity was young.

Ampudia

For a good off-the-beaten track Castilian experience, head west from Palencia five leagues to the town of Ampudia, unexpectedly dominated by an imposing **castle** ① *www. castillodeampudia.com, guided visits Apr-Sep Sat 1200, 1300, 1800 and 1900, Sun 1200 and 1300 plus 1800 and 1900 Jul-Aug; rest of year Sat only 1200, 1300; €3.50; if there are a few of you, or you are especially keen, T699 484 555 to arrange a visit at other times.* It's in top nick, bristling with castellation, but visits are limited, as it's still lived in. There's an ornate collection here too, with various rooms exhibiting a traditional pharmacy, dolls and toys, guns, and religious art among other things.

The **Colegiata de San Miguel Arcángel** ① *Jul-Sep daily 1030-1330, 1700-2000, Apr-Oct Fri-Sun 1100-1330, 1700-2000, Nov-Mar Sat-Sun 1030-1330, 1700-2000, free*, is a floorboarded Gothic and Renaissance affair, light and breezy and with a spiky tower that looks ready to blast off to join the archangel himself. Its known as the *Novia de los Campos* (Bride of the Plains; this area of the province is known as *Los Campos*). The main altarpiece is a Renaissance work; more interesting perhaps is the Gothic side chapel of San Ildefonso, containing the tombs of the men who paid for the building, and also a pretty Plateresque *retablo*.

Next to the Colegiata is the **Museo del Arte Sacro** ① *May-Sep Tue-Sun 1000-1330, 1600-1900, Oct-Apr 1100-1330, 1630-1830, closed early Jan-early Mar, €2*, quite a good museum of religious art. The town itself is very pretty, with wooden *soportales* raising the houses over the footpaths. It has a few appealing eating and sleeping options.

Medina de Rioseco

A little further west, and once quite an important wool and wheat merchants' town in the province of Valladolid, Medina de Rioseco still retains some historic atmosphere, and has benefitted from an excellent program of restoration and promotion of tourism. It now has plenty to offer and is well worth a look, especially on a Wednesday morning, when there's an entertaining livestock market. It lies on the main road between Valladolid and León, so makes a good stop if going between those cities too.

The most endearing aspect of the town is the pedestrian street Calle Lázaro Alonso, colonnaded in warped old wood. Following this from the main road, you'll come to one of Medina's churches, the **Iglesia de Santa Cruz**. More than a bit mausoleum-like from the outside, it houses the **Museo de Semana Santa** ① *Tue-Sun 1100-1400, 1600-1900 (1700-2000 in summer), weekends only Jan-Feb, €3*, devoted to Holy Week celebrations in different towns and villages of Castilla y León.

More beautiful is the church of **Santa María** ① *Tue-Sun 1100-1400, 1600-1900 (1700-2000 in summer), €2*, built from attractive white-ish limestone in the 15th and 16th centuries. Gothic in style, it's topped by a flamboyant baroque spire. Inside it's fairly ornate, with showy star vaulting and a big gilt *retablo*. Flashest of all is the intricately decorated funerary chapel of the Benavente family. The pretty little coloured organ provides a homelier touch. There's a small museum inside; the attendant has the keys to the **Iglesia de Santiago**, a squareish structure further down the hill. It also costs €2, but a combined ticket for all the town's attractions can be had for €7.

The recently completed **Museo de San Francisco** ① *C San Francisco 1, T983 700 020, www.museosanfrancisco.es, Tue-Sun 1100-1400, 1600-1900 (1700-2000 summer), €3*, is an innovative display of local history and religious art in a noble Franciscan monastery. Visits are by guided tour only – tours last about 45 minutes and leave on the hour.

On the edge of town, by the Canal de Castilla (see page 52), stands a huge **flour mill** ① *T983 701 923, summer daily 1100-1400, 1600-1900, winter weekends only, €2.50,* which holds an exhibition on the mill itself and also on the canal. From here, there are also one-hour boat trips (€5) running Tuesday to Sunday on the canal itself. From Thursday to Sunday, there are longer trips of 2½ and 3½ hours up to the seventh and sixth locks of this impressive waterway. Phone or check the town website (below) for times.

Tourist information is available at the town's **tourist office** ① *C San Francisco 1, T983 720 319, www.medinaderioseco.com, Tue-Fri 1000-1330, 1600-1800, Sat 1100-1300, 1600-1800, Sun 1100-1300*, in the Museo de San Francisco.

Camino de Santiago

Frómista

In northern Palencia, Frómista, as well as lying on the Camino de Santiago, is a compulsory stop on the Romanesque circuit. The reason is the **Iglesia de San Martín** ① *winter 1000-1400, 1530-1830, summer 0930-1400, 1630-2000, €1.50, €2 with San Pedro*, a remarkable 11th-century Romanesque church, one of the purest and earliest, derived almost wholly from the French model that permeated the peninsula via the Pilgrim Route. From the outside it's beautiful, an elegant gem standing slightly self-satisfied in the sunlight. The church managed to survive the Gothic and baroque eras without being meddled with, but a late 19th-century restoration brought mixed benefits. While the building owes its good condition to this, it also has lost some of the weathered charm that makes the Romanesque dear. That said, the purity of its lines make it well worth a visit. Inside, it's the capitals of the pillars that attract the attention. While some were sculpted during the restoration (they are marked with an R, with creditable honesty), the others are excellent examples of Romanesque sculpture. There are no Biblical scenes – many of the motifs are vegetal, and some are curious juxtapositions of people and animals, particularly lions and birds. The church is crowned by an octagonal tower as well as two distinctive turrets.

Nearby, **San Pedro** is an attractive Gothic building with a small museum. There's a small **tourist information centre** on the main crossroads in town.

Astudillo

Just off the Camino, southeast of Frómista, the town of Astudillo is a beautiful, out-of-the-way little place. All that remains of its medieval walls is the **Puerta de San Martín**, a striking gateway. The central square is an attractive tree-lined affair, and there are several noble *palacios* and mansions. On the small hill above town is a castle; the hill itself is honeycombed with old wine bodegas.

Villalcázar de Sirga

The Camino continues through an awesomely empty landscape before arriving at the village of Villalcázar de Sirga, which is built around a memorable church, **Santa María la Blanca** ① *May to mid-Oct daily 1030-1400, 1700-1930, mid-Oct to Apr Sat 1200-1345, 1630-1800, Sun 1200-1345, €1, pilgrims €0.20*. It's a majestic sight, a massive Gothic affair quite out of proportion to everything else around it. The exterior highlights include a carved rose window and a portal topped by a frieze depicting the Pantocrator with evangelists and apostles, and, below, Mary in the Annunciation and the Adoration. Inside, particularly noteworthy are the painted tombs of the Infante don Felipe, prince and brother of King Alfonso X, and his wife. Both date from the late 13th century.

Carrión de los Condes

Carrión de los Condes provides some relief after the hard slog across the Castilian plain, with a greener feel around the Carrión, the river on which the town lies. A couple of shabby churches can be found north of the main road, but the nicest part of town is around the plaza to the south of it. The **Iglesia de Santiago** is the town's showpiece, with an excellent late 12th-century façade, an unusual affair with zigzag columns and an actor doing a backflip among the figures on the archivolt. The Christ in Majesty has been described as the most impressive in Spain. There's also a small **museum** ① *Jun-Sep 1100-1400, 1700-2000, Oct-May Sat and Sun only, €1,* inside. Another church, **Santa María**, is a clean-lined affair with a large porch and some chessboard patterning. It's relatively unadorned inside apart from a massive gilt *retablo*. A statue of St Michael is camp even by his lofty standards; the archangel looks as if he's just stepped off the set of *Starlight Express*. On Thursday mornings, a market stretches between the two churches. There's a nice park by the river too. Just west of town, the monastery of **San Zoilo** has been converted into a beautiful hotel (see Where to stay, page 50).

La Olmeda and Quintanilla

Near Carrión are two of the little-known highlights of Palencia province, the Roman villas of La Olmeda and Quintanilla. **La Olmeda** ① *T979 119 997, www.villaromanalaolmeda.com, Tue-Sun 1030-1830, €5,* 18 km north of Carrión, near the town of Saldaña and just outside Pedrosa de la Vega, is the more impressive. Dating from the late first century AD, it was a sizeable building with defensive turrets, many rooms, and an attached bathhouse. Around the large central courtyard, rooms are decorated with geometrical and vegetal mosaic flooring, but in a larger room is a superb mosaic with Achilles and Ulysses as well as a hunting scene, with all manner of beasts in a flurry of complex activity. There are regular free guided tours (with English audio available), and multilingual information panels. There's also a café here.

A couple of kilometres away, **Saldaña** itself, an attractive if hard-bitten *meseta* town, has some of the finds from the two villas assembled in a **museum** set in an old church. There are some excellent pieces, particularly those found at a funerary complex by the Olmeda villa. Your entry ticket for Olmeda is valid here. Buses run to Saldaña via the turnoff for La Olmeda from Carrión de los Condes, and also head here from Palencia, Burgos and León.

Quintanilla, just off the N120 west of Carrión, has a large **villa** ① *Apr-Sep Tue-Sun 1000-1400, 1700-2000; Oct and Mar 1030-1330, 1600-1800; closed Nov-Feb; €3,* featuring some excellent mosaics as well as a hypocaust underfloor heating system for the cold Castilian winters. The entry fee is €6 if you're going to visit both villas.

Palencia listings

For hotel and restaurant price codes and other relevant information, see pages 11-17.

🔵 Where to stay

Palencia *p43, map p44*

Accommodation is very reasonably priced.

€€ Castilla Vieja, Av Casado del Alisal 26, T979 749 044, www.hotelcastillavieja.com. This hotel on the edge of the old town isn't interesting, but is modern, well equipped and fairly priced. The rooms are spacious, with polished wooden floorboards and decent bathrooms. The mini-suites, which have extra space and a lounge area, are only €20 more than the standard double. Parking available. There are usually cheaper rates available on the hotel website.

€€ Hotel Colón 27, C Colón 27, T979 740 700, www.hotelcolon27.com. Pleasant and welcoming with spacious rooms in the heart of town. Good value for the price (which is at the bottom end of this category), although there's some morning noise from the school opposite.

€€ Hotel Don Rodrigo, C Los Gatos 1, T979 700 937, www.hoteldonrodrigo.com. Quiet and light, this place offers solid value in the old town near the river. Rooms are unadorned but crisp and clean, and there's parking available. Bottom of this price category.

€€ Hotel Monclús, C Menéndez Pelayo 3, T979 744 300, www.hotelmonclus.com. This brick, slightly stuffy hotel is in the middle of town. The rooms are comfortable but sombre brown. It's quiet and central, with parking.

€ Hostal 3 de Noviembre, C Mancornador 18, T979 703 042. With surely the smallest lobby of any Spanish hotel, this is a good choice. Doubles are all exterior and comfortable, although the singles are cramped (though cheap). Parking available. Reception open 1900-2330 only; phone ahead at other times.

Ampudia *p46*

€€€ Casa del Abad de Ampudia, Plaza Gromaz 12, T979 768 008, www.casadelabad.com. An excellent accommodation and eating option is this beautiful and originally renovated 16th-century abbot's house in the main square. A riot of colour and subtle beauty, every room is different and comfortable, with price grades reflecting size and amenities. There's even a gym and sauna. The meals are delicious – the restaurant is of the highest class – and the wines are superb. Recommended.

€ Atienza, C Duque de Alba 3, T979 768 076, www.casaruralatienza.com. Another welcoming choice, this is a *casa rural* in an old workers' cottage with a restored wine bodega. The rooms are charming, meals are served and there's a peaceful garden.

Medina de Rioseco *p46*

€€ Hotel Vittoria Colonna, C San Juan 2, T983 725 087, www.hotelvittoriacolonna.es. A welcome addition to the Medina scene, this new hotel is on the main road in the centre of town and has plenty of comfortable rooms with parquet floors and welcoming beds. Bathrooms are decked out in modish grey and facilities, which include a restaurant, are excellent.

€ La Muralla, Plaza Santo Domingo 4, T983 700 577. Just at the bottom of C Lázaro Alonso, this is clean, airy and remarkably good value. Rooms without bathroom cost less.

Frómista *p47*

€€ Hotel Doña Mayor, C Francesas 8, T979 810 588, www.hoteldonamayor.com. This is in the heart of the village and features smallish, attractive, quirkily designed rooms with small balconies. It's a relaxed place with pleasant staff; the only real downside is the elevated price for this quality and that the restaurant isn't up to much.

€ Hostal San Telmo, C Martin Veña 8, T979 811 028, www.turismofromista.com. A great place to stay; a large, light and tranquil *casa rural* with large garden/courtyard and charming but cheap rooms.

Villalcázar de Sirga *p47*
€ **Hostal Las Cántigas**, C Condes de Toreno 1, T979 880 015, www.hostallascantigas.es. This excellent modern *hostal* is right by the church of Santa María la Blanca in this tiny and tranquil village. It makes a great rural base and is well priced. Rooms have bathroom, heating and there's a bar and restaurant.

Carrión de los Condes *p48*
€€ **Real Monasterio San Zoilo**, T979 880 050, www.sanzoilo.com. The best of several options. A characterful setting in an old monastery with a peaceful grassed garden. There's also a good restaurant with atmospheric beamed ceiling, offering quality local produce at fair prices.
€ **Hospedería Albe**, C Collantes 21, T979 880 913, www.hostalalbe.es. Hospitable, pleasant and cool, with charming rustic decoration. A couple of rooms have their own kitchenette and cost a few euros more. Prices are very fair.

Restaurants

Palencia *p43, map p44*
Palencia's not exactly a gourmet paradise and restaurants are a little thin on the ground here.
€€€ **La Encina**, C Casañe 2, T979 710 936, www.asadorlaencina.com. This Castilian *asador* is considered the city's best and most reliable restaurant. It's famous for its roast meats, but also for its *tortilla*, which has thrice been voted the best in the nation. They recite the dishes without prices, so the bill can come as a shock at the end, but the lamb is excellent.
€€ **Casa Lucio**, C Don Sancho 2, T979 748 190, www.restaurantecasalucio.com. A bright, traditional and warmly lit bar and restaurant dealing in standard Castilian fare with a spring in its step. There's excellent service, and a reliable selection of classics

like *rabo de toro* (bull's tail stew). Good value. Recommended.
€€ **El Perejil**, C San Bernardo 2, T979 745 775. Just off the main pedestrian drag, this is a rewarding place to stop for lunch or a glass of wine. The tapas under the glass counter in the small bar are eye-catching and tasty; the *comedor* serves an excellent lunch menu with plenty of choice.
€€ **La Fragata**, C Pedro Fernández de Pulgar 8, T979 750 129. There are 2 options on offer at this corner spot; well-prepared fish and seafood in the restaurant, or cheap, simple and effective *raciones* and *platos combinados* in the bar. Tue is hearty *cocido* day, and there's a daily lunchtime menu that's good value too.
€€ **Ponte Vecchio**, C Doctrinos 1, T979 745 215, www.pontevecchiopalencia.com. Closed Mon. Atmospheric and spacious Italian restaurant located opposite the church of San Miguel in a lovely stone building. The food is upmarket and excellent.
€€ **Taberna Plaza Mayor**, Plaza Mayor 1, T979 740 410. A warm wooden tavern right on the main square, with tiled bar and walls. Hang out in the bar and enjoy *raciones* of calamari and the like, or head upstairs to the restaurant, which looks down to the bar through a hole in the floor. There's a terrace outside in summer.
€ **El Coso**, C Eduardo Dato 8, T979 746 758. A characterful and yellow-tiled café that does a range of cheap meal options. It's very convivial and fills up in the evenings.

Cafés
Alaska, C Mayor 26, T979 742 835. A compact, historic café/bar bedecked with massive paintings, a popular terrace, and a toilet accessed by a tight spiral staircase. They also do good tapas and have free Wi-Fi.

Medina de Rioseco *p46*
€€ **Mesón la Rúa**, C San Juan 25, T983 700 519. A reliable choice for traditional Castilian food. The menu bristles with local

specialites such as *pichón* (squab) and hearty stews. The *menú del día* is great value at €10 and other prices are extremely fair. Recommended.

Villalcázar de Sirga *p47*
€€ El Mesón de Villasirga, Plaza Mayor s/n, T979 888 022, www.mesonde villasirga.com. Great Castilian cooking at this hearty local.

Carrión de los Condes *p48*
€€ Bodegón El Resbalón, C Fernán Gómez 17, T979 880 799. This dark and inviting spot is in an attractively refurbished traditional building. Stone and wood give a typical bodega feel, and the typical local cuisine matches it. The €10 *menú* is worth waiting for.

🍷 Bars and clubs

Palencia *p43, map p44*
Bar Maño, C La Cestilla 5, T979 740 210. A trendy modern bar that by day is also a restaurant, serving a bright contemporary *menú del día* and tasty tapas.
El Gato Negro, C San Marcos s/n, T979 743 343. Though it serves tasty free tapas by day, the 'black cat' comes into its own at night, when it becomes one of the city's most lively and atmospheric pubs for an after-dinner *copa*.

🎉 Festivals

Palencia *p43, map p44*
1st week of Sep Palencia has lots of fiestas, but the main one is **San Antolín**, with markets, stalls, bullfights, fireworks and concerts.

Ampudia *p46*
1st weekend of Sep Ampudia's fiesta includes bullfights.

🚌 Transport

Palencia *p43, map p44*
Bus For information, T979 743 222. Hourly buses to **Valladolid**, 4 a day to **Burgos** (1 hr 15 mins) and **Madrid** (5 daily, 3 hrs 15 mins). 4 a day to **Aguilar de Campoo** via **Frómista** and Osorno, hourly buses to **Dueñas** via **Venta del Baños**, 2 to **Ampudia**, 2 to **Cervera**, 2 to **Astudillo** and 3 to **Saldaña**.

Train Palencia is on the main line. Lots of trains go to **Frómista** (4 daily, 25 mins), **Aguilar de Campoo** (4 daily, 1 hr), **Madrid** (1¾-2¼ hrs, up to 12 daily), **Valladolid** (at least hourly, 30 mins), **León** (12 daily, 1 hr 10 mins), and other regional destinations.

Ampudia *p46*
Bus There are 2 buses daily to and from Palencia to **Ampudia**, and 1 to **Valladolid**.

Medina de Rioseco *p46*
Bus ALSA buses run here from **Valladolid** (20 a day) and **León** (8 a day). There are also services to **Madrid** and one to **Sahagún**.

Frómista *p47*
Bus and train There are regular services to **Palencia**.

Astudillo *p47*
Bus 2 daily buses to and from **Palencia**.

Carrión de los Condes *p48*
Bus Regular buses to **Palencia**.

North towards Santander

The northern part of Palencia province is an incredible haven of Romanesque architecture; every little village seems to have a round-arched gem tucked away. Fans of the style could spend many happy days exploring the area, based at Aguilar de Campoo. The Department of Tourism has a number of useful booklets and pamphlets on the subject, which it rightly regards as the province's chief attraction. It is working towards having several dozen more churches open to the visiting public within a few years.

Canal de Castilla

North of Frómista, the road heads north towards Santander. Alongside it stretches part of the Canal de Castilla. A major work, it was started in 1749 with the aim of transporting goods from the interior to the coast more easily. In those times of war and political turmoil it took over a century to complete. One branch begins at Valladolid, one at Medina de Rioseco, and they meet and continue north to Alar del Rey, from where the mountains made a continuation impossible and goods once again were put to the road. It was a significant engineering feat for its time but sadly saw only 20-odd years of effective use before it was rendered redundant by the railway. Long stretches of it have a canalside path to walk, and there are a couple of information centres along the way.

Monasterio de San Andrés de Arroyo

ⓘ *30-min tours at 1000 (not Mon), 1100, 1200, 1230, 1515, 1600, 1700, and 1800, €3, free Mon.* Make every effort to get to San Andrés de Arroyo, south from Aguilar de Campoo, and 8 km west of Alar del Rey. A working monastery populated by Cistercian nuns, it boasts a superb late 12th-century cloister, which you will be shown around by a friendly inhabitant. The cloister is double-columned and features some exceptionally intricate work, especially on the corner capitals. How the masons managed to chisel out the leaves and tendrils is anybody's guess. The far side of the cloister is more recent but features equally ornate work. The Sala Capitular is a Gothic affair with an ornate tomb supported by lions, in which rest the mortal remains of Doña Mencía Lara, a powerful local countess in her day. Traces of paint remain, a useful reminder that the bare Gothic style that we admire was often probably rather garishly coloured. The centrepiece of the cloister is a Moorish fountain originally from Granada.

Closer to the main road (2 km east) is the crumbly red Romanesque monastery **Iglesia de Santa María de Mave**. The keys are in the *hospedería* that's built into the monastery.

Aguilar de Campoo → *For listings, see pages 54-55.*

The lovely town of Aguilar sits where the Castilian plain gives way to the northern mountains of the Cordillera Cantábrica. Chilly, even snowy, in winter, its pleasant summer temperatures make it a place of blessed relief from the *meseta* heat. It makes an excellent base for exploring the area's Romanesque heritage. Aguilar is named after its 'eagle's nest', a slightly exaggerated description of the modest hill capped by a castle that overlooks the town. In latter days, however, the town has been known for biscuit making; the rich smells wafting through the streets make a visitor permanently peckish. While iconic Fontaneda biscuits, first made by a local family in 1881, are no longer produced here, there are still three biscuit factories here, producing a wide range of crunchy delights. The **tourist office** ① *Plaza de España, T979 123 641, Tue-Sat 1000-1345, 1600-1745 (1700-1845 summer), Sun 1000-1345, 1-hr guided walks leave Tue-Sun 1100, Tue-Sat 1700, €3*, is helpful.

The town sits on the Río Pisuerga and is centred on the long **Plaza de España**, which is where most things go on. At one end of the plaza is the **Colegiata de San Miguel** ① *T979 122 231, summer 1030-1330, 1700-2000, ring to visit at other times; guided tours Mon-Sat 1100, 1200, 1700, Sun 1300; €2*, which conceals a Gothic interior behind its Romanesque façade. Inside, there's a big *retablo*, a scary sleeping Christ with real hair, and a museum.

A number of **gateways** remain from the old walls; that on Calle Barrio y Mier has a Hebrew inscription, a legacy of the once substantial Jewish population, while the one behind the church is topped by griffins.

Across the river, the **Monasterio de Santa Clara** is home to a community of nuns that follow the Assisi saint. Its **Gothic church** ① *daily 1200-0100, 1800-1900*, can be visited. Delicious pastries can be bought inside.

The **Museo Ursi** ① *C Tobalina s/n, Oct-Dec Fri-Sun 1700-2000, Easter-Sep Fri-Sun 1230-1400, 1700-2000, €2*, is the workshop of the sculptor Ursicino Martínez, whose work, mostly from wood, is a blend of the sober, the abstract and the light-hearted.

Worth looking at is the Romanesque **Ermita de Santa Cecilia**, a chapel with a leaning tower below the castle. You'll have to get the key from the priest's house (the tourist office will direct you). The interior is simple; the highlight is a superb capital showing the Innocents being put to the sword by chainmailed soldiers. Above, up a path, little remains of the castle but its walls; the view is good, but the town looks better from lower angles.

Monasterio de Santa María la Real

On the road to Cervera, 1 km west is the **Monasterio de Santa María la Real** ① *Jul and Aug daily 1030-1400, 1600-2000 (guided visits 1100, 1230, 1630, 1800), Sep-Jun Tue-Fri 1600-1930; Sat and Sun 1030-1400, 1630-1930, €2, €5 guided visit*. The cloister is attractive enough, although bound to be disappointing after San Andrés de Arroyo, which is similar. The columns are doubled, but many of the capitals are missing (some are in Madrid). The Sala Capitular features clusters of multiple columns, their capitals impressively carved from a single block of stone. The **Museo Románico**, housed in the monastery, is useful for planning a Romanesque itinerary as it contains many models of churches in the province. You can stay here in a posada whose profits fund the Romanesque foundation whose HQ this is.

Cervera de Pisuerga

Some 25 km west of Aguilar is the quiet town of Cervera de Pisuerga, set in the foothills of the Cordillera Cantábrica. It's a fine base for outdoor activities; walkers will have a good time of it in the hills around here. The town's highlight is the Gothic **Iglesia de Santa María del Castillo** ① *Jul-Sep daily 1030-1330, 1700-2000, also Fri-Sun in late Jun and early Oct, €1,* imperiously enthroned above the town. It's not of huge interest inside, but worth checking out is the side chapel of Santa Ana, with polychrome reliefs adorning the walls above the *retablo*. There's also a small **Museo Etnográfico** ① *summer Tue-Sun 1100-1400, 1700-2000, spring and autumn Sat and Sun 1100-1400, 1700-2000; €2,* which is of moderate interest. The **tourist office** ① *Parque El Plantío s/n, T979 870 695, summer only Mon-Sat 1000-1400, 1700-2000, Sun 1000-1400,* on the edge of town, has lots of information on driving and walking routes.

North towards Santander listings

For hotel and restaurant price codes and other relevant information, see pages 11-17.

▣ Where to stay

Monasterio de San Andrés de Arroyo *p52*
€€ El Convento de Mave, T979 123 611, www.elconventodemave.com. A peaceful place to stay, apart from the odd goods train rattling by. There are various larger and more elaborate rooms costing substantially more (**€€€**). Closed Jan-Feb.

Aguilar de Campoo *p53*
€€ Hotel Valentín, Av Ronda 23, T979 122 125, www.hotelvalentin.com. This slightly larger-than-life complex can't be missed as you approach. On the main road on the edge of town, it has a disco, restaurant, shops and a hotel that manages to be quite calm and pleasant, with large, light rooms. It's been recently refurbished, and offers excellent value.
€€ Posada Santa María la Real, Av Monasterio s/n, T979 122 000, www.alojamientosconhistoria.com. These refurbished monastery buildings 1 km west of town make a characterful place to stay, but you can tell it's not run by hospitality professionals. The split-level rooms are attractive but the upstairs sleeping area can get very stuffy in summer, and a few other details are missing too. Nevertheless, there's decent-value food on offer and this can be a good bet if you bear in mind it's not luxurious.

€ Hostal Siglo XX, Plaza España 9, T979 126 040. A good choice, with cosy rooms with TV and shared bath above a restaurant. Grab one of the front rooms, which have access to enclosed balconies overlooking the square.

Camping
Monte Royal, Av Virgen del Llano s/n, T979 123 083, www.campingmonteroyal.com. Near the lake to the west of town, this is a campsite with all the trappings.

Cervera de Pisuerga *p53*
€€€ Parador Fuentes Carrionas, Ctra de Resoba s/n, T979 870 075, www.parador.es. Some 2 km above the town is this large pinkish parador, which enjoys a privileged natural setting. There are great views from all the balconied rooms (which cost a little more), particularly those in the front, overlooking a lake. It's a lovely spot.
€ Casa Goyetes, C El Valle 4, T979 870 568. In the heart of town, this attractive wood-beamed *casa rural* is a relaxing and comfortable base. It's excellent value, and the homely rustic interior is a delight.
€ La Galería, Plaza Mayor 16, T979 870 008. Right in the heart of this pretty village, this is a fine option with nice rooms on the charming square.

▣ Restaurants

Aguilar de Campoo *p53*
€€ El Barón, C El Pozo 14, T979 123 151, www.restaurantebaron.com. An excellent

restaurant set in an old stone building, with atmospheric decor. There's a good tapas bar, worthwhile *menú*, plenty of cheer and hearty local cuisine. Recommended.

Cervera de Pisuerga *p53*
€€ Casa Victor, Paseo Valdesgares 1, T979 870 390. The town's best eatery is a cheery place doing excellent roast meats, tasty croquettes and more-ish homemade desserts.

⊖ Transport

Aguilar de Campoo *p53*
Bus The bus station is next to the **Hotel Valentín**. Regular services run to **Palencia**, **Santander**, **León**, **Burgos** and **Cervera**. **Train** RENFE station is to the east of town and has frequent trains to **Palencia**, **Santander** and **Madrid**.

Cervera de Pisuerga *p53*
Bus Cervera is linked by bus to **Aguilar** and **Palencia** a couple of times daily.

León

León is one of the loveliest of Northern Spain's cities, with a proud architectural legacy, an elegant new town and an excellent tapas bar scene. Once capital of Christian Spain, it preserves an outstanding reminder of its glory days in its Gothic cathedral, one of the nation's finest buildings. After crossing the dusty *meseta* from Burgos, pilgrims arriving here should put their feet up for a couple of days and enjoy what León has to offer.

**Arriving in León → ** *Phone code: 987. Population: 135,119. Altitude: 870 m.*
Getting there and around León's bus and RENFE train stations are close to each other just across the river from the new town, a 10-minute walk from the old town. ▸▸ *See Transport, page 65.*

Best time to visit Like Burgos, León's high altitude results in freezing winters and roasting summers; spring and autumn are good times to visit, as there's little rain.

Tourist information León's helpful main **tourist office** ⓘ *T987 237 082, Plaza de la Regla s/n, oficinadeturismodeleon@jcyl.es, Oct-Apr Mon-Sat 0930-1400, 1600-1900, Sun 0930-1700, May-Sep daily 0900-2000*, is opposite the cathedral.

Background
León was founded as a Roman fortress in AD 68 to protect the road that transported the gold from the mines in El Bierzo to the west. It became the base of the *Legio Septima*, the seventh legion of Imperial Rome; this is where the name originates (although León means 'lion' in Spanish). The city was Christianized in the third century and is one of the oldest bishoprics in western Europe. After being reconquered in the mid-eighth century, León became the official residence of the Asturian royal line in the early 10th century; the royals were thereafter known as kings of León. The city was recaptured and sacked several times by the Moors until it was retaken for the final time by Alfonso V in 1002. León then enjoyed a period of power and glory as the centre of Reconquista pride and prestige; the city flourished on protection paid from the fragmented *taifa* states.

As the Reconquista moved further south, however, León found itself increasingly put in the shade by the young whippersnapper Castilla, which had seceded from it in the 10th century.

In 1230 the crowns were united, and León is still bound to Castilla to this day, a fact bemoaned by many – spraycans are often taken to the castles on the coat of arms of the region, leaving only the Leonese lion. When the Flemish Habsburg Carlos V took the throne of Spain, León feared further isolation and became one of the prime movers in the *comunero* rebellion. One of the most extreme of the *comuneros* was a Leonese named Gonzalo de Guzmán, who declared a "war of fire, sack and blood" on the aristocracy. The rebellion was heavily put down, and León languished for centuries.

The region's coal provided some prosperity in the 19th century, but it has really only been relatively recently that the city has lifted itself from stagnating regional market town to what it is today; a relatively modern and dynamic Spanish city.

Places in León → *For listings, see pages 62-66.*

León's **old town** is to the east of the River Bernesga and surrounded by the boulevards of the newer city. Walk up the pedestrianized Calle Ancha and prepare to be stunned by the appearance of the white Gothic cathedral, a jewel in Spain's architectural crown.

Cathedral
ⓘ *www.catedraldeleon.org, May-Sep Mon-Fri 0930-1330, 1600-2000, Sat 0930-1200, 1400-1800, Sun 0930-1100, 1400-2000, Oct-Apr Mon-Sat 0930-1330, 1600-1900, Sun 0930-1400, €5.*
Effectively begun in the early 13th century, León's cathedral is constructed over the old Roman baths; this, combined with the poor quality of the stone used and the huge quantity of stained glass, historically made the building fairly unstable. A late 19th-century restoration replaced many of the more decayed stones, an impressive engineering feat that required removing and replacing whole sections of the building.

Approaching the cathedral up Calle Ancha, its spectacular bulk is suddenly revealed. The main western façade is flanked by two bright towers, mostly original Gothic but capped with later crowns, the northern (left hand) one by one of the Churriguera brothers. Walking around the outside, there's some superb buttressing as well as numerous quirky gargoyles and pinnacles. Back at the main door, investigate the triple-arched façade, expressively carved. The central portal features a jovial Christ above a graphic Hell, with demons cheerfully stuffing sinners into cooking pots. To the right are scenes from the life of the Virgin; a brief biography of her son is on the left side.

As you enter through the wooden doors, look up at the back corner behind you. The leathery object hanging above the door is supposed to be the carcass of the *topo maligno* (evil mole) who was blamed for tunnelling under the building works and destroying the masons' labours. In reality, the Roman baths underneath were the cause of all the tunnels; while the mole was apparently captured and killed, the hanging carcass is really that of a large tortoise.

The beautifully untouched Gothic interior of the cathedral is illuminated by a riot of stained glass, a patchwork of colour that completely changes the building's character depending on the time of day and amount of sun outside. The sheer amount of glass is impressive; some 1700 sq m. The oldest glass is to be found in the apse and in the large rose window above the main entrance; some of it dates to the 13th century, while other panels span later centuries. There's a general theme to it all; the natural world is depicted at low levels, along with the sciences and arts; normal folk, including nobles, are in the middle, while saints, prophets, kings and angels occupy the top positions. Between midnight and 0100, the floodlights are turned off and the building illuminated from the inside, a spectacular sight. Ongoing restoration work means that you can visit a platform in the cathedral's interior (accessed outside, down the side of the building) which lets you get up close to some of the magnificent stained glass. It's an excellent experience, especially the visits at 2330 at weekends, which allow you to appreciate the glass under floodlights.

Another of the cathedral's appealing attributes is that, although there's a Renaissance *trascoro* illustrating the Adoration and Nativity, there's a transparent panel allowing a perspective of the whole church, a rarity in Spanish cathedrals. The *coro* itself is beautifully and humourously carved of walnut, although you'll have to join one of the frequent

León

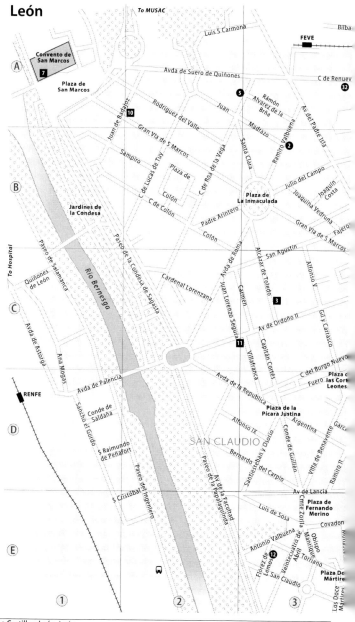

100 metres

100 yards

Where to stay 🛏

Hostal Albany **2** C5
Hostal Bayón **3** C3
Hostal Casco
  Antiguo **1** B5
Hostal Guzmán el
  Bueno **5** B4
La Posada Regia **6** C4
Parador de
  San Marcos **7** A1
París **8** C5
Pensión Blanca **11** C2
Q!H **4** B5
Quindós **10** A2
Reina **9** D4

Restaurants 🍴

Alfonso Valderas **1** C4
Café Europa **4** B5
Casa Condeso **11** B5
El Besugo **27** C5
El Gran Café **6** B5
El Palomo **7** C5
Ezequiel **5** A2
Fornos **3** B4
La Competencia **10** C5
La Esponja **8** B4
La Poveda **2** B3
La Ribera **30** B4
La Trébede **14** B4
Las Termas **9** C5
L'Union **12** E3
Nuevo Racimo
  de Oro **15** C5
Sabor de Grecia **32** A3
Vivaldi **33** C5

Bars & clubs 🍸

Cervecería Céltica **17** B5
El Capitán **18** C5
El Universal **13** C5
Glam **28** C5
León Antiguo **21** B4
Planet Móngogo **31** A4
Taxman **16** A5

guided tours to inspect it at close quarters. The *retablo* is an excellent painted work by Nicolás Francés, although not complete. Scenes from the lives of the Virgin and the city's patron, San Froilán, are depicted.

Much venerated is the 13th-century statue of the Virgen Blanca, in one of the apsidal chapels; there's also a replica of the elegant sculpture in the portal. Inside the north door of the cathedral is another Virgin, also with child; she's known as the Virgin of the Die, after an unlucky gambler lobbed his six-sider at the statue, causing the Christ-child's nose to bleed.

Also worth a peek are two excellent 13th-century tombs in the transepts. Holding the remains of two bishops involved in the cathedral's construction, they are carved with scenes from the prelates' lives; although heavily damaged, the representations are superb.

The **cathedral museum** ① *Oct-Apr Tue-Fri 1000-1330, 1600-1900, 1000-1330 Sat; May-Sep Mon-Fri 1000-1330, 1600-2000, Sat 1000-1200, 1400-1900, Sun 1000-1100, 1400-2000, €5, €2 cloister only*, is housed in the cloisters and sacristy. Most of the cloister is Renaissance in style, with several tombs of wealthy nobles and frescoes; note too the star vaulting. The museum, part of which is accessed up a beautiful Plateresque stair, has a good collection, with many notable pieces. Outstanding items include a Mozarabic bible dating from the 10th century, fragments of stained glasswork, and a superb crucifixion by Juan de Juni, portraying a twisted, anguished Christ.

Basílica de San Isidoro
① *Sep-Jun Mon-Sat 1000-1330, 1600-1830, Sun 1000-1330, Jul-Aug Mon-Sat 0900-2000, Sun 0900-1400, church free, Panteón €5, free Thu afternoon.*
As well as the Gothic cathedral, León also has a cracker of a Romanesque ensemble in the Basílica de San Isidoro. Consecrated in the 11th century over an earlier church, it was renamed in 1063 when Fernando I managed to get that learned saint's remains repatriated from Sevilla.

The complex is built into the medieval city walls, much of which is preserved. The façade is beautiful, particularly in the morning or evening light; it's pure Romanesque in essence, although the balustrade and pedimental shield were added, harmoniously, during the Renaissance, and there are Gothic additions in other parts of the building. Facing the building, the right-hand doorway is named the **Puerta del Perdón** (door of forgiveness); pilgrims could gain absolution by passing through here if they were too infirm to continue their journey to Santiago. The door is topped by a good relief of the Descent from the Cross and Ascension.

To the left is the **Puerta del Cordero** (door of the lamb), with an even more impressive tympanum depicting Abraham's sacrifice. Atop this door is the Renaissance pediment, decorated with a large shield surmounted by San Isidoro in Reconquista mode (like Santiago, this bookish scholar made surprise horseback appearances to fight Moors several centuries after his death). The interior of the church is dark and attractive, with later Gothic elements in accord with the Romanesque; large multifoil arches add a Moorish element. The *retablo* dates from the 16th century and surrounds a monstrance in which the Host is permanently on display (the basilica is one of only two churches in Northern Spain to have been granted this right). Below is a casket containing the remains of Isidore himself – or whoever it was whose bones were found in Sevilla long after the saint's burial place had been forgotten.

The real treasure of San Isidoro lies through another exterior door which gives access to the **museum**. On entering, the first chamber you are given access to is the Panteón Real, an astonishing crypt that is the resting place of 11 kings of León and their families. The arches, the ceiling and some of the tombs are covered with Romanesque wallpainting in a superb state of preservation (it's barely needed any restoration). There are scenes from the New Testament as well as agricultural life; if you're at all jaded with religious art and architecture, this sublime space will fix it. The short columns are crowned with well-carved capitals, mostly vegetal, but some with Biblical scenes or motifs derived from Visigothic traditions.

The next stop on the visit is the first of the two cloisters, above which rises the emblematic **Torre del Gallo** (tower of the cock), topped by a curious gold-plated weathercock that wouldn't look out of place at White Hart Lane. The original is now in the museum; recent studies have revealed that it was made in sixth-century Sasanian Persia.

The treasury and library is the other highlight of the visit to the museum. Although the complex was sacked and badly damaged by French troops in the Napoleonic Wars, most of the priceless collection of artefacts and books survived. More remains of San Isidoro reside in an 11th-century reliquary beautifully decorated in Mozarabic style; another reliquary is equally finely carved from ivory. The ornate chalice of Doña Urraca is made from two Roman cups and studded with gems. The library contains some beautiful works, of which the highlight is a 10th-century Mozarabic bible.

Convento de San Marcos

León's other great monument is the San Marcos convent by the river, which doubles as a sumptuous parador. Not a bad place to stay, you might think; so, no doubt, did generations of pilgrims who laid their road-dusted heads down here when it was administered as a monastery and hostel by the Knights of Santiago.

The massive façade is the highlight. It postdates the pilgrim era and is 100 m long, pure Plateresque overlaid by a baroque pediment, and sensitively dignified by a well-designed modern plaza. The church itself is attractive if rather unremarkable; more inspiring is the adjoining cloister with its figure-adorned arches. You can also access it from the parador. There are daily tours of the hotel, but it's easy enough to take a stroll around the ground floor areas; the bar, lounge and cloister are attractive and open to the public.

Next to the parador on the riverbank a crowd gather at weekends and on some weekday evenings to watch the curious game of *bolos*, in which old men toss a wooden ball at skittles aiming, not to knock them over, but to roll it in an arc between them.

Beyond the parador, cheerful coloured panels greet the visitor to **MUSAC** ⓘ *T987 090 000, www.musac.es, Tue-Fri 1100-1400, 1700-2000, Sat-Sun 1100-1500, 1700-2100, €5, free Sun afternoon*, an upbeat contemporary art museum with rotating temporary exhibitions of varying quality. There's a cute gift shop and good café-restaurant here.

Old town

On the edge of León's old town, the **Museo de León** ⓘ *Plaza Santo Domingo 8, T987 236 405, Tue-Sat 1000-1400, 1600-1900 (1700-2000 summer), Sun 1000-1400, €1.20*, opened its doors in early 2007 to some acclaim. It's a very impressive modern display that comprehensively covers the city's significant Roman, royal, and Jewish past, with good information in English too. Among the pieces on display is the famous Cristo de Carraza, an exquisite 11th century ivory crucifix.

Other sights in the old town include the nearby **Casa Botines**, a *palacio* built by Gaudí in subdued (for him) fairytale style. It now functions as an exhibition centre, but the top floors are a bank. The building's façade features St George sticking it to a dragon; a bronze sculpture of Gaudí observes his creation narrowly from a park bench outside. Next door is the elegant **Palacio de los Guzmanes**, a 16th-century Renaissance palace with a fine façade and beautiful patio. Across the square, the old Ayuntamiento is from the same period; next to it is the fine tower of **San Marcelo**.

Wandering around León's old quarter will reveal many time-worn architectural treasures and hidden nooks. The area north of Calle Ancha contains several, but the area south is the most interesting. This is the **Húmedo**, the 'wet' barrio, named after its massive collection of tapas bars, the most popular of which are around Plaza de San Martín, which hums with life most evenings and explodes at weekends. Near here is the beautiful **Plaza Mayor**, an extremely elegant porticoed 18th-century design that holds a fascinating and extremely traditional Wednesday and Saturday morning fruit and veg market. Delve a little further into the area and you'll come to the **Plaza de Santa María del Camino**, popularly known as Plaza del Grano (grain square) for its one-time wheat exchange. It's a lovely time-worn space with rough cobbles, wooden arcades and a pretty Romanesque church.

Valdevimbre

An excellent lunch or dinnertime excursion is to head some 20 km south of León to **Valdevimbre**, a historic winemaking village with spacious bodegas dug into the hills. Several of these have been converted into atmospheric restaurants with fine, well-priced food (see Restaurants, page 64). To get to Valdevimbre, turn off the N630 or A-66 motorway 18 km south of León. A taxi either way costs around €25.

León listings

For hotel and restaurant price codes and other relevant information, see pages 11-17.

⊖ Where to stay

León *p56, map p58*
€€€€ Parador de San Marcos, Plaza San Marcos 7, T987 237 300, www.parador.es. One of Spain's most attractive hotels, housed in the former monastery and pilgrim hostel of San Marcos. The furnishings are elegant but not over the top, and the building itself is a treasure. The rooms are comfortable and attractive, even if they don't quite live up to the rest of the building. The restaurant is excellent.
€€€-€€ Q!H Hotel, Av de los Cubos 6, T987 875 580, www.qhehoteles.es. This brand-new boutique hotel has an excellent location on a wide pedestrian street just a few paces from the cathedral (some of the rooms have great close-up views of it) but in a quiet zone. The rooms are decorated with comfortable modern style, and the staff are most helpful. There's a spa complex and café too.

€€ Hostal Albany, C Paloma 13, T987 264 600, www.albanyleon.com. Right by the cathedral, this excellent modern hostal offers compact, comfortable rooms, friendly staff, and a worthwhile restaurant and pastry shop on site. There's no parking particularly close by though.
€€ Hostal Guzmán el Bueno, C López Castrillón 6, T987 236 412, www.hostalguzman.es. This is a good choice in the old town, with attractive woody rooms in a spruce old building in the barrio of the Cid. They're a little dark because it's on a narrow street, but they are well equipped, and the management is friendly.
€€ Hotel París, C Ancha 18, T987 238 600, www.hotelparisleon.com. This is something of a León hub; a bright family-run hotel on the main pedestrian street near the cathedral. The rooms are well-equipped and very comfortable for the price – with minibar, good bathroom and pillow menu. There's also a good café, and atmospheric downstairs restaurant and tapas bar.
€€ Hotel Quindós, Gran Vía de San Marcos 38, T987 236 200, www.hotelquindos.com.

This is a very pleasant modern hotel near San Marcos, with inventively chic decor, modern art on the walls, rooms all decorated differently from each other and with plenty of colour, as well as an excellent restaurant.

€€ La Posada Regia, C Regidores 9, T987 218 820, www.regialeon.com. This is a superb, characterful place to stay in León's old quarter. Just off busy pedestrian C Ancha, this 14th-century building has enticing rooms with floorboards, pastel shades and many thoughtful touches; get one away from the street though, as there's a motorcycle shop next door. There's an equally charming new annexe opposite. The restaurant is good, but overpriced. Underground parking is very close by. Recommended.

€ Hostal Bayón, C Alcázar de Toledo 6, T987 231 446. This is a fine and homely choice, with comfy rooms with en suite or shared bath in a friendly *pensión*. It's got character and it's quiet and leafy with house plants.

€ Hostal Casco Antiguo, C Cardenal Landázuri 11, T987 074 000, www.h-cascoantiguo.com. This newish spot is attractively modern and enjoys a fabulous location in the heart of old León, very close to the cathedral but on a quiet street. The rooms aren't huge but have good bathrooms; an added plus are the ruins of a Roman camp in the basement.

€ Hotel Reina, C Puerta de la Reina 2, T987 205 200. This hotel was a faded beauty until enterprising new management took it over; now it is charmingly Spanish retro and offers excellent value. Rooms are bright and cheery, and come with or without old-fashioned bathroom (only 2 rooms use each shared one). There's a lift and roof terrace, and always a genuine welcome. Recommended.

€ Pensión Blanca, C Villafranca 2, T987 251 991/678 660 244. This is an exceptional budget option; the rooms are light and colourful, tastefully decorated with brand new furnishings. Rooms have private or shared bathroom; guests have use of a kitchen and there's free internet access and a friendly owner. Breakfast is included in the price, and you can have your laundry done. Highly recommended.

❼ Restaurants

León *p56, map p58*

Eating in León is a pleasure. Nearly all the tapas bars give a free snack with every drink; it's standard practice to order a *corto* (short beer) to take full advantage. The most concentrated tapas zone is around Plaza San Martín in the Barrio Húmedo; for a more sophisticated scene, head across C Ancha into the Barrio Romántico around Plaza Torres de Omaña.

€€€ Casa Condeso, Plaza Torres de Omaña 5, T987 170 613. The gold paint and turquoise frills around the lampshades mark this place as out of the ordinary, and the great *menú del día* (€15 weekdays) is equally memorable, with great modern cuisine in old-fashioned portions; it's worth phoning ahead for a spot in the attractive dining room. Recommended.

€€ Alfonso Valderas, Arco de Animas 1, T987 200 505. Famous for its *bacalao* (cod), this elegant but down-to-earth upstairs restaurant does it in myriad tasty ways. But don't be dissuaded if salt cod isn't your thing: the grilled meats are truly excellent, as are all the starters. Excellent service. Recommended.

€€ Candela, Pl San Martín 3, T987 201 327, www.restaurantecandelaleon.com. With an intriguing interior that incorporates a traditional 19th century house and an ancient road, this is a reliable choice for tasty Italian-influenced cuisine and an excellent-value *menú del día*.

€€ El Palomo, C Escalerilla 8, T987 254 225. A good little restaurant in the Húmedo area, with well-priced, high-quality fare and a friendly attitude. The cuisine is typically Leonese, with plenty of dishes to share as well as steaks and fine fish dishes. Order à la carte. Recommended.

€€ Ezequiel, C Roa de la Vega 4, T987 172 177, www.embutidosezequiel.es. Make a beeline for this combined chorizo shop and bar to try traditional Leonese cured meats. The tapas are incredibly generous and filling, but if you're still hungry, grab a table and try regional specialities like *botillo* or *cocido*. Good salads and warm-hearted service round out the experience. Recommended.

€€ La Poveda, C Ramiro Valbuena 9, T987 227 155. This traditional restaurant fills up fast, for the quality is very high. Dishes are mostly *raciones*, and are absolutely delicious – the *sesos* (brains) have incredible flavour and texture, and the octopus is as good as you'll get outside Galicia.

€€ Las Termas, C Paloma 13, T987 264 600, www.restaurantelastermas.es. An excellent lunch *menú* is the main reason to come to this spot near the cathedral. For €16, you get a wide choice of generously sized dishes. Keep your eyes peeled for rice dishes for 2, normally on Thu; they're prepared fresh to order, and are enormous and delicious. The desserts are always tasty too, as they own the pastry shop round the corner.

€€ Sabor de Grecia, C Renueva 11, T987 224 628. A welcoming family-run restaurant not far from San Isidoro, this is much visited for its short but very delicious menu of Greek cuisine. Dishes such as meatballs or broad beans ooze with flavour, and can be accompanied by a number of Greek wines. Recommended.

€ Fornos, C El Cid 8, T680 857 544. This longstanding León favourite in new premises specializes in traditional Leonese fare, accompanied by a range of wines. Grab a table and try the delicious *ensaladilla rusa*, calamari, the *mollejas*, or any of the other tasty *raciones*. Good tapas at the bar too.

€ La Ribera, C Fernando González Regueral 8, T987 270 408. The locals crowded into this place will show you that it's one of León's best tapas options. Once you squeeze your way to the bar, you'll find out why; as well as the home-made fried potatoes, you can enjoy some of the tastiest innards around:

tripe, kidneys and *asadurilla* to remember. If that's not your thing, try the delicious mussels or calamari. Recommended.

€ La Trébede, Pl Torres de Omaña 1. Decorated with everything from old farming implements to stuffed reptiles, this cosy neighbourhood bar is consistently busy. There's always an interesting tapa to go with your wine, and the chatty buzz makes this one of the town's best.

€ L'Unión, C Flórez de Lemos 3, T987 261 710, www.vegetarianoleon.com. Quality vegetarian places are thin on the ground in Spain, but this place certainly fits the bill. Simple decor, but excellent and innovative plates are served in generous quantity and can be washed down with organic wine. The *menú* is great value.

Cafés

El Gran Café, C Cervantes 9, T987 272 301, www.elgrancafeleon.com. This classic-looking café is a popular and atmospheric spot for an afternoon coffee, but it really hits its straps in the evenings, when there's regular live music. Tue jam sessions are lots of fun and pack the place out.

Valdevimbre *p62*

€€ La Cueva San Simón, T987 304 096. A spacious warren of a place with the main dining area in the fermentation chamber; try the *solomillo a la brasa*, morsels of tender steak that you rapidly cook on a sizzling grate that's brought to the table. This is one of several equally characterful restaurants in this small village, so just turn up and take your pick.

🎉 Bars and clubs

León *p56, map p58*

León's nightlife is busy; the **Barrio Húmedo** is the best place for concentrated action – wander around these streets and you'll find any number of bars that will suit you.

Cervecería Céltica, C Cervantes 10, T987 072 438. This large and bright bar has an excellent range of Belgian beers, and several draught options, all expertly poured. Always buzzy and cheerful.

Glam, C Platerías 10. The trendiest late-night spot with León's young, this spacious and extravagantly decorated *discoteca* is absolutely mobbed at weekends around 0200. The music is far from glam rock, usually centring around the latest pop and dance hits and enlivened by live acts and go-go dancers. Live bands sometimes play here too.

León Antiguo, Plaza Ordoño IV s/n, T987 226 956. A good bar with a friendly upmarket vibe and a nice outdoor terrace in the quieter part of the old town. Always busy and cheerful.

Planet Móngogo, Plaza Puerta Castillo 5. Open Tue-Sun from 1800. People come from all over Northern Spain to visit this unique bar/restaurant, which blends trash horror, psychobilly, and high-quality, low-priced 'Hell-Mex' food among a riot of voodoo, zebra stripes and leopard spots. It's a spot you won't forget in a hurry. Highly recommended.

Taxman, C Babia 6. By the car park behind the cathedral, this bar has a loyal following thanks to its excellent service, good coffee, and beautifully poured drinks. The theme is The Beatles, whose mugshots are everywhere, but they happily play other music on request.

❂ Festivals

León *p56, map p58*
Mar/Apr León's **Semana Santa** (Easter Week) is a very traditional, serious affair, with many mournful processions conducted by striking hooded *cofradías* (religious brotherhoods and sisterhoods). Carrying the *pasos* (floats bearing sculptures of Jesus and Mary) is thirsty work; relief comes in the form of *limonada*, a *sangría*-like punch; a throwback to Christian Spain's dark past is that going out to drink a few is traditionally known as *matar judíos* ('kill Jews').

Late Jun The feasts of **San Juan** (24 Jun) and **San Pedro** (28 Jun) are León's major fiestas of the year. There's a good range of activities over 10 days, including bullfights, concerts and high alcohol consumption.
Early Oct Fiesta de **San Froilán**, the city's patron, is the first weekend of Oct. There's a Moorish/medieval market, processions and dances; there's also a good Celtic music festival.

◎ Shopping

León *p56, map p58*
The main shopping street is **Av Ordoño II** in the new town; more quirky shops can be found in the old town.

Books
Galatea, C Sierra Pambley 1, T987 272 652, near the cathedral, has a surprising and high-quality selection of English-language fiction and non-fiction.
Iguazú, C Plegarias 7, T987 208 066. A good place to go for maps and travel literature.

Food
Don Queso, C Azabachería, is a good cheese shop. Nearby is a delightful shop that sells all the necessary ingredients to make your own sausages and chorizo.

◔ What to do

León *p56, map p58*
Mundileón, T987 212 266, www.mundileon. com. This agency is a good option for people without transport. They arrange a variety of tours around this fascinating province, in English or Spanish, and will pick up from any hotel in the city.

❍ Transport

León *p56, map p58*
Bus Within the province, **Astorga** (30-45 mins) is served hourly, **Sahagún** 2-3 times daily (1 hr), **Riaño** 3 times daily (1 hr 45 mins)

Ponferrada hourly (1-2 hrs), and Villafranca del Bierzo 3 times daily (2 hrs 30 mins).

There are 10 to 12 daily departures for **Madrid** (3½ hrs, €24), 8 to **Valladolid** (2 hrs, stops at Valladolid airport on request, €12), a similar number north to **Oviedo** (1 hr 30 mins, €11) and **Gijón**, 5-7 to **Zamora** (2 hrs) via Benavente, 2 to **Salamanca** (3 hrs), 4 to **Burgos** (2 hrs), 1 to **Palencia**, and 3 into **Galicia**.

Train From the RENFE station, trains run to **Madrid** 9 times a day (2¾-4½ hrs, from €35-45), north to **Oviedo** (2 hrs, €9-20) and **Gijón** 7 times, east to Barcelona 3 times daily (10-11 hrs) via **Palencia**, **Burgos**, **Logroño**, **Vitoria**, **Pamplona** and **Zaragoza**, and 2 daily westwards to **A Coruña** and **Santiago**.

A dozen trains run east to **Sahagún**, and several daily go west to **Astorga** and **Ponferrada**.

The FEVE station is on Av Padre Isla, northwest of the centre. The line runs to **Bilbao**; it's a scenic but slow journey via every village (1 daily, 7 hrs 40 mins, €25). The luxury train service, **Transcantábrico**, follows this route and onwards to Santiago. Leaving on Sat from Easter to Sep, it takes a week, with numerous stops for gourmet meals, or to be bussed off to various attractions.

⊙ Directory

León *p56, map p58*
Medical services Hospital Virgen Blanca, C Altos de Nava, T987 237 400. Call 112 in an emergency.

León Province

Although joined in semi-autonomous harmony with Castilla, the province of León is fairly distinct, and offers a different experience to the vast Castilian plain. In fact, it's got a bit of everything; a look at the map confirms that it's part *meseta*, part mountain and part fertile valley.

León was an important early kingdom of the Christian Reconquest, but soon lost ground and importance as the battlegrounds moved further south and power became focused around Valladolid and then Madrid. Mining has been a constant part of the area's history; the Romans extracted gold in major operations in the west of the province, while coal, cobalt and copper are all still extracted, although with limited future.

The west of the province is a region of hills and valleys known as El Bierzo. It's a busy, rural zone of grapevines, vegetables, mines and more; further exploration reveals superb natural enclaves and vibrant local fiestas.

The pilgrim route crosses León province, stopping in the towns of Sahagún, Astorga, Ponferrada and Villafranca del Bierzo as well as the capital; all good places to regain lost strength for the climb into Galicia and the last haul of the journey. The province's north includes part of the Picos de Europa.

Sahagún

Sahagún is one of those rare towns whose population is only a quarter of that it housed in the Middle Ages. These days it's a likeable enough place; wandering its dusty streets it's hard to imagine that Sahagún was ever anything more than what it is today – an insignificant agricultural town of the thirsty *meseta*. Sahagún's main attraction is its collection of *mudéjar* buildings. These differ from Aragonese *mudéjar* and are to some extent Romanesque buildings made of brick.

The area around Sahagún was settled by Romans and the town is named for an early Christian basilica dedicated to a local saint, Facundo (the Latin name was *Sanctum Facundum*). The town began to thrive once Santiago-fever got going, and it gained real power and prestige when King Alfonso VI invited a community of Cluny monks to establish the Roman rite in the area. They built their monastery, San Benito, on the site of the old Visigothic church; once Alfonso had granted it massive privileges and lands, it became one of the most powerful religious centres of Spain's north.

Sahagún's most famous son was a 16th-century Franciscan missionary to the Americas, Friar Bernardino, a remarkable character. His respect for Aztec culture made him a controversial figure at the time; he mastered the *náhuatl* language and wrote texts in it. He is commemorated in his hometown by a small bust near the Plaza Mayor.

The **Iglesia de San Lorenzo** is the most emblematic of Sahagún's *mudéjar* buildings; a church dating from the early 13th century and characterized by a pretty belltower punctured with three rows of arches. The interior is less impressive, remodelled in later periods. It's worth climbing the tower if restoration work permits.

The **Iglesia de San Tirso** dates from the 12th century and is similar, with a smaller but pretty tower. The interior has suffered through neglect, but it's worth popping in to see the floats from Sahagún's well-known **Semana Santa** celebrations, as well as a well-carved 13th-century tomb, later reused. A spectacular church on the hill, **Santuario de la Virgen Peregrina**, formerly a Franciscan monastery, is finally undergoing much-needed restoration; when it reopens it should be the crowning *mudéjar* glory of the town. Especially notable is the little chapel at the back of the church, where fragments of superb Mozarabic stucco work were found when the plaster that covered them began to flake off in the mid-20th century. The chapel was commissioned by a local noble in the 15th century to house his own bones.

By the church is what's left of the **Monasterio de San Benito**; a clocktower and a Gothic chapel. The portal also survived and has been placed across the road behind the building; it's an ornate baroque work from the 17th century with impressive lions. Nearby, in the still-functioning Benedictine **Monasterio de Santa Cruz** ① *guided tours Tue-Sat 1000, 1100, 1200, 1600, 1700, 1800, Sun during mornings only, €2*, is a small museum of religious art that also has architectural and sculptural fragments from the burned monastery.

Around Sahagún

If your legs aren't weary from peregrination, or if you've got a car, there's a good excursion from Sahagún. It's an hour's walk south to the **Convento de San Pedro de las Dueñas**, which preserves some excellent Romanesque capitals and attractive *mudéjar* brickwork. The keyholder is a curious old man named Pablo; if he doesn't appear, seek him out in the house below the castle by the main road.

The Maragatos

The matter of origin of the Maragatos has provoked much scholarly and unscholarly debate. They have been variously touted as descendants of Moorish prisoners, Sueves, Visigoths and Phoenicians, but no one is really sure. Until fairly recently they kept pretty much to themselves; it is still common to see them in their characteristic national dress. The men wear a red waistcoat, bowler-style hat and a black tunic, while the women have a shawl and a headscarf.

The Maragatos are famous for their *cocido*; served in reverse to the standard Spanish custom; the meal starts with the stewed meats; usually a bit of everything, chicken, lamb, sausage and chunks of pork from various parts of the pig. The chickpea and cabbage part of the stew follows on a separate plate, and is washed down by the broth after. There are many restaurants in Astorga serving it up, but some of the best are in the small villages of the *maragatería*, the surrounding district.

Head east from the convent for around half an hour to **Grajal de Campos**, with an excellent castle of Moorish origin but beefed up in the 15th and 16th centuries. It's a very imposing structure indeed. There's not a great deal to see inside, but it's fun to climb the crumbling stairs and walls. While you're in town, have a look at the nearby *palacio*, which has seen better days but preserves an attractively down-at-heel patio. From here, it's about an hour back to Sahagún.

Mansilla de la Mulas
Beyond Sahagún, the pilgrim trail continues to Mansilla de la Mulas. There are few mules around these days, and what remains of its once proud heritage are the ruins of its fortifications. Some 8 km north, however, is the lovely Mozarabic **Iglesia de San Miguel de Escalada** ① *Oct-Mar Tue-Sun 1040-1400, 1500-1750; Apr-Sep Tue-Sun 1015-1400, 1630-2000*. Dating from the 10th century, it was built by a group of Christian refugees from Córdoba. There's a pretty horseshoe-arched porch; the interior is attractively bare of ornament; the arches are set on columns reused from an earlier structure, and are beautifully subtle. A triple arch divides the altar area from the rest of the church. It's a lovely place and well worth the detour.

Valencia de Don Juan
West of Sahagún, and south of León, the chief attraction in this small town is its weird twisted ruin of a castle built in the 15th century, with strange-shaped battlements rising above green grass. The pretty bullring is also worth a look. The villages nearby are warrened with curious tomblike bodegas burrowed into the hills; they produce slightly effervescent red and rosé wine. South of here is Toral de los Guzmanes with a massive adobe palace. The road continues south of here into Zamora province.

West of León
The road (and the Camino de Santiago) west from León starts out through urban sprawl to the village of **Virgen del Camino**, where a modern church houses a respected Virgin. Beyond here, the village of **Hospital de Orbigo**, reached via a long medieval bridge, is a reasonably attractive little place famous for its trout soup, and the best option for pilgrims to stop over between León and Astorga. The bridge was the scene of a curious event in

1434. A local noble, iron chain around his neck and doubtless suffering some form of insecurity, decided to take up residence on the bridge for the fortnight leading up to the feast day of Santiago. Passing pilgrims were forced to either declare his chosen lady the most beautiful in Christendom or have a joust with the knight or one of his heavies: just what a penniless peregrine needed after another hard day's slog across the plains. The event became known as the *Paso Honroso*; how fair the fights were is not known, but the knights unhorsed over 700 pilgrims, killing one and wounding several more. Ah, for the days of chivalry. In early June, the event is commemorated in a fiesta, with everyone dressed in medieval costume, and jousts held on the vega below the bridge.

Astorga

While Astorga has an interesting history, nothing much goes on here now. However, it's a very pleasant, relaxed place with some attractive buildings and a peaceful small-town atmosphere. Astorga and its surrounding villages are particularly famous for being the home of the Maragatos (see box, above), a distinct ethnic group that for centuries were considered the bravest and most trustworthy of muleteers and guides.

As a major Roman centre for administering the gold-mining region further to the west, Astorga was known as Asturica Augusta, having been founded by Augustus during his campaigns against the never-say-die tribes of the northwest of the peninsula. Astorga was one of the earliest of Christian communities in Spain; the archbishop of Carthage, San Cipriano, wrote a letter to the presbyter and faithful of the town as early as AD 254. After the disintegration of the Empire, the area was settled by the Sueves who made the journey from Swabia, now in southwest Germany. They made Astorga their capital and fought constantly with the Visigothic rulers until Astorga finally fell for good in the sixth century.

Astorga's most important sight is its **cathedral** ⓘ *Mon 0900-1100, Tue-Sat 0900-1400, 1600-1800, Sun 1100-1400, cathedral free, but entry after 1100 includes the Museo Diocesano, €2.50*, on which construction began in the 15th century. The best view of the cathedral is to be had from below it, outside the city walls. Most of it is in late Gothic style, but the façade and towers are later baroque constructions and seem overlarge and ornate for the comparatively small town. The sculptural reliefs depict events from Christ's life, and are flanked by numerous cherubs and flights of Churrigueresque fancy. Inside, the marble *retablo* is impressive, while the highlight of the are the paintings of the temptations and trials of St Anthony, who is bothered during his hermitage by some memorable demons.

Next to the cathedral, the **Palacio Episcopal** ⓘ *Tue-Sat 1100-1400, 1600-1800, Sun 1100-1400; summer Tue-Sat 1000-1400, 1600-2000, Sun 1000-1400, €3 (€5 including Museo Diocesano)*, is something of a contrast. In 1887 a Catalan bishop was appointed to Astorga. Not prepared to settle for a modest prefab bungalow on the edge of town, he decided that his residence was to be built by his mate, a man called Gaudí. The townsfolk were horrified, but the result is a fairytale-style castle with pointy turrets. Little of the interior was designed by the man, as he was kept away by the hostility of the locals, but there are a couple of nice touches, notably in the bishop's throne room and chapel. Much of the (chilly) interior is taken up by the **Museo de los Caminos**, a collection of art and artefacts relating to the pilgrimage to Santiago. The garden is guarded by some scary angels. The **tourist office** ⓘ *Tue-Sat 1000-1400, 1600-1900, Sun 1000-1400*, is opposite the Palacio Episcopal.

Astorga's **Plaza Mayor** is attractive, and notable for the figures of a Maragato man and woman that strike the hour on the town hall clock. Some of the city's Roman heritage can be seen at the **Museo Romano** ⓘ *Tue-Sat 1000-1400, 1600-1800 (1700-1930 summer), Sun*

1100-1400, €3, constructed over some of the old forum by the Ayuntamiento. Finds from many of the archaeological excavations around the town are on display. There are many **Roman remains** of interest around the town; the tourist office will provide a map of the *Ruta Romana*; there are guided tours in the summer.

Another museum is the **Museo de Chocolate** ① *Tue-Sat 1600-1800 (1630-1900 summer), Sun 1000-1400, €2.50*, where you can learn how chocolate was, and is, made.

Around Astorga

Some 5 km from Astorga, **Castrillo de los Polvazares** is somewhat touristy, but it's the most attractive of the **Maragato villages**. Built of muddy red stone, it's been attractively restored, and you still expect the rattle of mulecarts down its cobbled streets. There are many other less-developed Maragato villages around that are worth checking out if you've got transport. There are around 40 or 50 of them in all; some of the nicest are **Murias de Rechivaldo**, **Luyego** and **Santiago Millas**. All have at least one hearty restaurant dishing up the famed **cocido**.

El Bierzo

The lands immediately west of Astorga mainly consist of low scrubby hills. There's little of interest until the Bierzo region in the west of the province. The Bierzo is crisscrossed by middling mountain ranges and pretty valleys. The Romans mined gold and other metals here, and some coal mines are still creaking on towards their inevitable closure. It's now mainly famous for red wine and vegetables; its peppers have DO (*denominación de origen*) status and are famous throughout Spain. There are many hidden corners of the region to investigate; it's one of Northern Spain's least known and most interesting corners that could merit a sizeable guidebook on its own.

Ponferrada

Although afflicted by rampant urban sprawl, industrial Ponferrada has a small, attractive old centre above the river Sil. It's a fast-growing and vibrant young city and capital of the Bierzo region, whose fruity red wines are growing in fame outside Spain. The main feature of the centre is a superb **Templar castle** ① *Tue-Sat 1030-1400, 1600-1800, Sun 1100-1400, open until 2030 Jul-Aug, €6, free Wed*, low but formidable, with a series of defensive walls and a steep underground passage descending to the river.

Some lovely buildings are preserved in the old town; check out the small lanes around the **Plaza de Ayuntamiento**, an attractive space in itself; nearby a pretty clocktower arches across the street. The **Basílica de la Virgen de Encina** sits in another square and is an attractive building. The **Museo del Bierzo** ① *Tue-Sat 1100-1400, 1600-1900 (1700-2030 May-Sep), Sun 1100-1400, €2.70*, set in an old *palacio* in the centre, is a good display, with items of interest from the region's Celtic cultures as well as the Templar period. There's a nice patio and cobbled courtyard. There's also a small **railway museum** ① *Tue-Sat 1100-1400, 1600-1900 (May-Sep 1700-2030), Sun 1100-1400, €2.70*, on the edge of the new town, with several lovable old locomotives. The **tourist office** is by the castle walls.

Valle del Silencio

One of the most charming spots in Northern Spain is this hidden valley south of Ponferrada. The treeless plains of Castilla seem light years away as you wind through grape vines into the narrow valley carved by the River Oza. Chestnuts and oaks, as well as abundant animal and bird life accompany the cheerful stream through villages that are utterly tranquil and rural. A circular walk around the valley, waymarked PR L-E 14, is an excellent way to spend a day; it takes about six hours.

The village of **Villafrancos** is one of the prettiest in the valley, with a delightfully picturesque stone bridge, and villagers going about their business as if the passing of centuries is a curious but inconsequential matter. There's a small bar here, but no accommodation available.

Perched below the hamlet of **San Pedro de Monte**, signposted down a side road, is a monastery, mostly in ruins but of a venerable age. You can visit its baroque church, which has a Romanesque tower. The Valle del Silencio road ends at **Peñalba de Santiago**, and you feel it's done well to get this far. Peñalba, a village of slate where three mountain ranges meet, has eked out an existence on chestnuts for centuries. Although the village is in good modern repair (restored a few years ago to beautiful effect), it's a grey beauty, with wooden balconies and an ends-of-the-earth feel. Enjoy a glass of home-made wine and a tapa of *cecina* at Cantina opposite the church, a bar steeped in tradition and the focus of village life.

The centrepiece of the village is a 10th-century **Mozarabic church** ① *Oct-Mar Wed-Sat 1040-1400, 1600-1750, Sun 1040-1400, Apr-Sep Wed-Sat 1015-1400, 1630-2000, Sun 1015-1400*, which belies its solid exterior with elegant horseshoe arches inside, as well as many fragments of wall painting.

It's about a four- to five-hour stroll from Ponferrada to Peñalba, through beautiful surroundings; much of the distance is a marked trail that follows the river. **▶▶** *See Transport, page 79.*

Molinaseca

Some 5 km southeast of Ponferrada, on the Camino de Santiago, this excellent stone village, famous for its *embutidos* – chorizo, salchichón, and the like – sits by a babbling river, scene of a frenetic water-fight during the village fiestas. It's full of bodegas that have been converted into bars, where the typical order is a cheap local wine that comes with a hunk of bread and slice of chorizo. It's particularly popular on Sundays with folk from Ponferrada. There's a pilgrim hostel here, and plenty of accommodation and eating options. For pilgrims it may make a more relaxing stay than Ponferrada itself.

Villafranca del Bierzo

West of Ponferrada, the Camino de Santiago heads west to Galicia and the road leads into dark wooded uplands. The next stop for most Santiago-bound walkers is Villafranca del Bierzo. An attractive town, it's a nice spot to gather strength and spirit before the long ascent into Galicia. In medieval times, many pilgrims were by this stage not physically capable of continuing into the harsher terrain and weather conditions. That being the case, if they reached the church here, they were granted the same absolutions and indulgences as if they had completed the whole journey to Santiago. The **Iglesia de Santiago** is where they had to go, at least from when it was built in the late 12th century. Although Romanesque, it's unusual in form, with a cavernous, barn-like interior with a calming feel. There's a crucifixion above the simple altar, with Christ looking very old and careworn; the side chapel is a more recent affair with an 18th-century *retablo*. The side door, the Puerta del Perdón, is what the pilgrims had to touch to receive all the spiritual benefits of their journey. It has some nice capitals around it, including one of the three wise men cosily bunked up in a single bed.

Nearby, the foursquare **castle** has big crumbly walls as well as a restored section. It's still lived in and therefore cannot be visited. There's a late **Gothic Colegiata** with some local architectural influences; near here make a point of walking down Calle del Agua, a superbly atmospheric street lined with old buildings. Villafranca's **tourist office** ⓘ *daily 1000-1400, 1600-1900 (2000 summer)*, is very helpful.

Las Médulas and around

The Romans found gold all over Bierzo, but here at Las Médulas they had to perform engineering wonders to get at it. Mining open-cast, they diverted river waters in elaborate ways and employed thousands of labourers in what was a massive ongoing operation. Las Médulas are the eerie and surreal remains of their toil, a large stretch of terrain sculpted into strange formations and crisscrossed by paths and tunnels, some of which are amazingly extensive. To get the full idea, it's best to head first to the best viewpoint in the area, near the village of **Orellán**; from here there's an amazing vista over the tortured earth. Pliny described one of the mining techniques as *ruina montium* (the destruction of a mountain); vast quantities of water were suddenly channelled through a prepared network of wells and sluices, literally blowing the whole hillside out and down the hill to the panning areas below. A few hills survived the process; these stand forlorn, sharp little peaks red among the heathery valleys.

Near the mirador is a network of galleries to explore (entrance €1.50); ponder Pliny's account of the labour as you walk through them: "The light of day is never seen for months at a time. The galleries are prone to collapse without warning, leaving workers buried alive. Any rocks that blocked their passage were attacked with fire and vinegar, but the smoke and fumes often choked people in the caves. So they were broken into smaller pieces with blows from iron mallets and carried out on shoulders day and night, handing them along a human chain in that infernal darkness." The incomprehensible thing is that these mines were not even particularly lucrative; recent estimates put the annual production of gold at around 25 kg; extraordinarily low from such a vast operation.

Once you've got the perspective, head for the village of Las Médulas itself, where there's a small visitor centre. From here, guided walks of the area lasting about 1½ hours run four times daily and cost €3, but you can strike off along the paths yourself at any time.

The area is some 24 km southwest of Ponferrada.

North of León → *For listings, see pages 75-79.*

The mountainous northern reaches of León province are little known except by locals, but merit plenty of exploration. It's a favourite destination of cavers and rockclimbers in summer and skiers in winter. A series of spectacular mountain passes join the province with neighbouring Asturias; these are often snowbound in winter. A car is the best way to nose around the area, although the **FEVE** trains and the odd bus makes its way out from León to many outlying villages in the zone.

Las Hoces and the Cuevas de Valporquero

A good day out from León could see you head north to the region of Las Hoces, two narrow gorges spectacularly carved from the grey stone. Take the LE-311 that follows the course of the Torio River and continue past Matallana de Torio up the first of the gorges, **Las Hoces de Vegacervera**. The villages in this area continue much as they have done for years, pasturing sheep in the summer and grimly hanging on through the cold winters. Look out for *madreñas*, a wooden clog worn over the shoes when tramping around the muddy fields, and the famous Leonese *mastín*, or mastiff, an enormous, shaggy, friendly beast.

Off the road through the gorge are the stunning limestone caves of **Valporquero** ① *www.cuevadevalporquero.es, mid-May-Sep 1000-1800, Oct-mid-Dec Thu-Sun 1000-1700, Mar-mid-May Thu-Sun 1000-1700, €8.50*, much of which remains to be discovered. Some of the chambers are amazingly large, and (in spring and autumn) there is an underground river plunging into the depths, as well as the fascinating limestone sculpture. Take warm clothing, non-slip footwear and some sort of waterproof to the caves, as it can get pretty wet if it's been raining.

Beyond the Valporquero cave turn-off, take a right turn up the LE-313 through the other gorge, the **Valdeteja**. Continuing through the gorge, take another right just after Valdeteja itself on the LE-321. About 6 km down this road, look out for a small paved area on the right. A path leads to a spectacular waterfall pounding through a hole in the rocky hill. Once you've followed the horseshoe shape through both gorges, the road ends at the village of **La Vecilla**, 4 km from the waterfall and serviced several times daily by **FEVE** trains from León. There are several accommodation options in this region.

Northeast to the Picos → *For listings, see pages 75-79.*

The northeastern section of León province is isolated and fairly poor, climbing steadily towards the Picos de Europa. Formerly a significant coal-mining region, little of that goes on here now; farming and sausage-making are the mainstays of the small towns in the area.

Boñar and around

Vegaquemada, a small village on the way to Boñar, has nothing of interest except a strange church in an Italianate style, with an ornate layered belltower and a porch with filigreed ironwork. ▶▶ *For the Leonese Picos, see below.*

Boñar is served by buses from León, but also has a train connection to Santander on the private **FEVE** network. From Boñar, the quickest route to the peaks is east via Sabero, a coalmining town amid low mountains that look to be melting.

Boñar itself is liveliest in winter as there's a **ski resort** nearby. It's a somewhat bleak place like much of this region, but there are a couple of decent places to stay.

Riaño

Forgive Riaño its slightly ugly, gawky appearance overlooking an often empty lake; the construction of the controversial dam and reservoir forced the town to reluctantly relocate to the top of the hill in the 1980s.

Although it's the southern gateway to the Picos, not an awful lot goes on here except hunting and people passing through. If you're wanting to explore this side of the range, **Posada de Valdeón** makes a smaller but more inviting and convenient base (see page 76).

There's a tourist kiosk at the entrance to the town, a couple of banks, a service station and a handful of places to stay.

Leonese Picos → *For listings, see pages 75-79.*

Although this part of the Picos range isn't as endowed with tourist facilities as the Asturian or Cantabrian sections, it contains much of the area's most dramatic scenery, with breathtaking mountain vistas suddenly revealed as you round a bend in the path or road. It's also colder and, in winter snowier, than the more northern sections. While Riaño (see above), is the area's biggest town, it's a bit far from the action and not especially charming;

a better bet is little Posada de Valdeón, spectacularly set in a lush valley surrounded by rocky peaks.

Valdeón Valley

West of Riaño, the Valdeón Valley is the main part of the Leonese Picos and a remote rural area famous for its strong blue cheese. The road climbs to the **Puerto de Pandetrave** at 1562 m, which suddenly reveals a superb view of the valley, dwarfed by the imposing stone masses of the Picos. The first village in the valley itself is **Santa Marina**, a very rural settlement of simple stone houses. It's a friendly village with a good campsite and a hostel.

Four kilometres further up the lovely grassy valley is the area's main settlement, **Posada de Valdeón**. This is the southern terminus for the popular walk along the Cares Gorge and is well equipped for such a small place, with hotels, a supermarket and bank, but no cash machine. The setting is spectacular, with the intimidating mass of Peña Bermeja behind it contrasting with the lush pasturelands around. The Picos de Europa National Park has an **information office** ① *T987 740 504, Mon-Fri 0900-1700, Wed 1400-1700 only*, in Posada from where it runs free guided trips during the summer months (phone for details). There are several places to stay.

North from Posada de Valdeón, a steep and narrow road makes its way to the village of **Caín**, a walk of just over 1½ hours. Jeeps run a shared-taxi service between the two towns. Not far from Posada, a fantastic view opens up as the valley seems to be swallowed up by lofty mountains; it's an awe-inspiring sight in good weather. The **Mirador de Pombo** is one vantage point to appreciate the vista; it's marked by a slender chamois and a confusing diagram of the peaks around. Before you reach here, the hamlet of **Cordiñanes** has a good rustic *pensión*.

Caín itself would be about as isolated as a rural village gets were it not for the number of walkers passing through the **Garganta de Cares**. As it is, there are a couple of restaurants, shops and a few lodging options.

León Province listings

For hotel and restaurant price codes and other relevant information, see pages 11-17.

⊖ Where to stay

Sahagún *p68*
If you're not walking the Camino, Sahagún is best seen as a day trip from León or Palencia, but there are decent places to stay.
€€-€ Hostal El Ruedo, Plaza Mayor 1, T987 780 075, www.restauranteelruedo.com. This is a good choice, on the main plaza with clean modern rooms, recently renovated and equipped to hotel standard, above an *asador*. There are only 4 rooms so you might want to book ahead during peak pilgrim season.
€ La Codorniz, C Arco, T987 780 276. Right opposite the tourist office, these rooms are unremarkable in decoration, but large, light and comfortable and the restaurant is decent.

Valencia de Don Juan *p69*
€€ El Palacio, C Palacio 3, T987 750 474. One of the best places to stay in town, this is set in a beautiful old mansion and has friendly Asturian management and a good bar (where you can try Asturian cider) and restaurant.

Astorga *p70*
€€ Hotel La Peseta, Plaza San Bartolomé 3, T987 617 275, www.restaurantelapeseta. com. Good rooms above what is widely considered one of Astorga's best restaurants. The rooms are excellent for this price, and the staff incredibly welcoming.

€ Pensión García, Bajada Postigo 3, T987 616 046. One of the cheaper choices in town, this is clean and decent, if fairly unremarkable.

Around Astorga *p71*
€€ Cuca la Vaina, C Jardín s/n, Castrillo de los Polvazares, T987 691 078, www. cucalavaina.es. If you're exploring the area, this is a top base in the village of Castrillo de los Polvazares, with a lively bar and excellent restaurant. The rooms are rustic and beautiful, with elaborately carved headboards, and much-needed heating in winter.
€ El Molino de Arriero, Av Villalibre 5, Luyego, T987 601 720, www.molinodelarriero. com. This is another welcoming *casa rural* with compact, simple rooms. Also serves good cheap meals. The bar gets noisy at weekends, but otherwise it's a very peaceful place.

Ponferrada *p71*
Few of Ponferrada's accommodations are in the old town; most are in the new zone across the river.
€€ Hostal La Encina, C Comendador 4, T987 409 632, www.hostallaencina.com. Parked right beside the castle, this is pricier than some of the many cheaper *hostales* around Ponfe, but worth it for the warm rustic decor and the amiable owner.
€€ Hotel Bierzo Plaza, Plaza del Ayuntamiento 4, T987 409 001, www. aroihoteles.com. This appealing modern hotel has an excellent location in central Ponferrada, on the town hall square and warm, professional service. The rooms are decorated with a light touch, and are good value for the price. There's a popular café downstairs. Recommended.

Valle del Silencio *p71*
Peñalba de Santiago
There are 2 accommodation options, both *casas rurales* available only to rent as a whole. Both need to be booked in advance.
Casa Elba, Arriba de la Fuente 2, T988 322 037, casaelba.blogspot.com. Very cosy, with 2 double rooms and 2 single beds, kitchen,

balcony, heating and lounge with log-fire. If there are a few of you, it's a bargain for daily or weekly rental.
Turpesa, Plaza de la Iglesia s/n, T987 425 566, casaturpesa.blogspot.com.es. Not quite as cosy as **Casa Elba**, but still a good deal for €180 a weekend or €500 a week. It sleeps 3.

Villafranca del Bierzo *p72*
There are several good places to stay in Villafranca.
€€€ Parador Villafranca del Bierzo, Av Calvo Sotelo-Constitución s/n, T987 540 175, www.parador.es. Recently renovated in neo-rustic style, this comfortable modern parador offers good views, a garden, outdoor pools, and a high level of service and food.
€€ Hotel San Francisco, Plaza Mayor/ Generalísimo 6, T987 540 465, www. hotelsanfrancisco.org. Closed Dec-Feb. This is a solid option on the attractive main plaza. As it's right in the centre, you pay a little for location, but it's an enjoyable place to stay.

Valdeón Valley *p75*
Santa Marina
€€ Casa Friero, C Amapolas 1, T987 742 658. A very good, if slightly pricey, *casa rural* in the village; kitchen facilities are available for guests' use. Sleeps 6 and is only available as an entire rental; €90 per day or €420 for a week.
€ La Ardilla Real, Plaza de la Esquina, T987 742 677, www.alberguelaardillareal.com. A friendly place in the heart of the village that offers simple but comfortable dormitory accommodation (€12 per person) and warming home-style meals.
Camping El Cares, 1 km out of town, T987 742 676. A campsite where you can rent horses to explore the valley.

Posada de Valdeón
€ Ezkurra, Plaza Cortina Concejo s/n, T987 740 547. A stay at this warm and welcoming *casa rural* feels like sleeping at a friend's place rather than staying at a hotel. There's plenty of comfort at very low prices, and

good information from the hospitable owner. Breakfast is delicious and features home-made *bizcocho*.

€ Hostal Campo, Ctra Cordiñanes s/n, T987 740 502. In the centre of the town, this friendly choice has big, warm and comfy rooms with modern bathrooms and views at a reasonable price. Fuel up for the hike with their delicious €4 breakfast.

€ Pensión Begoña, Plaza Cortina Concejo s/n, T987 740 516. Run by the same management as the **Hostal Campo**, this is a friendly option, cheap, fairly basic and likeable; rooms have clean shared bathroom and a down-to-earth walkers' vibe.

€ Posada El Asturiano, Ctra Cordiñanes s/n, T987 740 514. A favourite with many Picos regulars, this has warm and comfortable rooms just off the square and a reasonable restaurant. It's not quite so inviting in winter, when it feels a bit abandoned and musty.

El Valdeón, T987 742 605. Open summer only. The closest campsite is a couple of kilometres out on the road to Soto.

Caín

€ Casa Cuevas, Caín, T987 740 500, www.casacuevas.es. Recently refurbished, this walkers' spot offers comfortable, if a touch spartan, rooms, and is the village's best spot for a no-frills feed. There's a *menú* for €10; otherwise ask for *cabrito asado*, roast goat that is the region's speciality.

€ Posada del Montañero, Caín, T987 742 711. The nicest option, open Apr-Sep, a comfortable but overpriced inn with a good simple restaurant.

€ Rojo, C Santiago 8, Cordiñanes, T987 740 523. A rustic *pensión*, clean and comfortable with an unbeatable location if you're not scared of big, powerful mountains.

🍴 Restaurants

Sahagún *p68*

€€€ Restaurante Luis, Plaza Mayor 4, T987 781 085. Sahagún is famous for its *puerros* (leeks), and the best place to try them is here;

it's a great restaurant with a log fire, courtyard and a large fresco depicting market day. There's a *menú* at lunchtimes but it's much more interesting to go à la carte.

Astorga *p70*

€€ Hostal La Peseta, Plaza San Bartolomé 3, T987 617 275. See Where to stay, above. The best *cocido* in town.

€€ Parrillada Serrano, C Portería 2, T987 617 866, www.restauranteserrano.es. This is spacious and cosily stylish; there's a big range of dishes (including an excellent fish soup) and a good-value *menú*.

€ Cubasol, C Ovalle 10, T987 616 489. Traditional and no-frills place for cheap *raciones* of octopus, calamari, or sweetbreads. There's a cheap *menú del día* too.

€ Pizzería Venecia, C Matías Rodríguez 2, T987 618 463. Popular with all types of Astorgan, this is an inexpensive option with poor service and excellent pizza.

Cafés

Café Kavafis, C Mártires de Somiedo 5, T987 615 363. This cosy little place has internet access and books, including by the Alexandrine poet after whom it is named. The peaceful atmosphere changes at weekends, when it becomes a small disco, with good DJs.

Around Astorga *p71*

€€ Casa Juan Andrés, C Real 24, Castrillo de los Polvazares, T987 691 065, www.casajuan andres.es. Not the cheapest of the village's places, but this cosy place up the far end offers the best *cocido* in town in a beautifully decorated traditional courtyard house.

Ponferrada *p71*

There are many good tapas bars in Ponferrada, some in the old centre, and some around Plaza Fernando Miranda.

€€ Las Cuadras, Trasero de la Cava 2, T987 419 373. A good dark Spanish restaurant down the side of the castle with gutsy fishes and meats and a good set lunch. The tables are characterfully set around a central atrium.

€ El Bodegón, Travesía Pelayo 2, T987 411 019. Atmospheric central tapas bar in a spacious old stone wine cellar. A hearty dish of potatoes with sauce comes free with your drink.

€ Fragata, Av Montearenas s/n, Santo Tomás de las Olas, T987 401 231. It's worth tracking down this no-frills place on the edge of Ponferrada to gorge on some of Northern Spain's finest octopus, served in the traditional manner. Great value, but book ahead.

€ La Bodeguilla, Plaza Fernando Miranda 5, T987 411 119. One of the city's best tapas bars, this has wine-inspired decor, with wooden cases, hanging 'vines', and a soft padded bar. It's a popular meeting point for its delicious ham *pinchos*.

€ La Fonda, Plaza del Ayuntamiento 10, T987 425 794, with a nice covered terrace and excellent *alubias* (stewed beans) and generous meat dishes. *Menú del día* for €12.

Villafranca del Bierzo *p72*
€ Mesón Don Nacho, C Truqueles 2, T987 540 076, tucked off the main road just short of the square, is a cellar-type place offering an excellent *menú* for €10 full of hearty things like stews, tripe, and *caldo gallego*, a fortifying Galician soup.

€ Sevilla, Plaza Mayor s/n. Serves a good-value lunch *menú* with plenty of choice and lots of seating outside on the square. There's also internet access and friendly people running it.

Las Médulas and around *p73*
€ El Lagar, C Leirancos s/n, Orellán, T987 695 383. If you're visiting Las Médulas, the best lunch stop is this rustic spot in nearby Orellán. The food is no-nonsense and abundant; it's a very typical redoubt of Bierzo hospitality.

Las Hoces and the Cuevas de Valporquero *p73*
€ Venta de Getino, Getino, T987 576 424 www.restauranteventadegetinocasaamador. com. Not far north of the turn-off to the Valporquero caves, this typical rural restaurant makes a great lunch stop. The food is excellent and plentiful, and the family-run atmosphere very welcoming. There's a *menú del día* for €10 (€15 at weekends), but don't expect to be able to finish it all.

Boñar and around *p74*
€€ La Praillona, Av Constitución 41, T987 735 810, www.lapraillona.com. Quality Leonese mountain cuisine can be had at this well-run place. Ingredients are of high quality, and the traditional dishes come with a modern twist.

Valdeón Valley *p75*
Posada de Valdeón
€ Pensión Begoña, see Where to stay, above. Just about the best place to eat in the Leonese Picos, this simple mountain inn has fed former prime minister Zapatero and offers hospitable service and hearty no-frills traditional cooking. It's a set menu (€14) with limited choice – you might get trout, which abound in the streams around here, or stew made from freshly hunted boar or venison – but it's bound to be hearty and good.

🎵 Bars and clubs

Ponferrada *p71*
Ponferrada has a famously boisterous nightlife; in the streets behind the **Temple** hotel there are any number of *discobares* with all types of music. Later on, the action moves out to the large bars in the purpose-built complex known as **La Gran Manzana**.

A unique venue in the heart of the old town is **Sala Tararí**, C del Reloj 17, www. salatarari.com, an excellent bar with an inclusive feel, friendly folk, regular high-quality concerts, and a rocking Thu night jam session that's worth timing your visit to experience.

✦ Festivals

Astorga *p70*
Aug A Roman festival, togas and all.

Valdeón Valley *p75*
Posada de Valdeón
Sep 8 The Leonese Picos's biggest day is the fiesta of the Virgen de Corona in the Valdeón Valley.

✦ Transport

Sahagún *p68*
Bus A few buses stop in Sahagún but they are significantly slower than the train.

Train There are a dozen or so feasible daily trains linking **León** and Sahagún, a journey of 30 mins. Some of the trains continue to **Grajal**, 5 mins away, before heading onto **Palencia**.

Mansilla de las Mulas *p69*
Bus There are buses at least hourly from **León** to Mansilla (20 mins). 2 buses continue Mon-Fri, and 1 Sat to **San Miguel de la Escalada** (40 mins).

Valencia de Don Juan *p69*
Bus Buses run to Valencia from **León** 6-8 times a day (30 mins). A similar number head on to **Valladolid**.

Astorga *p70*
Bus There are 15 daily buses from **León** to Astorga. There are a few trains too, but the station is inconveniently situated 20 mins' walk from the centre.

Ponferrada *p71*
Bus Ponferrada's bus station is across the river from the old town; it's a bit of a trudge, but there are frequent city buses crossing the river. Many buses go to **León**, several a day go on west to **Villafranca**, and several continue into **Galicia**, mostly to **Lugo** and **Santiago**.

Train Trains run east to **León** via **Astorga** 6 times a day, and some go west to **A Coruña**, **Ourense** and **Vigo**. The train station is also across the river from the old town.

Valle del Silencio *p71*
Bus There are only 2 buses monthly from **Ponferrada** up the valley to Peñalba de Santiago, so drive, hitch or walk.

Villafranca del Bierzo *p72*
Bus Villafranca is served by ALSA buses from **León** and **Ponferrada**. Many buses continue into **Galicia**.

Riaño *p74*
Bus There are 3 buses daily (only 1 on Sun) from **León** to Riaño, one continuing to the **Picos de Europa**.

Valdeón Valley *p75*
Posada de Valdeón
Bus The southern part of the Picos is a bit problematic when it comes to transport. There's 1 bus Mon-Fri from **León** to Posada de Valdeón, and on to **Caín**, currently leaving León at 1830. There are 5 buses to **Riaño** from León Mon-Fri, 2 on Sat, and 1 on Sun.

Taxi There's a shared taxi service from Posada de Valdeón to **Caín**, at the head of the Cares Gorge walk.

Soria

One of Spain's smallest provincial capitals, Soria rules a province that's incredibly empty, one of the most sparsely populated in Spain. Although much of it is dry Castilian plains, the river Duero gives it the fullest attention, carving a big horseshoe shape through the province, eventually reaching the sea at Porto in northern Portugal (where it's named the Douro). In the north of the region are some craggy hills and tranquil hilly forests, but few trees remain in the south, for centuries a battleground between Christian and Moor. Dozens of castles are testament to this, as are the gracefully simple Romanesque churches built by the eventual victors. As the Reconquista progressed, however, Christian settlers moved south in search of less thirsty lands, leaving the province a little denuded.

Soria is little known in the travel community but is worth a day or two of anyone's time, particularly for its outstanding Romanesque architecture and strong community spirit. It's one of Castilla's friendliest places, and a good spot to get a feel for this part of central Spain, its landscapes, and its cuisine.

Arriving in Soria → *Phone code: 975. Population: 39,528.*

Getting there and around Soria is well connected by bus to other major cities in Northern Spain. The bus station is a 15-minute walk northwest from the centre of town. A yellow bus runs from Plaza Ramón y Cajal to the train station, a couple of kilometres south. The old town, where most sights of interest are to be found, is easily walkable, tucked between two attractive parks, the hilltop Parque el Castillo and the more formal Alameda de Cervantes. The pedestrianized main street changes name a couple of times but runs the length of the area. ►► *See Transport, page 86.*

Tourist information Soria's **tourist office** ① *C Medinaceli 2, T975 212 052, oficinadeturismo desoria@jcyl.es, mid-Sep to Jun Mon-Sat 0930-1400, 1600-1900, Sun 0930-1700, summer daily 0900-2000,* is just around the corner from Plaza Ramón y Cajal and is very helpful.

Background

Although nearby Numancia was an important Celtiberian settlement, Soria itself didn't really get going until the Middle Ages, when it achieved prosperity as a wool town. But its relative isolation (plus the fact that the sheep ate all the grass) led to its decline, along with that of the rest of Castilla. Once the coast was under central control, there was no percentage left in towns like Soria; the conditions that led to its rise ceased to exist after the Moors had been driven out. The *cabeza* (head) *de Extremadura* – this word formerly referred to the Christian borderlands in the Reconquista – became just another decaying provincial town. Happily, this meant that there wasn't enough money to meddle with its Romanesque architectural heritage too much, a fact that the city is surely grateful for today.

Places in Soria → *For listings, see pages 85-86.*

Iglesia de Santo Domingo
On the northern edge of the old town, by the main road through Soria, is the Santo Domingo church, built of beautiful pale pink stone, and possessing one of the loveliest Romanesque façades in Spain. The interior is simple; barrel-vaulted and with several interesting capitals that can be a little hard to inspect in the gloom. The portal is the highlight, though, with ornately carved bands depicting a number of Biblical scenes in appealing naïve sculpture. A small guide inside the doorway helps to identify the scenes; including the visitation of the angel to the Magi. The three seem more saucy than wise, all very cosy in bed under a single duvet.

Monasterio de San Juan de Duero and around
① *Jul-Sep 1000-1400, 1700-2000; Oct-Jun 1000-1400, 1600-1900, closed all day Mon and Sun afternoon, €0.60.*
Not far from the Iglesia de San Pedro, just on the other side of the river, this is Soria's best sight. Although it started as a humble church, a group of Hospitallers of Saint John of Jerusalem (later known as the Knights of Malta) set up base here on their return from the crusades. The simple church, damaged by fire over the years, preserves some excellent capitals and has decent Spanish display panels on the Romanesque in general. The cloister outside is a strange and striking sight. The knights blended four different types of arch around the square, the simple Romanesque, the Islamic horseshoe and two extroverted crisscross styles also derived from the east. Throughout the complex, the capitals are an expression of the returning knights' wonderment at the strange world they had seen beyond Christendom: strange beasts and plants, violent battles and weird buildings predominate; there's scarcely a Biblical scene in sight.

On the other side of the main road from San Juan, but on the same side of the river, a lovely riverside walk along the lazy Duero leads past the vine-swathed Templar church of **San Polo** (set in an apple orchard but closed to the public), to the hermitage church of **San Saturio** ① *Tue-Sat 1030-1400, 1630-1830 (1930 in spring and autumn, 2030 in summer), Sun 1030-1400, free.* The saint is a popular local figure who lived in the sixth century. The building is perched on sloping rock above a grotto where he lived as a hermit for 36 years. The chapel is attractively painted floor to ceiling with wall paintings of Saturio's life; there's an impressive bearded icon of him above the altar with very haunted eyes. In another chamber are more paintings of his doings; in one he appears to be boiling sea monsters. He's still the patron of Soria, and numerous offerings and requests are made by locals.

Around the Plaza Mayor
Back in town, above the Plaza Mayor, is another Romanesque treasure in lovely Sorian stone, the **Iglesia de San Juan de Rabanera** ① *Jul-Oct Tue-Sun 1100-1400, 1700-2000; winter closed, but you can sneak a quick look inside before and after Mass (times on the door).* Behind the plaza on the other side is the long and imposing **Palacio de los Condes de Gómara**, whose Plateresque façade features a high gallery with Ionic columns; it's now used by the local government.

A mock-Roman building by the lovely Alameda de Cervantes park houses the **Museo Numantino** ① *Tue-Sat 1000-1400, 1600-1900 (1700-2000 summer), Sun 1000-1400, €1.20.* The very good display, with information in English, is mostly devoted to Roman and Celtiberian finds from Numancia and the province.

Around Soria → *For listings, see pages 85-86.*

Some 6 km north of Soria, just outside the village of **Garray**, a windswept grassy hill is the site of **Numancia** ① *Tue-Sat 1000-1400, 1600-1800 (to 2000 Apr-Sep), Sun 1000-1400, €0.60.* The inhabitants, doomed to bear the unsatisfactory name of Celtiberians until we can be surer of their origins, weren't too keen to submit to Republican Rome when it came knocking in 153 BC. Despite being outgunned, they amazingly managed to resist for 25 years. Finally, the enforcer Scipio was sent from Rome to sort them out. Not one for mucking around, he decided to encircle the walled town with a massive wall of his own, heavily fortified with camps. The despairing inhabitants lasted another 11 months before succumbing. The Romans built their own town on the site, which became one of the most important pre-Roman towns of the region, but there's not a great deal to see these days. Many years later the Numancian resistance became a powerful symbol of Spanish heroism

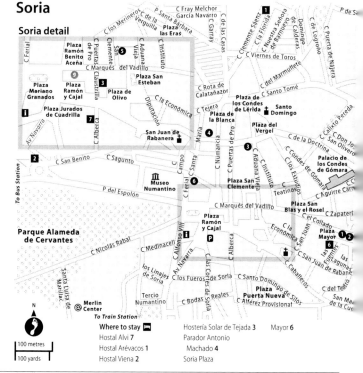

Soria

and somewhat ironically, was used by Franco, who surely would have better identified himself with the Romans. Even Soria's have-a-go football team is named after the town.

The spread-out site is by no means thrilling today; without your own transport you might be better confining yourself to a visit to the museum in Soria. The ruins include foundations of roads, houses, public baths and a large public building; more approachable are the reconstructed Celtiberian and Roman dwellings. A couple of monuments from 1842 and 1904 commemorate the long-dead heroism of the siege. Numancia is 500 m up a road on the right after passing the centre of the village. If you don't have a car, get a cab (about €12 each way); buses to Garray run at inconvenient times.

There are several good parts of the **Sorian hills** to explore north of the capital, towards the province of La Rioja. The N-111 barrels straight north to Logroño, but ascends a picturesque mountain pass on the way, before encountering some seriously craggy hills just over the border in Rioja province. West of the road is a large expanse of forested hills, with several numbered walks. The nicest village in the region is **Molinos de Duero**, a quiet little place with lovely stone houses. Nearby, the village of **Vinuesa** is another potential base, and has a small information centre on the region.

Twenty kilometres north and west of Vinuesa is the **Laguna Negra**, reached by a potholed road. From the car park, it's a couple of kilometres up the hill to the small lake,

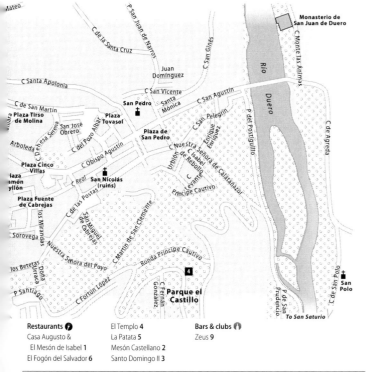

Restaurants
Casa Augusto &
El Mesón de Isabel **1**
El Fogón del Salvador **6**

El Templo **4**
La Patata **5**
Mesón Castellano **2**
Santo Domingo II **3**

Bars & clubs
Zeus **9**

beautifully opaque under jagged rocky peaks. There's a small information centre here, which can provide details about other walks in the vicinity.

Another good route north of Soria is on the R-115 northeast by bus or car into dinosaur country. **Yanguas**, on the Sorian side of the border, is an extremely peaceful place to stop and the numerous dinosaur footprints are well worth investigating.

East of Soria, the **Dehesa de Moncayo** is another pleasant hillforest on the Aragonese border, while the town of **Agreda** is nice enough but has little to offer compared with Tarazona, further on. However, for a couple of decades it played an important part in Spanish history; a nun in the monastery, Sor María de Agreda, became a regular correspondent with the mighty King Felipe II, and gave him much political advice and spiritual comfort over many years.

South of Soria → *For listings, see pages 85-86.*

Almazán

If you're desperately in search of ugly Castillian towns, then Almazán will be another disappointment; a tranquil, friendly, furniture-making centre with attractive preserved sections of walls overlooking the Duero, and a couple of Romanesque churches. Ascending from the bus station or the main road, you'll pass through an attractive arch and find yourself in the main plaza. The tourist office can be found here, as can the sober Palacio de los Hurtado de Mendoza. More striking is **San Miguel** ⓘ *Tue-Sun 1100-1400, 1600-1800, free*, the Romanesque church, slightly strangely capped with a brick belltower in Mudéjar style. Inside, it's cool and pleasant. A sculptural relief, sadly badly damaged, depicts the murder of Thomas Becket in Canterbury Cathedral. The story behind this unexpected subject is that it was carved at the behest of Eleanor, who married king Alfonso VIII; it was her father, Henry II, who was responsible for the turbulent priest's death. His daughter was probably trying to help him out with atoning for the deed.

Medinaceli

Medinaceli is a curious place, with a modern roadside town that has moved away from its roots – the old town sits atop a hill a couple of kilometres away. It's the old town that merits a visit, so if you're coming by public transport you'll have a bit of a walk ahead. It's either 3.5km by road, or you can strike at the hill directly, more strenuous but potentially quicker and more interesting.

Atop the hill, the old town is attractive but somewhat unreal. Although some people live here (half of them in a retirement home), it's not a real town any more; hotels, restaurants, and craft shops are the only things open, and the whole place has the feel of an open-air museum. Still, it's very picturesque. As well as a number of stately houses and palacios, also worth noting is a Roman triumphal arch dating from the 2nd century AD, probably wondering where the rest of the Roman town got to.

East of Medinaceli, and almost in Aragón is Santa María de la Huerta, a village that grew around a large Cistercian monastery. It's worth a peek for its lovely cloister, but it's not an inviting place to overnight.

Soria listings

For hotel and restaurant price codes and other relevant information, see pages 11-17.

◐ Where to stay

Soria *p80, map p82*

€€€ Parador Antonio Machado, Parque del Castillo s/n, T975 240 800, www.parador.es. Soria's parador is an attractive modern building peacefully set at the top of a park-covered hill above town. It's named after the famous poet, and selections of his work line the wall. The nicest rooms are suites that overlook the river and don't cost a great deal more, but it's all very comfortable, and is well staffed.

€€ Hostería Solar de Tejada, C Claustrilla 1, T975 230 054, www.hosteriasolardetejada.es. This is a great place to stay in the heart of Soria. Original decoration is backed up by warm-hearted service. The rooms, all different, are attractive and brightly coloured, and a solar and lunar theme runs throughout. Free Wi-Fi. Recommended.

€€ Hotel Soria Plaza Mayor, Plaza Mayor 10, T975 240 864, www.hotelsoriaplazamayor.com. With an excellent location on the tranquil square in the heart of the old town, this hotel has plenty to offer. There are just 10 rooms, decorated in dark but elegant style, with floorboards and a/c. The ones at the top of the building are not for space freaks, but are very appealing with their sloping roof.

€ Hostal Alvi, C Alberca 2, T975 228 112, www.hostalalvi.com. Extremely central, and efficiently run, this hostal has compact rooms on the upper floors of a municipal building. The exterior rooms have much more light, although there is a little bit of traffic noise as cars echo their way up this narrow street. Interior rooms are perfect for lighter sleepers.

€ Hostal Arévacos, C Clemente Sáenz 8, T975 212 832, www.hostalarevacos.com. Friendly family-run *hostal* offering comfortable modern rooms and easy parking a short distance from the town centre. Free Wi-Fi and a laundry service are among the facilities.

€ Hostal Viena, C García Solier 1, T975 222 109, www.hostal-viena.com. A short walk from the centre, this old-fashioned but hospitable *hostal* is set above a café. It's a bargain really for what you get; rooms with or without bathroom are showing their age but comfortable; all have TV and are pretty quiet. You should be able to park free somewhere nearby.

Around Soria *p82*

€€€-€€ Real Posada de la Mesta, Plaza Cañerias s/n, Molinos de Duero, T975 378 531, www.realposada.com. This is a great place to stay in this elegant village; a beautiful, large, old stone mansion with great decoration in heavy rustic style. They serve tasty gourmet meals. A highlight are the seasonal truffle-hunting outings. Recommended.

⊘ Restaurants

Soria *p80, map p82*

Soria's eating and drinking is focused around Plaza Ramón Benito Aceña, at one end of C Mayor, and Plaza San Clemente.

€€€ Mesón Castellano, Plaza Mayor 2, T975 213 045, www.mesoncastellanosoria.com. On the main square, and Castilian it certainly is, with large portions of heavy dishes such as roast goat, balanced by a decent house salad and some good Ribera del Duero reds. They'll also give you a very tasty free tapa if you drop in for a glass of wine.

€€€ Santo Domingo II, Plaza del Vergel 1, T975 211 717, www.santodomingo2.es. An elegant wood-and-curtains type of Spanish restaurant, with mixed Basque and Castilian fare. There are *menús* for 2 or more, which are good value.

€€ **El Fogón del Salvador**, Pl del Salvador 1, T975 230 194, www.fogonsalvador.com. There's nothing quite like the warm lighting and enticing aromas of a Castilian *asador*. This is one of the town's best, with extremely succulent meat brought to your table on its own little charcoal grill, and plenty of lighter dishes to back it up: in season, the grilled vegetables are a treat.

€€-€ **Casa Augusto/El Mesón de Isabel**, Plaza Mayor 4, T975 213 041, www.casaaugusto.com. These 2 connected restaurants are among the city's best. In **Casa Augusto** (€€), you can try traditional Sorian fare such as the tasty *pecho de cordero* or a variety of stews. It's decorated in traditional Castilian style, with excellent service. Adjoining it, **El Mesón de Isabel** (€) is a cheaper, bistro-style place with cheap set meal deals and comfort plates like meatballs and stuffed vegetables. The ambience is pleasant, with a large number of clocks and a romantic feel.

€ **El Templo**, Callejón del Pregonero 2, T975 215 162, www.bareltemplo.com. This central bar and restaurant stands out for the warm personal service and well-priced *raciones*; things like calamari and salads come in abundant quantity and quality. There are also more substantial dishes like steaks.

€ **La Patata**, Plaza San Carlos 1, T975 213 036. Popular for its good-value *raciones* and toasted bar-top snacks. They take a pride in their *patatas bravas*, served with a spicy home-made sauce.

🎶 Bars and clubs

Soria *p80, map p82*
The main nightlife starts in C Zapatería and C Real. Later it progresses away from the centre to the **Rota de Calatañazor** zone, where there are several *discobares* and *discotecas*.
Zeus, Plaza Ramón Benito Aceña s/n, T975 231 048. A smart café/bar on 2 floors. It's a good option at any time of the day; morning coffee to late-night drinks; they cater to all.

✳ Festivals

Soria *p80, map p82*
Late Jun Sanjuanes, Soria's main festival. with an array of bullfights, processions, fireworks and wine drinking.
2 Oct San Saturio's feast day is a big event.

⊖ Transport

Soria *p80, map p82*
Bus
7 daily buses to **Madrid** (2½ hrs), 6 to **Logroño** (1 hr 30 mins), several to **Vitoria** and to **Pamplona**, some via **Tafalla** and **Olite**. 6 buses (3 on Sun) to **Zaragoza** via **Tarazona**. Heading west, 1 daily heads Mon-Fri to **Berlanga**, 3 daily to **Calatañazor** and **El Burgo de Osma**, and another 3 to **Aranda de Duero** and **Valladolid**.
There are buses from Soria to Almazán and Medinaceli more or less hourly.

Train
The main rail destination is **Madrid** (2 daily, 2¾ hrs, €22), serviced via **Guadalajara** and **Almazán**.

Along the Duero: west from Soria to Valladolid

Travelling along the Río Duero you roughly follow the long-time frontline of the Reconquista. There are more castles than you could poke a battering ram at, although many are ruinous. The land is dry and sun-beaten except along the riverbanks, which give their name to one of Spain's best wine regions, the Ribera del Duero. Peñafiel, with its fine *mudéjar* architecture and vibrant festival, makes a convenient base for exploring the Duero region, which has many bodegas to visit as well as a wine museum. Within easy reach of Berlanga is one of Castilla's more remarkable monuments, the Ermita de San Baudelio. Further west, one of the oldest dioceses in the peninsula, dating from at least AD 598, El Burgo de Osma, once an important Castilian town, makes a worthy stopover, while nearby, the castle of Gormaz stands proud and forlorn on a huge rocky hill. North of here, the spectacular Cañón del Río Lobos provides top walking and vulture-spotting opportunities.

Calatañazor

Some 25 km west of Soria is the village of Calatañazor. This pretty but tiny place, with its cobbled streets, toppling castle and pretty Romanesque chapel, was the unlikely venue for the fall of the great Muslim warlord Al-Manzur, who was defeated here in a battle in 1002, the millennium of which was celebrated with *fiestas* and cultural events. Now home to only 30 inhabitants, Calatañazor – whose name derives from the Arabic 'Qal'at an-Nusur', which means castle of the vultures – is a picturesque place to stay. It's a touch touristy, but far enough off the beaten track that it's not really a problem; even in peak season, the day trippers disperse pretty soon after lunch. A small **tourist office** is at the bottom of the town, opposite the pretty 12th-century chapel, **Ermita de la Soledad**. In the heart of the village is the larger **Nuestra Señora del Castillo**, with a Romanesque portal and small museum. To get to Calatañazor, Burgo de Osma-bound buses from Soria will drop you at the turn-off on the main road, a 10-minute walk away.

Berlanga de Duero

Dominated by its impressive castle, Berlanga stands on a slope above the town, which is a likeable jumble of narrow lanes and old buildings set around an attractive plaza. In the centre is the reasonably interesting late-Gothic **Iglesia de Colegiata de Santa María**.

The **castle** ① *summer Tue-Sat 1100-1400, 1600-1930, Sun 1100-1400, €1, at other times ask for key in the tourist office (weekends) or Ayuntamiento (0830-1500 weekdays)*, originated as an Arab fortress, although most of it was built in the 15th and 16th centuries. The walls are preserved in a reasonable state, but little remains of the castle buildings or the elaborate gardens that once surrounded them. It is nevertheless picturesque.

Ermita de San Baudelio

ⓘ *Wed-Sat 1000-1400, 1600-1800 (2000 summer), Sun 1000-1400, €0.60.*

Some 8 km south of Berlanga is one of Castilla's more remarkable monuments. On a hillside that until the 19th century was covered in oak forest, the little chapel, Ermita de San Baudelio, was constructed at the beginning of the 11th century. It was close to the border that separated Muslim and Christian lands, and the design is a superb example of Mozarabic architecture. A horseshoe-arched doorway leads into an interior dominated by a central pillar that branches into extravagant ribs that recall a palm grove. There's even a tiny gallery, reached by an unlikely looking stair. Even more inspiring is the painted decoration, added 150 years later. Incredibly, an American art dealer was permitted to remove most of it in the 1920s (what he took is mostly now in the Metropolitan Museum in New York, although some has been repatriated to the Prado in Madrid). However, there's still enough left to excite: an Islamic hunting scene on the bottom half of the walls sits below a Biblical cycle; both preserve radiant colours and elaborate, sharp imagery.

El Burgo de Osma

El Burgo de Osma grew in the Middle Ages, and a large stretch of the wall is still well preserved; a vigilant sentinel on this wall almost changed the course of world history when he lobbed a boulder at a passing shadow one night in 1469. He narrowly missed killing the young prince Fernando, rushing by night to his furtive wedding with Isabel in Valladolid.

The **cathedral** ⓘ *Easter-Oct 1030-1300, 1600-1900, Nov-Easter 1030-1300, 1600-1800 Tue-Fri and Sun 1100-1300, 1600-1800, Sat 1030-1330, 1600-1930, €2 (€4 for guided tour)*, was started in the 13th century but has been sorely afflicted by later architects who just couldn't leave it alone, and added chapels left, right and centre, as well as an ugly appendix that houses the sacristy. The interior is richly decorated; the *retablo* is a good piece by Juan de Juni, much of whose other work can be seen in Valladolid's sculpture museum. A guided tour will take you to the cloister and museum, the highlight of which is a superb, ornately illustrated manuscript, a copy of the *Codex of Beatus de Liébana* dating from 1086, which has been described as "one of the most beautiful books on earth". The beautiful tomb of San Pedro de Osma, who raised the Romanesque edifice, is also memorable.

The large **Plaza Mayor** has an impressive old building, a former hospital that now houses both the **tourist office** ⓘ *T975 360 116, www.burgosma.es, 1000-1400, 1600-1900, closed Tue-Wed winter*, and **Antiqua Osma** ⓘ *summer Thu-Sat 1130-1400, 1630-1930; rest of the year Sat and Sun only 1100-1400, 1600-1900*, a fun little archaeological museum with finds and reconstructed scenes from the Iberian and Roman town of Uxama, whose fragmentary ruins can still be seen to the west of town. The courtyard is also used for art exhibitions.

A more earthy note is struck by the **Museo del Cerdo** ⓘ *C Juan Yagüe, www.elmuseodelcerdo.es, 1200-1400, 1630-1900*, or Museum of the Pig, run by a local restaurant. The western part of Soria province is anything but New Age; stag-hunting is a popular pastime, and the eating of vegetables frowned upon. The *matanza*, when the free-range pigs are driven in from the wild and converted into ham and chorizo, is a major town event every winter.

Castillo de Gormaz

ⓘ *The castle is little visited, and is permanently open (and free); buses run from El Burgo de Osma to Quintanas de Gormaz, from where it's a 1-hr walk, including a lengthy climb.*

Some 15 km south of El Burgo de Osma, Gormaz castle, built by the Moors around AD 950 is about the oldest, and certainly one of the largest, castles in western Europe, and was one of the 'front teeth' defending Al-Andalus from the Christians. While not a lot remains inside, it's well worth a visit just to see its walls, which are nearly 1 km in length and utterly commanding, visible for miles around. The Muslim origin of the citadel can be seen in the Caliph's gate, an ornate horseshoe portal. Although it seems totally impregnable even today, it was taken barely a century after being built, by Alfonso VI. He promptly gave it to El Cid; never let it be said that old Fonsi wasn't good to his friends.

Don't confuse Gormaz castle with the castle atop the town of San Esteban de Gormaz, a town on the N122 west of Burgo de Osma.

Cañón del Río Lobos

Tucked away in the wooded hills of northwestern Soria province, this beautiful gorge is worth seeking out. The Lobos river has carved its way down through soft limestone to form a spectacular canyon that winds its way some 25 km from near the village of Hontoria del Pinar in Burgos province southeast to Ucero, situated 15 km north of Burgo de Osma. The sculptured, concave cliffs are the domain of vultures and other birds of prey, such as the golden eagle and peregrine falcon; juniper and holm oak shade the canyon floor.

A walking trail runs the length of the valley. The river's gradient is gentle, so it's not a strenuous hike, but it's a hot one in summer, so take plenty of water. There are three places you can access the canyon trail: at either end, or on the SO960 road southwest of the town of San Leonardo de Yagüe, which itself is on the N234 running northwest from Soria to Burgos.

The main access point is near Ucero. It's a small, picturesque place nestled among crags, one of which bears a ruined castle. Just beyond the village is a **park information point** ⓘ *T973 363 564, open 1000-1400, 1600-1900, open all day at weekends and to 2000 in summer, closes 1700 in Jan and Feb*, with displays on the ecology and maps of the trail. About 1.5 km further on, there's a left turn that takes you to a large car park at the beginning of the canyon trail. From here it's 25 km to the other end. A short stroll from here takes you to the **Ermita de San Bartolomé**, a pretty Romanesque chapel a couple of kilometres up the trail (€1 entry). If you're going to walk the whole canyon, be aware that there's no bus link back. Many people walk the first half, return to their cars, and walk the second half the next day from the mid-point car park.

Aranda de Duero

"That's red Aranda. I am afraid we had to put the whole town in prison and execute very many people." (Remark made by the Conde de Vallellano to Dr Junod, Red Cross representative in Spain during the Civil War.)

A cheerful and solid Castilian working town, Aranda was spared the decline of the region by its location on an important crossroads. It's a busy place also set on a junction of rivers that still functions as a market town and supply centre for the surrounding area. Aranda's pride is roast lamb, for which it is famous throughout Spain; every eatery in town seems to be an *asador*, and the smell of cooking meat pervades the air.

The main sights are two attractive churches. **Iglesia de Santa María** has a superbly ornate portal still preserving some colour from the original paint job; scenes from the Virgin's life are portrayed, including the *Nativity* and the *Adoration of the Magi*. Nearby, the **Iglesia de San Juan** has a striking, many-layered portal set around Christ and, appropriately enough, a lamb. The **tourist office** ① *Tue-Sat 1000-1400, 1600-1900, Sun 1000-1400*, is on Calle de la Sal.

Peñaranda

East of Aranda is the sweet little town of **Peñaranda**, all cobbled streets and elegant buildings. There's a 14th-century **castle** on the hill above town, while in the heart, on the **Plaza Mayor**, the hulking **Iglesia de Santa Ana** isn't particularly loveable. Opposite is the more stylish **Palacio de Avellaneda** ① *Oct-Mar 1000-1400, 1500-1800, Apr-Sep 1000-1400, 1600-1930, tours on the hour*. Topped with a bust of Hercules, it was built by the counts of Miranda in the 16th century. The Plateresque façade is suitably grand, and attractively topped by a carved wooden roof. Inside there's an elegant galleried patio, and salons and stairways decorated in rich style. There's a **tourist office** ① *Tue-Sun 1000-1400, 1700-2000 (1600-1900 winter)*, in the centre.

Further along, near the village of **Peñalba de Castro**, are the bare hilltop ruins of **Clunia** ① *Tue-Sun 1100-1400, 1600-2000 (1500-1700 winter), €4*, once a significant Roman town. It's far from a world-class attraction, but has the remains of a theatre, bathhouse and several dwellings.

Ribera del Duero → *For listings, see pages 92-95.*

Peñafiel

Peñafiel is the main town of the Ribera del Duero wine region, and a good place to start your exploration of the zone. The square-jawed **castle** that sits on the hill above town was one of the Christian strongholds that flexed its muscles at the Moorish frontline, and the town grew up around it, although the settlement of Pintia nearby had been important in pre-Roman times. Peñafiel is now an attractive place by the river; there are even some trees, a rare enough site in the Castilian *meseta*.

Nicknamed 'the Ark' because it resembles a ship run aground, the citadel in Peñafiel was important because it occupied a crucial strategic ridge above the Duero. The castle is long and thin, so narrow as to almost resemble a film-set cut-out until you get close and see how thick the curtain walls are, reinforced with a series of bristling towers. Part of the castle now holds the **Museo de Vino** ① *www.museodelvinodevalladolid.com, Easter-Sep Tue-Sun 1100-1430, 1630-2030, Oct-Mar Tue-Sun 1130-1400, 1600-1900, €3 castle tour, €6 museum plus castle tour, €9 for a tutored tasting session of 4 wines*, a modern display covering all aspects of wine production. Much of it is rather unengaging – the information panels seem like sections from a textbook on agriculture – but things get more interesting with an array of aromas that you can inhale before revealing whether you sniffed correctly or not. Information is in Spanish, but there's an English/French audio guide. The cost of admission includes a guided tour around the other, unadorned, part of the castle. You can also pay extra for a tasting session.

The castle isn't Peñafiel's only point of interest. Down in the town, have a look at the excellent **Plaza del Coso**, a spacious square still used for markets and bullsports. With its beautiful wooden buildings and sand underfoot, it's an unforgettable sight. The town's major fiesta is superb (see page 95). Another highlight is the beautifully ornate brick *mudéjar* exterior of the **Iglesia de San Pablo** ① *daily 1200-1330, 1730-1830, €2*. Converted from fortress to monastery in the 14th century, the interior is in contrasting Plateresque style.

Peñafiel's **tourist office** ⓘ *Plaza San Miguel de Reoyo 2, T983 881 715, www.turismo penafiel.com, Oct-Mar 1000-1400, 1630-1900, Apr-Sep 1030-1430, 1700-2030*, is a good source of information. In the same building is a radio museum.

Around Peñafiel

The area east of Peñafiel is worth exploring, even for non-vinous reasons. A good place to start is the small town of **Roa**, whose **tourist office** ⓘ *Mon-Sat 1030-1400, 1630-2030, Sun 1030-1400*, has a wealth of information on the region.

The hill on which the town sits was inhabited in pre-Roman times but lay fallow for centuries until repopulation in the 10th century. Good sections of the medieval walls are preserved, and there's an attractive walk along them, with views across the Valley of the Duero. The church of **Nuestra Señora de la Asunción** is the centrepiece of Roa, and preserves Romanesque and Gothic elements, although the majority is in early Renaissance style. The star vaulting in the interior is especially impressive. Another interesting building in the town is a well-preserved *alhóndiga*, used for storing and trading grain in the Middle Ages.

Roa's most famous inhabitant was Cardinal Cisneros (known in English as Ximenez), powerful archbishop and regent of Spain for a period. He died here in 1517, the day a letter arrived from the new king that dismissed him from his post. The smiling bust of him that looks over the city walls is a charitable interpretation of the authoritarian cleric.

North of Roa, the village of **La Horra** preserves a series of what appear to be conical cairns. Visible all over the region, they are actually air-vents and indicate the presence of an undergound wine bodega. All the region's wine was once made in these cellars and the build-up of fumes from the fermentation necessitated the chimneys, which were sometimes also used to tip grapes down.

East of here, **La Aguilera** has an unexpectedly large church complex, the **Santuario de San Pedro Regalado** ⓘ *Mon-Sat 0900-1300, 1700-2000, Sun 1700-2000*. With an ornate interior and impressive flying buttresses, the church is dedicated to a 15th-century saint from Valladolid who spent his life as a monk here, preaching and performing the occasional miracle. He is the patron saint of bullfighters, as he once tamed a fierce bull that had escaped from the square in Valladolid; it's not uncommon for matadors to come here to give thanks for a lucky escape.

The attractive town of **Gumiel de Izán** nearby has a church with an impressive Renaissance façade and a large wooden *retablo* detailing the life of Christ, while the village of **Baños de Valderados** has the remains of a **Roman villa** ⓘ *Jul-Aug 1030-1400, 1600-2000, T947 534 229 to arrange a visit at other times*, with four reasonably preserved mosaïcs.

Wineries

Though the Ribera del Duero has a long history as a wine region – Vega Sicilia, the royal family's favourite tipple, was founded in 1864 – it's been since it was granted DO status in 1982 that the world has really sat up and taken notice, with its red wines winning rave reviews from experts and the public. The wines are based on the Tempranillo grape, although here it's called *Tinta del País*. Many consider the region's top wines superior to anything else produced in the country, and prices for wines such as Peter Sisseck's Pingus are stratospheric. Dealing with the cold Castilian nights gives the grapes more character, while traditionally a long period of rotation between oak barrels and larger vats has been employed. Ribera soils are also characteristic, and are probably responsible for the wines' very distinctive soft fruity nose. Most wineries can be visited, although they require a call in advance. Visits are rarely possible in August or during the vintage in late September to early October.

The excellent Pesquera is produced by **Bodegas Alejandro Fernández** ⓘ *T983 870 037, www.grupopesquera.com*, in the village of Pesquera de Duero west of Peñafiel. Visits need to be arranged by calling a week in advance; they are available in English, and free. In Pedrosa de Duero, near Roa, the tiny **Hermanos Pérez Pascuas** ⓘ *T947 530 100, www. perezpascuas.com*, makes the tasty Viña Pedrosa. **Condado de Haza** ⓘ *T947 525 254, www. condadodehaza.com*, another quality producer, is in an attractive building at the end of a long driveway between Roa and La Horra. **Vega Sicilia** is not open to the public.

In Peñafiel itself, a handy bodega to visit, clearly signposted off the main road, is **Protos** ⓘ *C Protos 24, T983 878 011, www.bodegasprotos.com, 1000-1400, 1600-1900*, a cooperative founded in 1927 whose mellow wines are very competitively priced for their quality. Ring in advance to arrange a visit.

About 17 km west of Peñafiel, it's hard to miss the giant complex of **Bodegas Arzuaga Navarro** ⓘ *T983 681 146, www.arzuaganavarro.com, visits bookable by phone, €5*, with a five-star hotel and enormous restaurant complementing the winery, which produces the excellent, juicy Arzuaga wines.

Just east of Sardón de Duero, on the main road some 25 km west of Peñafiel, is perhaps the most beautiful of the wineries, **Abadía Retuerta** ⓘ *T983 680 314, www.abadia-retuerta. com, Mon and Fri 1000 and 1200, from €10 depending on wines tasted, book by phone or website; you can buy wine here Mon-Sat 1000-1400, 1600-2000*, which stands next to a gorgeous 12th-century Romanesque monastery. The winemaking facilities themselves are modern and the wines aren't actually under the Ribera del Duero denomination, but they are outstanding, some blending Tempranillo and Cabernet Sauvignon to great effect, and there are examples for every budget.

Along the Duero: west from Soria to Valladolid listings

For hotel and restaurant price codes and other relevant information, see pages 11-17.

⬤ Where to stay

Calatañazor *p87*
Tourism is the village's only future and there are several good sleeping options.
€€ Casa del Cura, C Real 25, T975 183 642, www.posadarealcasadelcura.com. An upmarket *casa rural* with small but nicely decorated rooms, an attractive modern interior and a good restaurant with a large terrace. Reception is in the **Hostal Calatañazor** across the road.
€€-€ Hostal Calatañazor, C Real 10, T975 183 642, www.calatanazor.com. Good rooms and a restaurant decorated in Berber style. Value in the heart of the village.

Berlanga de Duero *p87*
€€ Hotel Fray Tomás, C Real 16, T975 343 033. Named after the town's most famous

son, a missionary priest, the rooms are pleasant enough, though a little staid and dull. However, the restaurant is good and the prices are more than fair.

El Burgo de Osma *p88*
€€€ Hotel Termal Burgo de Osma, C Universidad 5, T975 341 419, www. castillatermal.com. Behind a magnificent Plateresque façade, this modern hotel offers substantial elegance and comfortable rooms alongside a picturesque pool and spa area, with lots of treatment options on offer.
€€ El Fielato, Av Juan Carlos I 1, T975 368 236, www.hospederiaelfielato.es. On the corner of the main road and the principal pedestrian street, this recommendable place offers spotless, comfortable rooms equipped with hotel-standard conveniences.
€€ Hostal San Roque, C Universidad 1, T975 341 221. A grubby exterior conceals a clean, modern and very decent option on

the main road through town. The rooms have good bathrooms and you more or less have the run of the place.

€€ Hotel II Virrey, C Mayor 4, T975 341 311, www.virreypalafox.com. A plush but courteous hotel in traditional Spanish style. Facilities include gym and sauna, and the rooms are comfortable enough, although some are pokier than the grand decor would suggest; you might prefer to opt for a suite (**€€€**), which doesn't cost too much more.

€€ Posada del Canónigo, C San Pedro de Osma 19, T975 360 362, www.posada delcanonigo.es. An excellent place to stay, just inside the southern gate of the city wall. Decorated with care and style, the rooms are romantic and feature plush beds and floorboards. The *posada* also has an excellent restaurant.

Castillo de Gormaz *p89*
€€ Casa Grande, T975 340 982, www. casagrandegormaz.com. This excellent *casa rural* is in the village of Quintanas below the imposing fortress of Gormaz. It offers great views of the castle and is set in a spick and span yellow mansion. The rooms are delightful, with rustic touches; and there's a lounge with a fireplace. Also available for complete hire.

Cañón del Río Lobos *p89*
€€ Posada Los Templarios, C de la Iglesia s/n, Ucero, T975 363 528, www. posadalostemplarios.com. In a noble stone house in the village of Ucero, this is the top place to base yourself for walking the Cañón del Río Lobos. Smart modern-rustic decoration is allied with excellent facilities. Recommended.

Aranda de Duero *p89*
See Peñafiel, below, for rural tourism in the villages between Aranda and Peñafiel. Nearly all Aranda's accommodation is set away from the centre on the main roads. Exceptions include:

€€ Hotel Julia, Plaza de la Virgencilla s/n, T947 501 250, www.hoteljulia.es. This central hotel is a comfortable place full of interesting old Spanish objects. The rooms are excellent for this price, and there's friendly management and plenty of comfort. Free Wi-Fi.

€ Pensión Sole, C Puerta Nueva 16, T947 500 607. This *pensión* in the older part of town is a good budget option. It has good small clean rooms that are aging but comfortable; they all have TV and you can choose between simple en suite or shared bathroom.

Peñaranda *p90*
€€ Posada Ducal, Plaza Mayor s/n, T947 552 347, www.laposadaducal.com. Right on the main square, this beautiful *casa rural* was once the servants' quarters of the nearby palace. The accommodation has likely improved since those days; now it makes an excellent choice, with attractively rustic decoration and a decent restaurant too.

€€ Señorío de Velez, Plaza Duques de Alba 1, T947 552 201, www.hotelvelez.com. This hotel is a sound place to stay in the heart of town. Set in an attractive stone and adobe building, the rooms are clean and acceptable, if a touch overpriced. There's a nice terraced restaurant too.

Ribera del Duero and Peñafiel *p90*
If you've got a car, you might like to take advantage of the large numbers of *casas rurales* and *posadas* in the area between Peñafiel and Aranda, particularly around Roa and Gumiel de Hizán. The tourist office will provide a list; prompt them to make sure they give you it for both the provinces (Valladolid and Burgos) that this area straddles. The website www.toprural.com is also a good starting point, and the regional government website www.turismocastillayleon.com has an extensive list.

€€€€ Bodegas Arzuaga Navarro, T983 681 146, www.arzuaganavarro.com. Despite the bulky building and unappealing main road location, this is a luxurious base in one of the Ribera's best wineries. The rooms are most commodious, and all come with jacuzzi. Opportunities for tasting can be arranged, and the restaurant specializes in game and roast lamb. You can roam the extensive vineyard and grounds.

€€€ Convento las Claras, Pl Alonso s/n, T983 878 168, www.hotelconventolasclaras. com. In the centre of Peñafiel, just across the river from the heart of things, this excellent new convent conversion provides an historic place to stay and a comfortable base for the Ribera wine country. Rooms, set around a courtyard, are spacious and comfortable, and there's a good restaurant and spa facilities. Service is a little naïve but that will hopefully improve.

€ Hostal Campo, C Encarnación Alonso s/n, T983 873 192, www.hostalcampo.com. This *hostal* has comfortable and clean new rooms a short stroll from the centre on the other side of the main road. The main problem is a slightly depressing location near the sugar refinery. All rooms have bathroom and modern comforts; it's run out of the down-at-heel **Bar Campo** on the road to Pesquera.

€ Hostal Chicopa, Plaza de España 2, T983 880 782. This place has 2 important things going for it: price and location. Set right in the centre of the old town above a bar/ restaurant, these simple rooms go for a song. Some have their own bathroom, others share; it's pretty basic, but it's not a dive.

🍴 Restaurants

El Burgo de Osma *p88*
€€€ Virrey Palafox, C Universidad 7, T975 340 222. This restaurant is run by the same management as the **Hotel Virrey**, and is unashamedly devoted to meat, which is superbly done. On Feb and Mar weekends, the **Fiesta de la Matanza** takes place; pigs are slaughtered and devoured in their entirety.

€€ El Burgo, C Mayor 75, T975 341 249. Only open at weekends, this restaurant is a temple to meat. The food is great, but some of the steaks are laughably large, so be firm with the pushy owner who is sure he knows what you want.

€ Café 2000, Plaza Mayor 7, T975 340 446. A good cheap place to eat and snack, with a terrace on the main square and a decent €10 *menú*. As everywhere, meat is the way to go here rather than fish.

Cañón del Río Lobos *p89*
€ La Parrilla de San Bartolo, Ctra de San Leonardo s/n, Ucero, T975 363 516. On the main road through the village, this doesn't look much from the outside, but it's worth investigating for its excellent meat dishes at very reasonable prices.

Aranda de Duero *p89*
The local speciality is roast lamb, washed down with a bottle of red from the local Ribera del Duero. The lamb's not cheap or particularly subtle, but it's delicious and the portions are huge. A quarter lamb (easily enough for 2) costs around €40, and an eighth about €20; there are heaps of places to try it along the main pedestrian street Isilla, and around the Plaza Jardines de Don Diego on the road through the middle of town.

€€ Asador Ciprés, Plaza Jardines de Don Diego 1, T947 507 414. Many *arandinos* vouch for this *asador* as the town's best. Traditional service and delicious lamb combine well with the region's wines. If there's any room left, you can try another local speciality, *empiñonado*, a pine-nut sweet.

€€ El Lagar de Isilla, C Isilla 18, T947 510 683. One of several memorable *asadores* in town, this is perhaps the most atmospheric, with beams and old grape presses decorating this former wine bodega (dozens of which are dug out under the town). Lamb is cooked in the traditional wood oven and there's a great wine list and a friendly tapas bar out front. Make sure you go down to see the cellars.

Peñafiel *p90*

€€ Molino de Palacios, Av de la
Constitución 16, T983 880 505. This
is a lovely *asador* romantically set in
an old watermill on the river. The
speciality is predictable, namely roast
lamb, but there are also plenty of game
and wild mushroom dishes.

€ Restaurante María Eugenia, Plaza
España 17, T983 873 115. Friendly family-
run place decorated with heavy Spanish
furniture and decent landscapes. Good
seafood and huge steaks.

Cafés

Café Judería, a relaxing place for a coffee
or drink, nicely set in the park of the same
name by the river.

☺ Festivals

Aranda de Duero *p89*
Sep Aranda's annual fiesta, in the 2nd week
of Sep, is a cheerfully drunken affair.

Peñafiel *p90*
14-18 Aug The town's major fiesta is worth
attending. There are *encierros*, where bulls
run through the streets, followed by *capeas*
in the plaza, which is basically bull-dodging,
sometimes with the aim of slipping rings
over the horns. The homeowners sell off
balcony seats, but interestingly some
families still have hereditary rights to these
seats, even if the house isn't theirs.

☺ Transport

Calatañazor *p87*
Bus
There are 1-3 buses a day from **Soria**
to Calatañazor (25 mins). Other **Linecar
Valladolid**-bound buses can drop you
off just below the village.

Berlanga de Duero *p87*
Bus
There is 1 bus daily from **Soria** to Berlanga
from Mon-Fri (70 mins).

El Burgo de Osma *p88*
Bus
The bus station is on the main road; there are
4-6 services to **Soria** (1 hr) and 3 to **Aranda
de Duero** (45 mins) and on to **Valladolid**.

Aranda de Duero *p89*
Bus
Aranda has good bus connections, being at
the junction of major north–south and east–
west routes. The bus and train stations are
across the Duero from the old part of town.

About 4 buses a day go to **Madrid** (2 hrs)
and 6-7 to **Burgos** (1 hr 15 mins). There are
6 a day to **Valladolid** (1 hr 15 mins), 3 to
El Burgo de Osma (45 mins) and on to
Soria (1 hr 30 mins) and **Zaragoza** (3 hrs
45 mins) and 2 to **Roa**.

Train
Trains go to **Madrid** (1 daily, 2-3 hrs),
and **Burgos** (1 daily, 1 hr).

Peñafiel *p90*
Bus
There are 6 buses a day from Peñafiel
to **Valladolid** (45 mins) and **Aranda de
Duero** (30 mins), 3 of which continue to
El Burgo de Osma, **Soria** and **Zaragoza**.

Valladolid

Valladolid, the capital of the Castilla y León region, is not outstandingly beautiful but it is a pleasant, strollable place with a very significant history. It was the principal city of Spain for most of the early 16th century and its streets are redolent with the memories of important people who walked them and events that took place in them. These days it's still an important, slightly posh administrative centre, but a fairly relaxed and friendly one; perhaps it looks down the road to sprawling Madrid and breathes a small sigh of relief, as it was odds-on favourite to be named capital at one time.

Arriving in Valladolid → *Phone code: 983. Population: 317,864. Altitude: 690 m.*

Getting there Many visitors to Northern Spain arrive in Valladolid; there's a **Ryanair** connection to the city from London Stansted as well as Brussels Charleroi and some Spanish destinations. Valladolid is a major transport hub, only two hours from Madrid by road, and just an hour less by the new fast trains. As the capital of Castilla y León, it has excellent connections right around the region, as well as with the rest of Northern Spain. The bus and train stations are close together, about a 10-minute walk south of the centre. They can be reached by local buses Nos 2 and 10 from Plaza de España, or No 19 from Plaza Zorilla. ►► *See Transport, page 106.*

Getting around Situated on the east bank of the Pisuerga, Valladolid's old centre is fairly compact. At the southern end of this part, the large park of Campo Grande is flanked by two long avenues, Paseo de Zorilla, the main artery of the new town, and the mostly pedestrianized Acera de Recoletos. Nearly everything of interest is within an easy walk of the Plaza Mayor.

Tourist information The new **tourist office** ① *T983 219 310, www.asomateavalladolid. com, oficinadeturismodevalladolid@jcyl.es, mid-Sep to Jun Mon-Sat 0930-1400, 1600-1900, Sun 0930-1700, summer daily 0900-2000,* is in a big glass building by the park on Paseo de Campo Grande; you pass it if you are walking from the train station into town. It has all manner of information on the city and province. There's also a **tourist kiosk** ① *Tue-Sun 1000-1400, 1700-2000,* on Plaza Fuente Dorada, and an information desk at the airport.

Background

A site of pre-Roman settlements, Valladolid's profile grew with the Reconquista; it was well placed on the frontline to become an important commercial centre, driven in part by the Castilian wool trade. Although Fernando and Isabel married here in 1469 – a secret ceremony that profoundly changed the course of world history – it was in the 16th century that Valladolid became pre-eminent among Spanish cities. With a population of nearly 40,000, it was a massive place in a hitherto fragmented land, and de-facto capital of Spain; while the court was constantly on the move, the bureaucracy was based here. It was, as it

Torquemada and the Spanish Inquisition

"The hammer of heretics, the light of Spain, the saviour of his country." Sebastián de Olmedo.

Founded by Fernando and Isabel in 1478, the Spanish Inquisition was unusual in that it did not report directly to the Pope but followed a more nationalistic course. Born in 1420, Tomás de Torquemada entered a Dominican monastery in his youth and was appointed as Grand Inquisitor in 1483. He pursued his tasks with considerable energy, both reforming the administration of the Inquisition and giving it its uniquely Spanish direction. Under Torquemada there was a paranoid obsession that the conversions of Muslim and Jewish *conversos* had been insincere; this was to dominate the Inquisition's activities.

Given a remit to extract confessions under torture, the Inquisition was initially content to seize the estates of those Jewish *conversos* it considered to be insincere. This enabled it to quickly build up considerable resources. Later it employed the full range of punishments available including execution by public burning following a theatrical *auto de fe* or trial of faith. It is estimated that during Torquemada's direction there were around 2000 executions, the overwhelming majority of them Jewish *conversos*.

He was instrumental in ensuring that the Jews were expelled completely from Spain in 1492. It is reputed that when he found Fernando in negotiations with Jewish leaders over a possible payment to the Crown in order to remain, he compared Fernando's actions with those of Judas. The Jews were duly expelled, with disastrous long-term results for the country.

Torquemada's pursuit of Jewish *conversos* was largely responsible for the development of the cult of *sangre limpia* or pure blood that was to continue to obsess Spain throughout the 16th century. Based on the idea that only those of pure Christian blood could participate fully in the state, it was to cost Spain the services of most of its intellectual class, debilitating its development for centuries.

Torquemada stepped down from his role in the Inquisition in 1497. After his directorship it began to diversify into other areas including the maintenance of doctrinal purity and a concern with private morality. It was to retain a formidable grip over Spanish life until its formal abolition at the beginning of the 19th century. Torquemada retired to a monastery where he kept a unicorn's horn close at hand as an antidote to any attempt at poisoning him. He died of natural causes in 1499.

is now, a city of administrators and lawyers: "courtiers died here waiting for their cases to come up" (JH Elliott, *Imperial Spain*).

Valladolid played an important part in most significant Spanish historical events, and was home for periods to people as diverse as Columbus, Cervantes and the inquisitor Torquemada. It was a major centre of the Spanish Inquisition (see box, above); *autos de fe* and burnings were a regular sight in the plaza.

In the year 1550-1551, a significant and famous theological debate took place here between the liberal theologian Bartolomé de las Casas and the historian and philosopher Juan Ginés de Sepúlveda. The former was arguing for an end to indigenous slavery and forced conversions in Spain's American colonies, while the latter deemed the *indígenos* inferior, being incapable of reason and therefore without rights. Las Casas' view prevailed, effectively ending the doctrine of racial purity in the colonies. Las Casas

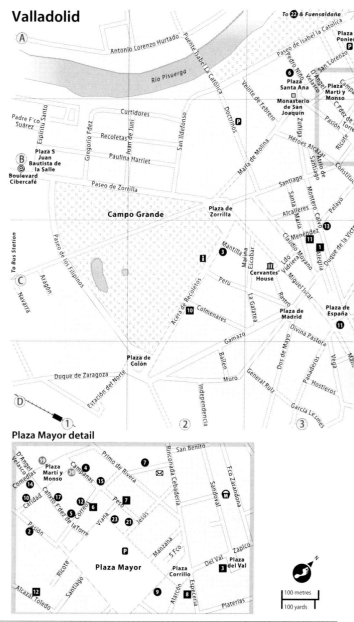

Valladolid

Plaza Mayor detail

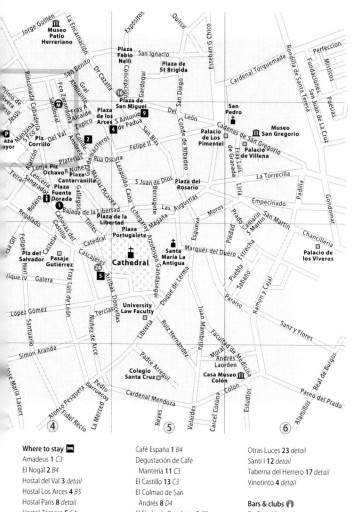

Where to stay 🛏

Amadeus **1** *C3*
El Nogal **2** *B4*
Hostal del Val **3** *detail*
Hostal Los Arces **4** *B5*
Hostal Paris **8** *detail*
Hostal Zamora **5** *C4*
Hostería La Cueva **6** *detail*
Imperial **7** *detail*
Meliá Recoletos **10** *C2*
Mozart **11** *C3*
Olid Meliá **9** *B5*
Roma **12** *detail*

Restaurants 🍴

Bar La Sepia **21** *detail*

Café España **1** *B4*
Degustación de Café
  Mantería **11** *C3*
El Castillo **13** *C3*
El Colmao de San
  Andrés **8** *D4*
El Figón de Recoletos **3** *C2*
Jero **7** *detail*
La Balconada **15** *detail*
La Criolla **5** *detail*
La Parrilla de San Lorenzo **6** *A3*
La Tasquita II **10** *detail*
Lion d'Or **9** *detail*
Los Zagales **2** *detail*
Méson La Sorbona **22** *A3*
Mil Vinos **14** *detail*

Otras Luces **23** *detail*
Santi I **12** *detail*
Taberna del Herrero **17** *detail*
Vinotinto **4** *detail*

Bars & clubs 🍸

Be-Bop **19** *detail*
El Soportal **16** *A5*
La Comedia **20** *detail*
La Española Cuando Besa **24** *C4*

was hardly an enlightened humanist, though; he suggested the labour problem be solved by enslaving Africans instead.

Felipe II was born in Valladolid, but surprisingly chose Madrid as his capital in 1561. The city lost importance after that, but had a brief reprise. A scheming adviser of Felipe III wanted to keep him away from the powerful influence of his grandmother, and persuaded him to move the capital northwards in 1601. The glory years were back, but only for five years, after which the court moved back to Madrid. Valladolid remained fairly prosperous until the collapse of the wool and grain markets, but enjoyed renewed wealth in the early part of the 20th century. The Falange held their first national meeting here in March 1934 and when war broke out Valladolid became an important and brutal Fascist stronghold; it is estimated that over 9000 Republican civilians were shot here behind the lines.

One of Spain's most important post Civil War writers, the late Miguel Delibes, was a *vallisoletano*. His work deeply reflects the Castilian landscape but is also often bitingly anti-Francoist; much of his journalistic life was spent battling the censors while working for the liberal *El Norte de Castilla*, the regional paper. *The Hedge* is perhaps his best-known translated work; a vicious satire on totalitarian Spain.

Places in Valladolid → *For listings, see pages 102-106.*

Valladolid's centrepiece is its large **Plaza Mayor**, attractively surrounded by the terracotta façades of buildings. It was here that *autos de fe* and burnings were conducted during the Inquisition's long tenure in the city. Most of Valladolid's buildings of interest are to the north and east of the plaza. The **cathedral**, topped by a statue of Christ standing tall above the city, seems a little crowded-in. The façade is baroque, the interior fairly bare and disappointing, although the **museum** ⓘ *Tue-Fri 1000-1330, 1630-1900, Sat and Sun 1000-1400; €2.50*, is worthwhile, with some excellent carved tombs among the usual assorted saints and Virgins.

Behind the cathedral stands the Gothic **Iglesia de Santa María la Antigua**, slightly down-at-heel but sporting an attractive tower. Also nearby is the **Pasaje Gutiérrez**, a belle époque shopping arcade with some pleasingly extravagant decoration. The **university law faculty**, also next to the cathedral, is worth a look for its camp baroque façade guarded by strange monkey-like lions on columns. Across the road, it's faced by a friendly looking Cervantes. Another university building is the lovely **Colegio de Santa Cruz**, a block away, with an ornate Plateresque door; it boasts an attractive central patio with the names of honorary graduates painted on the walls.

North of the cathedral, along Calle Las Angustias, is an interesting collection of buildings. The **Palacio de los Pimentel** was the building that saw the birth, in 1527, of Felipe II, likely to have been a rather serious little boy. His statue faces the palace from across the square, which also holds the **Iglesia de San Pedro**, with a very tall and ornate Gothic façade; the level of intricacy in the stonework is stunning.

Following the pedestrian street at the side of the San Pedro church, you'll soon come to an even more amazing façade. Looking like a psychedelic fantasy in stone, it's an outrageously imaginative piece of work. A pomegranate tree perhaps represents knowledge, while the hairy men represent nature and the value of hermitry. Like much sculpture from centuries ago, it's impossible to really unlock the meaning, but it's certainly a step away from the typical. It belongs to the **Colegio de San Gregorio**, a building commissioned by Fray Alonso de Burgos to house the college he founded, and also to house him after his demise. Now re-opened after a lengthy and beautifully-realized restoration, the building contains the **Museo San Gregorio** ⓘ *Tue-Sat 1000-1400, 1600-1930, Sun 1000-1400, €3*. The collection is what was formerly known as the National Sculpture Museum. It's a fairly specialized ensemble, excellent in its field, which is basically Spanish religious sculpture from the 16th-18th centuries. Look out for a portrait of an appropriately brooding Juana I as well as an excellent *retablo* of San Jerónimo, the highlight of which is the tiny lion; the painter obviously had only a limited notion of what they were like. An excellent collection of polychrome wooden sculptures by Alonso Berruguete show his mastery at depicting real emotion in that difficult medium, while a curious Zurbarán painting, *La Santa Faz*, displays that superb artist's passion for the subtleties of white cloth. Further highlights include a very creepy *Death* by Gil de Ronza, a range of Mannerist sculpture in alabaster, a gory *Martyrdom of St Bartholomew*, and a Rubens painting of *Democritus and Heraclitus*, who resembles a retired fairground boxer. A couple of interesting curios are an ensemble depicting all the events of a bullfight, and an amazing assembly of Neapolitan dolls, forming a 620-piece Nativity scene. There's a good system of information sheets in English.

Opposite, the Palacio de Villena (admission free) is part of the same museum and used for high-quality temporary exhibitions. The plan is to focus on aspects of Spanish art, bringing in key works from overseas galleries.

Other buildings of note in this part of town are the **Palacio de los Viveros**, where Fernando and Isabel married in 1469, having only set eyes on each other four days before. It now holds an archive and the university library, and isn't hugely interesting. Beyond here is the **Casa Museo Colón** ① *C Colón s/n, Tue-Sun 1000-1400, 1700-2030, €2*, a replica of Columbus' son's house, where the explorer is said to have died, far from the sea and a discontented man. The museum displays a lot of pre-Hispanic American material as well as various displays on his seafaring exploits.

Moving south from the Plaza Mayor down Calle Santiago the street ends at **Plaza de Zorrilla**, with an energetic fountain. José Zorrilla was a 19th-century poet born in the city, although he spent much of his life in Mexico. On the other side of the plaza stretches the pleasant and busy park of **Campo Grande**. Numerous pro-Republican civilians were shot here during the Civil War, many dying with the words 'Long live the Republic' on their lips.

Cervantes spent three years living in Valladolid, some days of it at his Majesty's leisure on suspicion of being involved in a murder. What was probably his house, a pretty vine-covered building on Calle Miguel Iscar, is nearby; it contains a **museum** ① *www.museocasacervantes. mcu.es, Tue-Sat 0930-1500, Sun 1000-1500, €3*, part of which recreates the living conditions of the day, and part of which holds a reasonably interesting collection of 19th- and 20th-century Spanish painting and sculpture.

West of the **Plaza Mayor**, a series of attractive streets around Calle Correos holds some excellent eating and drinking options. Beyond, towards the river, is the ugly **Monasterio de San Joaquín** ① *Plaza Santa Ana 4, Mon-Fri 1000-1330, 1700-1900 (2000 summer), Sat 1000-1430, free*, fronted by a strangely hag-like Virgin. In the monastery museum is a collection of religious art, of which the highlight is three Goyas in the church itself.

Finally (though there are several other museums in town that we haven't space to list here) the **Museo Patio Herreriano** ① *C Jorge Guillén 6; T 983 362 908, www.museopatio herreriano.org, Tue-Fri 1100-1400, 1700-2000, Sat 1100-2000, Sun 1100-1500, €3 (€1 on Wed)*, is a contemporary art museum built around a huge Renaissance patio that is elegant but rather cold and formal. The permanent collection is housed in various galleries possessed of little levity; there are some good works here (sculptures by the beachcombing Angel Ferrant and the Basque Jorge Oteiza stand out), but the worth of a visit depends largely upon the temporary exhibitions, which are frequently excellent. There are also regular concerts and other cultural events.

Near here, an artificial beach allows summer sunbathing on the banks of the Pisuerga; a small compensation for Valladolid's deep inland location.

Valladolid listings

For hotel and restaurant price codes and other relevant information, see pages 11-17.

⬛ Where to stay

Valladolid *p96, map p98*

Valladolid is full of accommodation; the tourist office can provide a complete listing.

€€€€ Meliá Recoletos, Acera de Recoletos 13, T983 216 200, www.melia.com. With a peaceful location on the park between the station and the centre, very close to the tourist office, this great modern hotel is just about the city's best. Rooms are large and light, with excellent bathrooms and facilities; the hotel's staff are well informed and most helpful. Cheaper prices available via the website.

€€€ Hotel Amadeus, C Montero Calvo 16-18, T983 219 444, www.hotelamadeus. net. A modern hotel on a central pedestrian street, smartly catering mostly for business travellers. This is good news, because they offer smart weekend rates if you book ahead. The rooms have all the facilities, including cable TV and internet point. The beds are large and comfortable. Parking available.

€€€ Hotel Imperial, C Peso 4, T983 330 300, www.himperial.com. Located in a 16th-century *palacio* in the heart of the old town, this has considerable old-Spain charm. The bedrooms are very attractive, the furnishings plush and there's a beautiful if formal bar/lounge with a pianist. It's also right by the tapas zone.

€€€ Hotel Mozart, C Menéndez Pelayo 4, T983 297 777, www.hotelmozart.net. The sister hotel to the **Amadeus** is set in a noble 19th-century mansion and has a classy feel. The rooms are large and light with windows looking out over the pedestrian streets below. The hotel has its own garage, plenty of charm, and excellent weekend and summer rates (**€€**).

€€ Hostal París, C Especería 2, T983 370 625, www.hostalparis.com. Bang in the heart of town, this appealing *hostal* is really a hotel in disguise and offers neat-as-a-new-pin rooms that are compact but comfortable and, despite the busy street, pretty quiet. Bathrooms are similarly good, and the staff helpful. Free Wi-Fi. Location great. Recommended.

€€ Hotel El Nogal, C Conde Ansúrez 10, T983 340 333, www.hotelelnogal.com. An intimate modern hotel near the old market. It's a friendly choice and well located. The rooms are a touch cramped but have a/c and otherwise comfortable and light.

€€ Hotel Roma, C Héroes del Alcázar de Toledo 8, T983 354 666, www. hotelromavalladolid.com. Slightly old-fashioned rooms but a helpful attitude and parking make this a good option if location is important to you. It's set in the main shopping zone just a few paces from the picturesque Plaza Mayor.

€€ Olid Meliá, Plaza San Miguel 10, T983 357 200, www.melia.com. This well-located hotel is one of the city's most luxurious even if the decor is hardly cutting edge these days. It could do with a refit, but the rooms are spacious and light, and neither they nor the bathrooms lack comfort. You pay a little extra for a superior room or one with a balcony. The hotel has gym and parking facilities; there are occasional enticing discounts advertised via the website.

€ Hostal del Val, Plaza del Val 6, T983 375 752, www.hostaldelval.com. A sound budget option, this *hostal* is very close to the heart of town. The rooms are good for the price; some are equipped with their own bathroom.

€ Hostal Zamora, C Arribas 14, T983 303 052. Right by the cathedral, this is cheap but acceptable, with OK heated rooms with tiny bathrooms. Late sleepers will be woken by the bells tolling for mass.

€ Hostería La Cueva, C Correos 4, T983 330 072, daniel25sanchez@hotmail.com. This *pensión* has small, attractive rooms above a restaurant on Valladolid's nicest little street. The better ones have compact en suite bathrooms, but there are rooms with just a washbasin available too.

€ Hostal Los Arces, C San Antonio de Padua 2, T983 353 853. This is a fine budget choice, with large (if noisy at weekends) rooms, comfortable beds and a decent atmosphere. Shared bathrooms are good; rooms with en suites available.

🍴 Restaurants

Valladolid *p96, map p98*
Valladolid is a gourmet's paradise. The zone of restaurants and tapas bars is in the small streets just west of the Plaza Mayor. Most of the options below function as both; the quality throughout this area is laudably high, with elaborate tapas creations accompanied by excellent local Rueda and Ribera wines the norm.

€€€ El Figón de Recoletos, Av Recoletos 5, www.elfigonderecoletos.es. This sleek traditional *asador* is confident in what it does best. While there are always daily specials, there are only 4 main dishes on the menu; the quarter roast lamb is enough for 2; the grilled kidneys are unspeakably delicious if innards are your thing. Reserve ahead if you want suckling pig; reserve somewhere else if you're vegetarian.

€€€ Los Zagales, C Pasión 13, T983 380 892, www.loszagales.com. Hanging hams by the dozen adorn this atmospheric and well-frequented spot just off the Plaza Mayor. Popular as an after-work tapas option, it's also a restaurant, whose classy and delicious fare includes pricey but quality meat, and a range of gourmet salads.

€€ Jero, C Correos 11, T983 353 508. One of the most enjoyable of the bars in this tapas district, this upbeat spot specializes in *pinchos* of the most elaborate kind, taste combinations from some fantasy land. Each has about 10 different ingredients, with quails' eggs just the start: They even have elaborate dessert platters when you're done

and a *comedor* for proper sit-down meals. Recommended.

€€ La Criolla, C Calixto Fernández de la Torre 2, T983 373 822, www.restaurantelacriolla.es. A likeable and attractive restaurant, full of intimate nooks and adorned with quotes from *vallisoletano* writers. The fare is based around simple traditional dishes, which have been given an attractive modern boost. There's a terrace in summer and a good tapas bar, which always has an intriguing daily special; you can also order an *espejo* – a mixed tapa selection. Quality food ranges from fish to game to roast meat, all with engaging presentation.

€€ La Parrilla de San Lorenzo, C Pedro Niño 1, T983 335 088. www.parrilladesan lorenzo.es. Closed Jul. A romantic meaty restaurant with various atmospheric vaulted chambers in the depths of a convent building. The menu's like a medieval parchment and illustrates various traditional Castilian dishes like roast lamb, as well as fish dishes like monkfish tail, or cod salad served in a caramel basket with sweet fruity sauce. Prices are fair.

€€ Mesón La Sorbona, Paraje El Barrero, Fuensaldaña, T983 583 077. Just north of the city, the village of Fuensaldaña is in the rosé wine district of Cigales. It's got a barrio of atmospheric traditional bodegas on the edge of town, many of which have been converted into restaurants, a popular lunch or dinner escape. This is about the best of them; jugs of local wine, simple salads, tortilla and good grilled meats are the way to go.

€€ Mil Vinos, Plaza Martí y Monso s/n, T983 344 336, www.milvinos.com. Looking like a TV studio with its designer furniture and floor-to-ceiling trendy glass, this bar claims to offer 1000 wines (it falls short), many of which are available by the glass. There's excellent service, with staff more than happy to recommend a wine. It's also a restaurant, with a short but decent menu of grilled meat and fish as well as plenty of cheeses. The wines can also be bought at market prices. Free Wi-Fi.

€€ **Otras Luces**, Plaza Mayor 22, T983 380 705, www.otrasluces.es. Offering a spacious terrace on the Plaza Mayor, this place tries to do a bit of everything, and makes a pleasurable choice for breakfast coffee, an evening drink, or good-value set lunch. The sizeable menu is divided by points of the compass – the north (Galician, Cantabrian, and Castilian dishes) is more reliable than the hit-and-miss Moroccan and East Asian offerings. Best are the organically minded burgers and salads. Service could improve.

€€ **Santi**, C Correos 1, T983 339 355, www.restaurantesanti.es. Superbly situated in the courtyard of a historic inn, named **El Caballo de Troya** after its large painting of the same name, although the Trojan horse looks surprisingly sprightly. The restaurant serves good-quality Castilian fare; there's also a *taberna*, which is an atmospheric place for a drink; it serves tapas and *raciones*, but you're better off eating in the restaurant.

€€ **Vinotinto**, C Campanas 4, T983 342 291. This high-ceilinged bar is lined with shelves of wine bottles, but the real focus is the open *parrilla*, where delicious cuts of meat, including tasty little lamb tapas skewers, sizzle over the coals. There's a *comedor* downstairs to eat, but it's more fun to eat at the wooden tables in the bar where it's all happening. There's another bar, **Vinotinto Joven**, more *pincho*-focused, opposite. Recommended.

€ **Bar La Sepia**, C Jesús 1, T983 330 769, www.barlasepia.es. This Valladolid classic, decorated in wood and brick, is down a side street just off the Plaza Mayor. You can smell the enticing aromas from a block away and when you sample the taste and texture of the *sepia* (cuttlefish) – it comes grilled with a garlic sauce – you'll understand why they're always busy.

€ **El Colmao de San Andrés**, Detrás de San Andrés 3, T691 111 476. This striking ensemble of eclectic furniture and objets d'art feels more like an antique dealer's or second-hand shop than a bar. A loyal local crowd keep things buzzing every night, sipping wine and munching snacks of smoked cod

or salmon on toast. It's one of the city's most characterful spots. It's off Calle Mantería behind the San Andrés church.

€ **La Balconada**, C Correos 3, T983 342 114. This small mezzanine restaurant is brightly coloured and very reasonably priced. The brief menu includes *tablas* to share with friends, a good house salad enlivened by warm prawns, or a tender *solomillo* steak which is great value.

€ **La Tasquita**, C Caridad 2, T647 629 279. The main reason to come to this *cervecería*, apart from its cheerful bar staff, is for excellent *pinchos*, with winning combinations atop slices of toast. Ranging from roast beef to prawns, or octopus with paprika, they're all delicious and it's seriously difficult to not stay to try another.

€ **Taberna del Herrero**, C Calixto Fernández de la Torre 4, T983 342 310, www.lataberna delherrero.es. This deservedly popular place sets out its stall to provide wholesome and traditional Castilian fare at popular prices. It succeeds superbly. *Raciones* of such delicious staples as *croquetas*, *lacón*, or a variety of stews are ridiculously cheap and filling (most plates €4-6, and a *menú del día* for €12.50). On Thu, a hearty *cocido* stew will beat the winter chills. Eat at blocky wooden tables or the solid bar. Deservedly popular.

Cafés

Café España, Plaza Fuente Dorada 8, T983 371 764, www.cafeespana.es. A traditional central café decorated with black and white photos. They have regular live music ranging from flamenco to jazz; check their website for upcoming performances.

Degustación de Café Mantería, C Mantería 1, T983 210 763. A most likeable café just off the Plaza de España, this narrow spot has an inclusive buzz and debatable art on the walls. The boss works his socks off, making strong, punchy coffees, and elaborately preparing little rolls with ham, olive oil, and tomato.

El Castillo, C Montero Calvo 1, T983 308 841. This is an old-fashioned spot with a row of outdoor tables on a pedestrian street. It's the

place to come for hot chocolate and *churros* (fried doughsticks) – a very traditional morning or late afternoon treat.
Lion d'Or, Plaza Mayor 4, T983 342 057. Open from 0900 until very late. A lovely old café in the main square, complete with fireman's poles and gilt-framed mirrors. It's very popular in the early evenings with people of a certain age, who have no doubt been coming here every afternoon for several decades; you can see why.

🍷 Bars and clubs

Valladolid *p96, map p98*
There are various zones of bars in Valladolid; some around Plaza Martí y Monso, known as **La Coca**, some smartish ones around Plaza San Miguel, more bohemian wine bars and nightspots around the cathedral, and a riot of student nightlife around C Paraíso by the university. Several *discobares* are on and around C Padre Francisco Suárez, between Paseo Zorilla and the river.
Be-Bop, Plaza Martí y Monsó 1. Sleek and stylish, this upmarket jazz bar and café is a favourite of romancing executives, perhaps because it's so dark that when you enter all you can see are the backlit spirit bottles behind the bar.
El Soportal, Plaza San Miguel s/n, T983 371 940. A modern, dark and moody café/bar with a horseshoe bar and plenty of seats. There's hospitable service and a busy, smart crowd at weekends, when it opens very late.
La Comedia, Plaza Martí y Monso 4, T983 340 804. This is a reliable choice; a good lively bar with outdoor seating when weather permits. It fills with a fairly smart pre- and post-dinner crowd – there's even a cigar menu – and is lively and buzzy. There's no draught beer, but several good wines and tasty mixed drinks. Open until fairly late and decorated with past stars of the silver screen.
La Española Cuando Besa, C Arribas s/n, T983 398 379. Offbeat spot by the cathedral

that feels like you're inside the trunk of a tree. 3 narrow levels and an upbeat, 'anyone-welcome' atmosphere.

🎭 Entertainment

Valladolid *p96, map p98*
Cines Roxy, C Mario de Molina 6, T983 351 672. A small but handy art deco cinema.
Teatro Calderón, C Las Angustias s/n, T983 426 444, www.tcalderon.com.The city's main theatre, with mainstream drama and dance in a beautifully ornate interior. Seats in the gods can go for as little as €10, but there's not a lot of leg room.

🎉 Festivals

Valladolid *p96, map p98*
Mar/Apr Semana Santa (Easter week) is fairly serious; hooded brotherhoods parade floats through the streets to the mournful wailing of cornets and tubas.
Early Sep Feast of the **Virgen de San Lorenzo**, the streets fill with stalls selling wine and tapas, there are bullfights, concerts and more.

🛍 Shopping

Valladolid *p96, map p98*
Valladolid's main shopping area is the pedestrian zone between Plaza Mayor and Plaza Zorilla, particularly along C Santiago.
Oletum, C de Teresa Gil 12, T983 213 560. A wide range of books with a good English-language section.

🏆 What to do

Valladolid *p96, map p98*
Football Real Valladolid is the city's football team. Their stadium, **Estadio José Zorilla**, Av Mundial 82 s/n, T983 360 342, www.realvalladolid.es, is to the west of town.

🚌 Transport

Valladolid *p96, map p98*
Air
Valladolid's airport (VLL), T983 415 500, is 12 km northwest of town. Buses run between the bus station and the airport to connect with flights (20 mins, €3). ALSA (www.alsa.es) buses running between Valladolid and León will stop here if you have pre-booked the ticket. A taxi from Valladolid to the airport costs €20.

As well as **Ryanair** flights to **London** Stansted and **Brussels** Charleroi, there are international connections to **Paris** and **Lisbon**, as well as domestic ones to **Barcelona** and **Málaga**.

Bus
Intercity buses go from Valladolid to nearly every major city in Spain. These services include: **Madrid** hourly (2¼ hrs), **León** 8-9 daily (2 hrs), **Barcelona** 2 daily (10½ hrs), **Segovia** 7-12 daily (1 hr 50 mins), **Zamora** 7-10 daily, **Palencia** hourly, **Bilbao** 3 daily (4 hrs), **Santander** 2 daily (4 hrs) and **Zaragoza** (5 hrs) via **Soria** (2¾ hrs) 2 daily.

Other destinations include **Aranda** (5 daily), **Roa** (2 daily), **Medina del Campo** (8 daily), **Rueda** (7 daily), **Medina de Rioseco** hourly (30 mins), **Simancas** half-hourly and **Tordesillas** hourly.

Car hire
There are a few car hire agencies at Valladolid airport; AVIS, T983 415 530, www.avis.com; Europcar, T983 560 091, www.europcar.com; Hertz, T983 415 546, www.hertz.com.

Taxi
T983 207 755.

Train
Services run to **Madrid** 12-15 daily (slow trains 2½ hrs, €23, fast trains 1 hr, €37) via **Medina del Campo** very regularly, to **Palencia** more than hourly (35 mins), and less frequently to most mainline destinations.

ℹ️ Directory

Valladolid *p96, map p98*
Medical services Hospital Universitario, T983 420 000, emergency T112.
Police T092 in an emergency.

West of Valladolid

Wandering the arid plains and dusty towns of western Castilla these days, it seems difficult to believe that this was once a region of great prestige and power. In the 15th and 16th centuries, towns like Tordesillas and Toro were major players in political and religious life, while Medina del Campo was a huge city for the time and one of Europe's principal trading towns, a sort of Wall Street of the *meseta*. Times have changed, and these places are backwaters, but poke about their streets with a rudimentary idea of Spanish history and you'll find them surprisingly rewarding. The excellent dry wines of Rueda or the hearty reds of Toro will banish any remaining dust from the journey across the scorched plains.

Tordesillas and around → *For listings, see pages 111-113.*

Heading west from Valladolid, after 8 km you come to **Simancas**, a pleasant medieval town whose spectacular castle was set up as an archive for royal documents by Carlos V and Felipe II. A couple of rooms in it are devoted to temporary exhibitions, but that's as much of the interior as you'll see unless you want to consult the archive, which you can do Monday-Friday 0815-1430 on presentation of a passport.

Beyond Simancas on the N620 you reach the town of **Tordesillas**, a place with an interesting history which boasts an imposing *mudéjar* monastery, and the attractive, arcaded 17th-century Plaza Mayor that would look even better if it were pedestrianized.

In 1494 Tordesillas was the location for the signing of a famous treaty between Spain and Portugal, two major maritime powers at the time. The treaty itself was signed in a building that now holds the **tourist office** ① *Tue-Sat 1000-1330, 1600-1830 (1700-1930 summer), Sun 1000-1400*, and the Museo del Tratado, which displays relevant original and facsimile documents, most interestingly the maps showing the proposed division and how knowledge increased over time.

Background

The area around Valladolid was the centre of much of Spain's political activity in the 15th and 16th centuries, and Tordesillas was an important power. Columbus had just got back from the Americas, and there were colonial issues to be sorted out. The 1494 treaty between Spain and Portugal was basically designed to leave Africa for Portugal and the Americas for Spain, but the canny Portuguese suspected or knew of the location of the tip of what is now Brazil, so they pushed the mid-ocean dividing line far enough over to give them a foothold in South America. It had to be re-evaluated within a lifetime, but the idea of two countries meeting to divide the world gives some idea of their control over the Atlantic at the time.

Not too long afterwards, Tordesillas gained an unwilling resident in Juana La Loca (see box, page 109) who was imprisoned here, along with her daughter and the embalmed corpse of her husband. She remained an icon of Castilian sovereignty, and it was due to her presence that Tordesillas became the centre of the *comunero* revolt against the reign of her foreign son Carlos in the early 16th century. The town was viewed with suspicion thereafter and quickly became the backwater that it remains today.

Real Monasterio de Santa Clara

ⓘ *Access to convent by guided tour only; some English-speaking guides at weekends. Tue-Sat 1000-1400, 1600-1830, Sun 1030-1500; Arab baths Tue, Thu-Sat 1000-1200, 1600-1700 (Oct-Mar 1600-1615), Sun 1030-1200, 1530-1600; combined ticket €7, free for EU citizens Wed and Thu afternoons.*

The Real Monasterio de Santa Clara, where Juana la Loca was incarcerated, is an excellent construction, built in *mudéjar* style, still home to a community of Clarist nuns. It was originally built as a palace by Alfonso XI, and he installed his mistress Doña Leonor here. After the king died of plague, Leonor was murdered on the orders of Pedro (the Cruel), the new king. Following the deaths of Pedro's longtime mistress as well as his son, he ordered his illegitimate daughter to convert the palace into a convent in their memory. The *mudéjar* aspects are the most impressive: a chapel with superb stucco work and attractive scalloped arches, and especially the small patio, an absolute gem with horseshoe and scalloped multifoil arches. Another chapel, the **Capilla Dorada**, also has a fine *mudéjar* interior. The cloister is neoclassical in appearance. The high chapel has a very elegant panelled *mudéjar* ceiling. Some fine alabaster tombs in late Gothic style can be seen in the Saldaña chapel, built by the state treasurer of John II and holding his remains, his wife's, and possibly Beatriz of Portugal, Pedro's daughter.

Urueña

North of Tordesillas, some 4 km from the N-VI motorway, Urueña is a small gem of a town. The fantastic walls that surround the village are the main attraction; their jagged teeth and narrow gateways dominate the plains around; on a clear day you can see kilometres from the sentries' walkway along the top. Urueña has been designated as a 'book town', and several bookshops and an exhibition on the history of the book can be found in its narrow streets; regular book launches, workshops, and writing and calligraphy courses are held here. About 1 km below the town is the lovely Romanesque **Iglesia de Nuestra Señora de la Anunciada**, unusually built in the Catalan style. The distinguishing feature 'Lombard arches', a feature that resembles fingers, traced around the apses. Arrange a visit (€1) with the **tourist office** ⓘ *town hall, Plaza Mayor 1, T983 717 445, turismouruena@wanadoo.es.*

Some 9 km south of here, the rustic sleepy village of **San Cebrián de Mazote** ⓘ *May-Oct Fri 1700-1930, Sat-Sun 1100-1400, 1700-1930,* is named for its fine Mozarabic church. It's well worth a look; call the keyholder if it's shut (T629 000 215).

Rueda

Between Tordesillas and Medina del Campo, the straggling town of Rueda is of little interest except for its white wine production. Rueda whites are consistently among Spain's best, and are mostly made from the Verdejo grape, a local variety (not to be confused with Verdelho) which produces wines with a distinctive lemony aroma and crisp finish. Several bodegas in the area can be visited, but the white wine process is not nearly as interesting

Juana la Loca

There are few more tragic figures in the turbulent history of Spain than Queen Juana, who has gone down in history with the unfortunate but accurate name of 'the Mad'. The daughter of the Catholic monarchs Fernando and Isabel, she was sent off in style from Laredo in a fleet of 120 ships bound for Flanders and marriage to Felipe, heir to the throne. Felipe was known as *El Hermoso* (Philip the Fair) and poor Juana made the unthinkable mistake of falling in love with her arranged husband. He didn't feel the same way, making it clear he intended to spend his time with mistresses. This sent Juana into fits of *amorous delirium* and hunger strikes; Felipe complained that she refused to leave him alone.

When she was 27, her mother Isabel died and Juana inherited the throne of Castilla. Her husband died shortly after their arrival in Spain, and this pushed the queen over the edge. She took possession of the corpse and had it embalmed,

refusing to let it be buried or approached by women. She roamed the countryside for years with Felipe, whom she occasionally put on a throne. Deemed unfit to rule, she was finally persuaded to enter a mansion in Tordesillas, where she was locked up, her husband with her. Her daughter Catalina was another unfortunate companion – Juana refused to let her be taken from her, and when she was rescued, her mother went on a hunger strike to ensure her return. The wretched Juana lived in rags for 47 years in Tordesillas; she had occasional lucid moments and was a constant focus for those dissatisfied with the new 'foreign' monarchy of the Habsburgs. Many historians (largely Protestant) have implied that her incarceration was a conspiracy, but there can be little doubt that she was mentally unfit to rule the nation. In 1555 she finally passed away at the age of 76. She is buried in Granada alongside the husband that she loved not wisely but too well.

---

as that of reds, so you're better off picking up a few bottles at the cellar door, and saving your visiting time for the Ribera del Duero east of Valladolid, or for Toro. One of the best wines here is made by **Marqués de Riscal**, located by the motorway just north of the town. About eight buses a day running between Medina and Valladolid stop here.

Medina del Campo → *For listings, see pages 111-113.*

In the early 16th century, Medina del Campo, 25 km south of Tordesillas, was one of the biggest cities in Spain, and its massive trade fairs drew merchants from around Europe in droves. Today, there are few remnants of Medina's past glories. The vast plaza is one of them, and there are some beautiful *palacios* around, but the modern town is ramshackle and poor. The **tourist office** ① *T983 811 357, www.turismomedina.net, Tue-Sat 1000-1400, 1630-1900, Sun 1100-1400,* is on the square by the large church.

Background

Medina was originally an important centre for the export of wool, but diversified to become, for a while, the pre-eminent commercial city of Spain. Queen Isabel often ran Castilla from here, and she actually died in a house overlooking the square. In the *comunero* uprising of 1520 to 1521, Medina was burned to the ground by attacking royalist forces. The town's fairs recovered, but as financial activity began to surround the court once it was settled in Madrid, Medina lost influence. The commerce was greatly harmed by the royal bankruptcies of the late 16th century, and Medina drifted into obscurity.

Places in Medina del Campo

One of the nicest of the many palaces is the Renaissance **Palacio de los Dueñas** ① *Mon-Fri 0900-1445; closed for part of Jul-Aug,* with a beautiful patio and staircase adorned with the heads of the monarchs of Castilla.

On the square, another palace, the **Palacio Real** ① *Tue-Sat 1000-1400, 1600-1900 (1700-2000 summer), Sun-Mon 1100-1430, €2,* is where Queen Isabel left this life in 1504. There's a recreation of her room and an interpretative display on the period.

The **Castillo de la Mota** ① *www.castillodelamota.es, Mon-Sat 1000-1400, 1545-1800 (1900 summer), Sun 1000-1430, €4,* is an impressive *mudéjar* castle across the river from town. The keep has been recently renovated and opened for guided visits. Tours also run of the whole complex, though there's not a great deal to see except the magnificent walls.

The **Museo de las Ferias** ① *C San Martín 26, T983 837 527, www.museoferias.net, Tue-Sat 1000-1330, 1600-1900, Sun 1100-1400, €2,* is situated in an old church and has an interesting look at the commerce of the great trade fairs and how they influenced the art and politics of the period; there's a large collection of related documents and art.

Toro → *For listings, see pages 111-113.*

Toro sits high above the River Duero between Valladolid and Zamora, from either of which it can easily be visited on a day trip, if you don't fancy spending the night. Its name means 'bull', but its emblem is a stone pig dating from Celtiberian times, which sits at the eastern entrance to the city. The city was repopulated during the Reconquista and changed hands a couple of times. A significant battle occurred near here in 1476 between the Catholic Monarchs and Portuguese forces supporting the claim of Isabel's rival, Juana (not the mad one), to the throne of Castilla. The heavy defeat suffered by Alfonso V, the king of Portugal, was a boost to the joint monarchs, and he gave up interfering three years later. The prolific playwright Lope de Vega also made Toro famous by naming one of his plays, *Las Almenas de Toro,* after its battlements. These days Toro is more famous for wine: it produces reds with a worldwide reputation. The **tourist office** ① *Plaza Mayor 6, T980 694 747, turismo@toro ayto.es, Tue-Sat 1000-1400, 1600-1900 (2000 summer), Sun 1000-1400,* is on the main square.

Places in Toro

There are several churches in town with *mudéjar* and Romanesque elements, but the highlight is the **Colegiata** ① *Mar-Sep Tue-Sun 1030-1400, 1730-1930, Oct-Feb Tue-Sun 1000-1400, 1630-1830, €1 for cloister and sacristy,* near the Plaza Mayor. The interior is graced by a high dome with alabaster windows and a baroque organ, but the real highlight is the Portada de la Majestad, a 13th-century carved doorway decorated with superbly preserved (and well-restored) painted figures in early Gothic style; the character expressed through such apparently simple paintwork is remarkable. In the sacristy is a celebrated painting, *La Virgen de la Mosca* (the Virgin of the Fly); the insect is settled on her skirt.

Overlooking the river is the **Alcázar**, a fort dating from the 12th century built on a Moorish fortification. Juana la Beltraneja, pretender to Isabel's Castilian crown, resisted here for a while; she must have enjoyed the views, which stretch for miles across the *meseta*.

Wineries

Most wineries are happy to show visitors around, but all need to be phoned beforehand. In terms of wine quality, one of the best is **Bodegas Fariña** ① *Camino del Palo, T980 577 673, www.bodegasfarina.com*, who market their wine as Colegiata and Gran Colegiata. **Covitoro** ① *Ctra Tordesillas, T980 690 347, www.covitoro.com*, the local wine cooperative, also produce some good bottles, with *Gran Cermeño* a well-priced, oak-aged red. These are a short walk along the main road east of town. Characteristic of the new wine techniques being applied in Toro, **Viña Bajoz** ① *T980 698 023, www.vinabajoz.com*, 6 km east of Toro on the main road in Morales de Toro, is a great cooperative that produces some excellent Tempranillo reds, and even some fruity Malvasia whites. There's a wine shop here with many available for tasting, as well as some other local gourmet food items. There are plenty of other wineries within easy reach of Toro; the tourist office will supply a list. Toro wines received DO (*denominación de origen*) status in 1987.

West of Valladolid listings

For hotel and restaurant price codes and other relevant information, see pages 11-17.

● Where to stay

Tordesillas *p107*

€€€ Parador de Tordesillas, Ctra Salamanca 5, T983 770 051, www.parador.es. Not the most characterful, but still a good option. It is located outside the town in a mansion surrounded by pine trees. The rooms are attractive, and there's a swimming pool.

€ Hostal San Antolín, C San Antolín 8, T983 796 771, www.hostalsanantolin.com. A good choice, just down from the Plaza Mayor. Rooms are excellent value for this price, and it's very professionally run. The restaurant is also one of Tordesillas' best.

Camping

Camping El Astral, Camino de Pollos 8, T983 770 953, www.campingelastral.es. A decent campsite by the River Duero across the bridge from town (follow signs for the parador). On-site pool and bungalows also available.

Urueña *p108*

€ Pozolico, C Santo Domingo 9, T983 717 481, www.pozolico.com. The simplicity of this *casa rural* is appealing; it also has a most friendly owner and an excellent

garden, plus views of the walls from a couple of the rooms. Chilly in winter.

€ Villa de Urueña, C Nueva 6, T626 847 133, www.villadeuruena.es. Run out of the restaurant of the same name on the main square, these are 2 *casas rurales* with simple doubles inside the walls. The **Casa de los Beatos** is the more and characterful building, but both are pleasant.

Medina del Campo *p109*

Medina perhaps appeals more as a day trip from Valladolid, but there are many places to stay.

€€€€ Palacio de las Salinas, Ctra de Salinas s/n, T983 804 450, www.balneario delassalinas.com. The most opulent of the town's choices, this is a massive palace 4 km west of town. Set in huge gardens, it's also a spa hotel and has plenty of comfort for a relaxing stay. Prices normally include breakfast, and half- and full-board rates are available.

€ Hostal Plaza, Plaza Mayor 34, T983 811 246, www.hostal-la-plaza.es. Right on the main square, this *hostal* offers excellent value. It has well-priced, spacious rooms with en suite bathroom as well as a restaurant.

Toro *p110*

€€ Juan II, Paseo Espolón 1, T980 690 300, www.hoteljuanii.com. This hotel is on the edge of the old town above the cliff dropping down to the river. The rooms are comfortable; some have great views, and there's some good old-fashioned Spanish hospitality in the air.

€€ Posada Reja Dorada, C Rejadorada 13, T980 694 979, www.palaciorejadorada.com Constructed around a columned patio, this lovely stone palace has an intriguing story attached to it, from the 15th-century Civil War. Recently refurbished, it's now a lovely boutique inn, with spacious, elegant rooms that seek to recreate the period with elegant beds stately fabrics and, in some cases, canopies. The café is open to the public. Recommended.

€ Doña Elvira, C Antonio Miguelez 47, T980 690 062. Although it's rather unattractively situated by a petrol station on the main road at the edge of the old town, this is the best budget option, with clean en suite rooms at a pittance, and rooms with shared bath for even less. There's some noise from the road, but it's not too bad.

🍴 Restaurants

Tordesillas *p107*
Hostal San Antolín, see Where to stay above, is a good eating option too.

€€€ El Torreón, C Dimas Rodríguez 11, T983 770 123. This restaurant has a lofty reputation hereabouts and is a favourite weekend lunch choice for Valladolid bureaucrats. It specializes in meat and is famous for a great steak tartare as well as home-made foie. There's a hearty, traditional Castilian atmosphere.

€€ Palacio del Corregidor, C San Pedro 14, T983 796 849, www.palaciodelcorregidor. com. Housed in a fine old *palacio*, this friendly restaurant specializes in good paellas and fish baked in salt. The paella should be ordered earlier in the day; if not, be prepared to wait.

Medina del Campo *p109*
€ Mónaco, Plaza Mayor 26, T983 801 020. The town's most characterful spot, this is a lively bar that has some great *pinchos*, and an upstairs restaurant with some excellent, rich, meaty plates and a good *menú* for €10.

Toro *p110*
Toro has a few cheap and cheerful places to eat around the Plaza Mayor.

€€€ La Viuda Rica, C Rejadorada 7, T980 691 581, www.laviudarica.com. The 'wealthy widow' has brought confident, expensive modern cuisine to this classic Castilian town, with an open kitchen, and stylishly prepared dishes that aren't afraid to break with tradition. Various set menus and plenty of Toro wines.

€€ Juan II, Paseo Espolón I, T980 690 300. To its great credit, this spot doesn't feel remotely like a hotel restaurant, and it's priced very fairly indeed. There's a large dining area, a terrace and a range of excellent Castilian fare.

€ Restaurante Castilla, Plaza Mayor 19, T980 690 381. This simple and friendly place has decent hearty local cuisine and tapas. You're much better eating outside if the weather's fine, as the cramped *comedor* can get pretty stuffy. They also have cheap rooms.

🍸 Bars and clubs

Toro *p110*
Carpe Diem, Plaza Mayor 5, T607 601 880. This is the town's best drinking option and a stylish spot.

La Bodeguilla del Pillo, C Puerto del Mercado 34. A local-style wine bar, full of character. Nearly every Toro wine is available by the glass.

🎉 Festivals

Tordesillas *p107*
Mid-Sep The fiesta includes the Toro de la Vega: a bull runs through the town to the countryside outside, where hundreds of people try, and usually succeed, to spear it to death.

⊖ Transport

Tordesillas *p107*

Bus Services between **Valladolid** and **Zamora** stop at the bus station just north and west of the old town. 7-10 weekdays, 3-4 at weekends, plus other services to major cities.

Medina del Campo *p109*

Bus There's a bus terminal next to the train station, but most buses to **Madrid** and **Valladolid** leave from a bar called Punto Rojo on C Artilleria near the Plaza Mayor. About 15 departures for Valladolid daily and 5 for Madrid.

Train Many trains to **Madrid**, **Valladolid**, **Palencia**, and **Salamanca**, as well as 3 a day to **León**, and 1 to **Lisbon**.

Toro *p110*

Bus Services between **Valladolid** and **Zamora** stop on the main road, a handier option than the train. 7-10 a day on weekdays and 3-4 at weekends.

Zamora

Like so many other towns along the river Duero, Zamora was a fortress of the Reconquista frontline, although before that it was a Celtic, Carthaginian, then Roman settlement. In the Middle Ages, the city was formidably walled and famous for its resilience during sieges; the saying 'A Zamora, no se ganó en una hora' (Zamora wasn't taken in an hour) dates from these times and is still used widely.

Today the city is a relaxed and peaceful provincial capital famous for ceramics and antiques. The centre is attractive with, incredibly, a couple of dozen Romanesque churches, which are at ease with some very harmonious modern urban architecture. The city still preserves large sections of its walls around the old centre, which perches high on the rocky bank of the Duero. Zamora province is famous for its wines, with many villages riddled with traditional underground bodegas, and for its wide variety of artisanal cheeses.

Arriving in Zamora → *Phone code: 980. Population: 66,293.*

Getting there and around The train station (a beautiful building) and bus station are inconveniently situated a 20-minute walk to the north of town. Local buses run to them from Plaza Sagasta near the Plaza Mayor, or it's a €5 cab fare. Nearly all the sights of interest are within the walled old town, of elongated shape but still just about walkable. → *See also Transport, page 121.*

Tourist information The city **tourist office** ⓘ *Plaza Arias Gonzalo 6, T980 533 694, daily 1000-1400, 1600-1900 (1700-2000 Mar-Sep)*, is at the cathedral end of town and is very helpful. At the other end of the old town is the similarly helpful **regional office** ⓘ *C Príncipe de Asturias 1, T980 531 845, oficinadeturismodezamora@jcyl.es, mid-Sep to May Mon-Sat 0930-1400, 1600-1900, Sun 0930-1700, Jun to mid-Sep daily 0900-2000*. City tours (€5 per person) run at weekends from March to June and October to November, and daily from July to September. Most guides will be able to summarize in English as they go along. Ask at the tourist office about summer kayaking trips on the Duero below town (€10 per person).

Places in Zamora → *For listings, see pages 119-121.*

Where they are preserved, the **city walls** are impressive and worth strolling around. There are a few noble entrances preserved around the perimeter. Zamora's most enchanting area is the western end of the walled town, a narrow, quiet zone of picturesque streets, noble buildings and little gardens culminating in the city's castle and cathedral.

The **castle** ⓘ *Tue-Sun 1100-1400, 1730-2200, free*, founded in the 11th century, has a muscular keep that's largely modern inside and has been converted into a space for art

The fighting bishop of Zamora

In an age that saw the central state increase its power over the individual, Antonio de Acuña, Bishop of Zamora during the *comunero* revolt, stands out as a swaggering medieval throwback of an individualist whose complete lack of self awareness led to him becoming a central figure of resistance to Carlos V. Born to a wealthy Castilian family who were used to dispensing patronage, Acuña had come to the attention of Fernando and Isabel, who appointed him their ambassador to Rome in 1506.

After Isabel's death, Acuña saw an opportunity to further his own interests and deserted Fernando in preference for Felipe el Hermoso (Philip the Fair). By pledging his absolute loyalty to the Pope he was able to secure his appointment to the bishopric of Zamora despite the opposition of top local bigwig Rodrigo Ronquillo, whose objections were brushed aside when Acuña seized the bishopric by force. His Triumph-of-the-Will-style antics saw him temporarily in charge but at the expense of making a host of powerful enemies.

Although his appointment was eventually confirmed by Fernando, Zamora became a centre of intrigue with Acuña at its centre. When he was eventually expelled from the city at the start of the *comunero* revolt, he raised an army of 2000 men and found himself on the side of the rebels while his implacable enemy Ronquillo was a leading royalist commander. He conducted a series of daring but essentially meaningless campaigns in the *meseta* around Valladolid before deciding in 1521 to march on Toledo where in a great display of showmanship he persuaded the populace to declare him bishop.

It soon became apparent that his individualistic acts of empire building were no substitute for an effective political and military strategy and after the defeat of the *comuneros*, Acuña was forced to flee. But he was captured and held captive in Simancas Castle where Carlos hoped he would be quietly forgotten about.

But in 1526, while attempting to escape, Acuña killed one of his gaolers. Carlos cunningly appointed Ronquillo as custodian of Simancas Castle. Ronquillo wasted no time in settling old scores and sentenced the erstwhile bishop to be tortured and executed. His body was then displayed from the castle walls as warning to others who thought they could challenge royal power.

Although the Pope went through the motions of complaining about this breach of protocol, in reality he recognized that Acuña was a son of the Church who had signally failed to bring any credit or advantage to the Papacy. Eventually the whole matter was quietly forgotten.

---

exhibitions. The gardens around it house information panels; at the entrance to the area is the **Museo de Baltasar Lobo** ⓘ *Tue-Sun 1200-1400, 1800-2100, free*, housing a number of the sensuous forms sculpted by the Zamoran artist whose name it bears.

Next to it, Zamora's **cathedral** ⓘ *catedraldezamora.wordpress.com, Tue-Sun 1000-1400, 1630-1830, summer 1000-1400, 1700-2000, €4*, is an interesting building, especially its dome, which is an unusual feature, with scalloped tiling and miniature pagodas that wouldn't look out of place on a southeast Asian temple. In the squarish interior, you can admire the finely carved stone retrochoir as well as the 16th-century walnut choir itself. The side chapels all have elegant *rejas*, while the stone *retablo* depicts the Ascension. The highlight, however, is the **museum**, and its small collection of superb Flemish tapestries.

Dating from the 15th and 17th centuries, they are amazing for their detail, colour and size (some of them are around 35 sq m). They depict scenes from antiquity: the conquests of Hannibal, the Trojan War and the coronation of Tarquin.

Zamora has an extraordinary number of Romanesque churches, a pleasing collection, particularly as several of them avoided meddlesome architects of later periods. The **Iglesia de La Magdalena** ① *Wed-Mon 1000-1300, 1700-2000, free*, is one of the nicest, with an ornate portal carved with plant motifs. Inside, it's simple and attractive, with a high single nave, and a 13th-century tomb with an unusually midget-like recumbent figure. Most of the worthwhile churches have the same opening hours.

In the **Plaza Mayor**, the **Iglesia de San Juan**, constructed in the 12th to 13th century, has a thistly façade and a big gloomy interior with unusual arches that run the length of the nave, rather than across it. The alabaster windows are an attractive feature.

The pretty **Iglesia de Santa María la Nueva** is increasingly inaccurately named as its Romanesque lines are going on 900 years old. It has some fine carved capitals outside;

Zamora

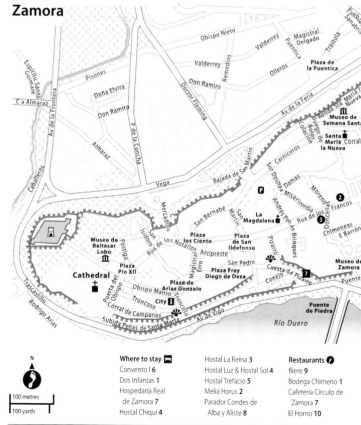

inside it's a simple temple with high barrel vaulting, a stone baptismal font, and the faded remains of some frescoes; you can just about make out scenes from the life of Christ and Mary. Next door is a museum detailing the traditions of Zamora's Semana Santa, while, further to the east, look out for the façade of the **Palacio de los Momos**, carved with penitents' chains seemingly at odds with the grandeur of the mansion.

The **Museo de Zamora** ⓘ *Plaza de Santa Lucía 2, T980 516 150, Tue-Sat 1000-1400, 1600-1900 (summer 1700-2000), Sun 1000-1400, €1.20,* is housed in two connecting buildings: a 16th-century *palacio*, and a modern construction designed by Emilio Tuñón and Luis Moreno Mansilla, which has won many plaudits since its opening in 1998. The museum was conceived as a chest that would hold the city's valuables; it's imaginative without being flamboyant, and fits quietly into the city's older lines. The collection covers everything from the Celtic to the modern, and is fairly interesting: Roman funeral stelae, gilt crosses from the Visigothic period, and especially a very ornate gold Celtic brooch are all things to catch the attention.

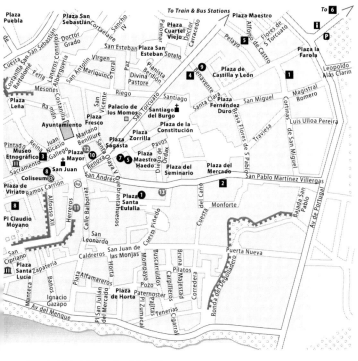

El Rincón de Antonio 2
La Rúa 3
Los Caprichos
 de Meneses 8
Serafín 5

Bars & clubs 🍸
Bodega Quinti 11
La Cueva del Jazz 13
Ocellum 12

On Plaza Viriato is the Museo Etnográfico **museum** ① *Tue-Sat 1000-1400, 1700-2000, Sun 1000-1400, €3,* which holds an ethnographic display of traditional Castilian life, bolstered by regular temporary exhibitions. A little further on lies the **Museo de Semana Santa** ① *Plaza de Santa María la Nueva s/n, Tue-Sat 1000-1400, 1700-2000, Sun 1000-1400, €3,* which has an interesting display illustrating the history of Zamora's famous Holy Week processions.

From parts of the old town, there are magnificent views over the ramparts and down to the Duero River and its picturesque old bridge. From **Plaza Troncoso**, just near the city tourist office, is one of the best, while **Calle Pizarro**, off Rúa de los Francos, is also worthwhile, especially at night. Another interesting street is the steep **Calle Balborraz**, which plunges down from the Plaza Mayor, and is an alluring assembly of character-laden buildings and intriguing shops.

Around Zamora

West of Zamora, the N122 heads towards the Portuguese castle town of **Bragança**, 100 km away. The road passes the massive and attractive reservoir of the Esla River. Some 10 km off the road (from a point 12 km west of Zamora), the church of **San Pedro de la Nave** was moved in the 1930s to protect it from submersion by the rising waters. It's a 17th-century Visigothic structure with lofty doors and some excellent capitals inside, as well as a frieze with various Christian motifs. The keyholder, María Angeles Refoyo, lives in the corner house where the road bends through the middle of the village.

North of Zamora, off the N630 just before the village of Granja de Moreruela, lie the impressive ruins of the **Monasterio de Moreruela** ① *Wed-Sun 1000-1400, 1700-2000 (winter 1530-1830), free.* Built by the Cistercians in the 12th century on a beautiful wooded site, the church and cloisters survive only in outline. Fortunately, the apse and chevet survive intact and convey an impression of the monastery's former glory. It's a romantic spot that you'll almost certainly have to yourself.

Puebla de Sanabria and Parque Natural Lago de Sanabria
Northwest of Zamora, via the unenthralling service centre of Benavente (which has a parador), the A52 heads west into Galicia. It's an attractive route that passes the beautiful **Parque Natural del Lago de Sanabria**. The lake is a hauntingly beautiful glacial feature with several good swimming beaches. The nearest town, **Puebla de Sanabria**, just off the motorway, is an exceptionally attractive place and makes a good stopover, with plenty of character in the narrow streets around its attractive 12th-century church and blocky castle.

Around the lake itself are several small villages with *casas rurales* and other accommodation options. The pretty hamlet of **San Martín de Castañeda** has in a restored monastery, an information centre on the natural park with exhibits on the history, geology, and geography of the area. There are several excellent walks around the lake and surrounding hills; horse riding is also a popular activity.

From Puebla de Sanabria, a beautiful road winds its way south through a spectacular hilly pass and on to Bragança in Portugal, about a 45-minute drive away.

Zamora listings

For hotel and restaurant price codes and other relevant information, see pages 11-17.

⬤ Where to stay

Zamora *p114, map p116*

€€€€ Dos Infantas, Cortinas de San Miguel 3, T980 509 898, www.hoteldos infantas.com. This is a modern and stylish option in the centre of town. It usually offers surprisingly reasonable online rates (**€€**) for large rooms, which are equipped to business hotel standards. There's parking available as well.

€€€€ Hotel Horus, Plaza del Mercado 20, T980 508 282, www.hotelhorus.com. In a stately brick building behind the market, this features attractive art nouveau fittings, helpful staff, and comfortable, classically decorated rooms; the superiors are on the top floor, with sloping attic ceilings. Facilities are excellent, and you're close to the main pedestrian drag but in a quiet zone. Excellent online rates if you book in advance.

€€€ Parador Condes de Alba y Aliste, Plaza de Viriato 5, T980 514 497, www.parador.es. This is a great place to stay in the heart of the old town, in a noble palace built around a beautiful courtyard. The rooms are large and attractively furnished in wood (the new wing is equally comfortable although not quite as atmospheric), while the pool out the back helps with the summer heat.

€€€ Hotel Convento I, Ctra la Estación s/n, Coreses, T980 500 422, www.hotelconvento. es. The stern façade of this former seminary 9 km from Zamora in the village of Coreses gives way to an opulent interior; this spa hotel bristles with columns, cherubs, frescoes, stained glass, pharaohs, and other baroque excesses. You'll either find it over-the-top or delightful, and the swimming pool area has to be seen to be believed. There's a full range of spa treatments available, and various weekend deals that include meals.

€€ Hotel Trefacio, C Alfonso de Castro 7, T980 509 104, www.hoteltrefacio.com. Good mid-range option, with modern rooms that have excellent bathrooms in the heart of the town. The management are warm and friendly and facilities are good. The superior rooms are a few euros more but are substantially larger and face the street, which is a quiet one.

€ Hostal La Reina, C Reina 1, T980 533 939, www.hostallareina.es. Superbly situated behind the church of San Juan on the Plaza Mayor, this cheery option has rooms with bathroom that are simple enough, but very good at this price.

Around Zamora *p118*

€€€ Parador Puebla de Sanabria, Ctra Lago 18, Puebla de Sanabria, T980 620 001, www.parador.es. A good modern option, but on the other side of the river from the attractive town centre. Helpful, friendly staff and a decent restaurant.

€ Hostal San Francisco, Alto de San Francisco 6, Puebla de Sanabria, T980 620 896, www.hostal-sanfrancisco.com. With a great location in the old town, this *hostal* is comfortable, heated and has good views. Offers plenty of value.

Camping

There are 3 campsites around the Lago de Sanabria. **El Folgoso**, Ctra Puebla-San Martín Km 13, T980 626 774, www.campingelfolgoso.com, is a pretty wooded site near the village of El Vigo and a short walk away from a lakeside beach.

⑦ Restaurants

Zamora *p114, map p116*

€€€ El Rincón de Antonio, Rúa de los Francos 6, T980 535 370, www.elrinconde antonio.com. Zamora's culinary star is an attractive restaurant with a stone interior and a big glassed-in terrace. The cuisine is innovative and excellent; the *mollejas* (sweetbreads) are heaven, as is the *rodaballo* (turbot). There's a huge range of delicious Zamoran cheeses on the trolley, and scrumptious sweets. If you're not that hungry, they do excellent miniature gourmet plates in the bar for €2 a shot; a great way to sample some wonderful textures and flavours without busting the bank. Highly recommended.

€€€ Los Caprichos de Meneses, Plaza San Miguel 3, T980 530 143, www.loscaprichosdemeneses.com. On the main square, this is a gourmet option that doesn't disappoint. Meneses is the extravagantly moustached boss, and he suggests that you choose a main course, and let them decide on the starters and desserts for you. This works well, but the grilled octopus is a treat you mightn't want to miss. Mains include succulent lamb, and several enticing *bacalao* choices, and desserts are rich and beautifully presented. Recommended.

€€ Biere, C Benavente 7, T980 517 178. Cheerfully thronged at lunchtime, this airy café-restaurant attracts crowds for its excellent set lunches. For €12 (or €21 at dinner time) you get a wide choice of dishes featuring both heavy Zamoran classics and lighter options for those hot summer days.

€€ La Rúa, Rúa de los Francos 19, T980 534 024. This likeable and comfortably decorated restaurant is solid for a range of choices, with simple *platos combinados*, a good *menú del día* and some great *zamorano* cuisine. However, it's the rices that give it its good name; the speciality, a paella-like rice with lobster, *arroz con bogavante* (€20 per person; best to order it beforehand), comes in a huge deep dish, sizzling with intent to satisfy.

€€ Serafín, Plaza Maestro Haedo 10, T980 531 422. Good hearty Zamoran and Castilian fare at reasonable prices, with a pleasant terrace outside. As well as the café, it also has a more upmarket restaurant, serving dishes such as *arroz a la zamorana*, a hearty rice with various porcine morsels.

€ Bodega Chimeno, Plaza Santa Eulalia 4, T980 530 925. Tucked away in the old town, this place looks like an apartment entrance from outside, but inside it's gloriously traditional, with wooden tables and barrels, a range of Toro wines by the glass, and surprisingly elaborate tapas like duck ham alongside more earthy offerings like canned tuna or chunkily-cut jamón.

€ Cafetería Círculo de Zamora, C Santa Clara 2, T980 530 534. On the 1st floor of a restored art deco building, this venerable Zamoran institution serves up good-value snacks and meals all day. There's also disabled access.

Around Zamora *p118*

€€€ El Empalme, N-525 Km 352, Ríonegro del Puente, T980 652 016. On the *ruta nacional* about halfway between Benavente and Puebla de Sanabria, this place seems like a standard roadside diner but is in fact famous throughout Spanish gourmet circles for the quality of its dishes prepared using locally sourced wild mushrooms of various varieties. There's also plenty of game in season.

€€ La Casona de Sanabria, Ctra Nacional N525, Puebla de Sanabria, T980 620 000, www.lacasonadesanabria.com. Puebla de Sanabria's best eating option is actually just outside the town, on the main road across the river near the big roundabout. It's an enormous hotel-café complex, but the restaurant is worth seeking out for huge and delicious dishes such as *codillo* (pork knuckle), roast lamb, and excellent octopus. Local wild mushrooms and cut-price wagyu beef are other options. The *menú del día* is perfectly adequate, but it's worth ordering off the *carta* here.

€ Café Bar Remate, C Arrabal 3, Puebla de Sanabria, T980 620 920. Though it doesn't look much from the outside compared to the other choices in town, this is a top spot for simple eating, with lovingly prepared traditional dishes such as *callos* (tripe) or octopus served in a pleasant *comedor*.

🍸 Bars and clubs

Zamora *p114, map p116*
The bulk of Zamoran nightlife is centred on the boisterous **C de los Herreros**, a narrow curving street off the Plaza Mayor, whose steep length is made of one bar after another; basically you just have to stroll down and see which one you fancy. There are some quieter bars around the Plaza Mayor too, and a few secluded options throughout the old town.
Bodega Quinti, C de los Herreros 23. One of the more atmospheric of bars on this street, this underground bar is in a claustrophobic but smart brick vault. It's better earlier in the night as it gets too packed later on.
La Cueva del Jazz, Plaza Seminario 3, T980 533 436, www.lacuevadeljazz.es. Legendary Zamora jazz den in an atmospheric cellar. They have regular live music; most concerts are now in a new venue at C Puerta Nueva 30.
Ocellum, Plaza Mayor 8, T980 514 848. This high-ceilinged café/bar is popular at several points of the day. Its terrace is a great spot for an afternoon coffee after walking the pedestrian zone of the city; later, it gets busy for after-dinner drinks, then becomes a *discoteca*, with a huge selection in the DJ booth and a downstairs dance floor.

🎉 Festivals

Zamora *p114, map p116*
Mar/Apr Zamora's **Semana Santa** (Holy Week) is one of the most famous and traditional in Spain. Book a room well in advance if you fancy a visit. Although there's plenty of revelry in the bars and streets, the main element is the serious religious processions of hooded *cofradías* (brotherhoods) who carry or accompany giant floats; it's effectively a week-long series of funeral processions; they are very atmospheric and traditional, accompanied by mournful music that communicates both the sadness and the bitter glory. One of the most beautiful is the procession on Sat evening, when the much-loved Virgen de la Soledad

is carried through the streets, preceded by a sisterhood carrying flickering candles.
End Jun Zamora's main fiesta is **San Pedro**, with streetlife, fireworks and bullfights. At the same time, the Plaza de Viriato holds an important ceramics fair; a picturesque sight indeed with thousands of vessels of all shapes and sizes arranged under the trees; they range from traditional plain earthenware to imaginatively painted decorative pieces.

🛍 Shopping

Zamora *p114, map p116*
Zamora is full of shops dealing in antiques and ceramics; there are also characterful shops along the main pedestrian streets selling wine, delicious local cheeses and hams.

⊖ Transport

Zamora *p114, map p116*
Despite Zamora's proximity to the Portuguese border, there are currently no public transport connections with it; you have to go via Salamanca or Madrid.

Bus
Some 7 buses a day run north to **León** (2 hrs) via **Benavente** (4 at weekends); 7-10 run to **Valladolid**, some stopping in **Toro** and **Tordesillas** (3 at weekends); 6 service **Madrid**; a massive 13 cruise south to **Salamanca** (40 mins-1 hr, 6 on Sun), and 5 go to **Oviedo** (3 hrs 30 mins), among other northern Spanish destinations.

Train
Trains are few: 2 a day run to **Madrid** (2 hrs, €31); more go to **Medina del Campo** (55 mins), and 2 to **Puebla de Sanabria**.

❶ Directory

Zamora *p114, map p116*
Police The police station is in the Plaza Mayor in the old town hall.

Salamanca and around

Salamanca has a strong claim to being Spain's most attractive city. A university town since the early 13th century, it reached its apogee in the 15th and 16th centuries, the Golden Age of Imperial Spain. The old town is a remarkable assembly of superb buildings; a day's solid sightseeing can teach you more about Spanish architecture than you thought you ever wanted to know – Plateresque and Churrigueresque were more or less born here. By night, too, it's a good spot; today's university students just don't seem to tuck up in bed with a candle, hot milk and a theological tract like they used to, and bar life is busy seven days a week, bolstered by the large numbers of tourists and foreign students learning Spanish. If you can handle the heat and the crowds, there are few better places in Spain to spend a summer evening than the superb Plaza Mayor; sit at an outdoor table and watch storks circle architectural perfection in the setting sun.

Arriving in Salamanca → *Phone Code: 923. Population:155,619. Altitude: 780 m.*
Getting there Salamanca is about 200 km west of Madrid. The bus station is west of town along Avenida Filiberto Villalobos. There are plenty of buses from Madrid, Valladolid and other Castilian cities. New motorways and the straight *meseta* roads make for easy driving access; it's about an hour from Valladolid, for example, and forty minutes from Zamora. There are also several train connections. ▸▸ *See also Transport, page 134.*

Getting around You won't have much cause to stray from the old town, which is very walkable. The bus and train stations are a 15-minute walk from the centre.

Best time to visit If you visit in summer you are guaranteed heat, tourists and outdoor tables. In many ways this is the nicest time to come, but the students aren't about (although there are always plenty of foreign-language students) and the nightlife is correspondingly quieter. Like the rest of Castilla, Salamanca gets cold in winter, but never shuts down and accommodation is cheap.

Tourist information There are two handy tourist offices, one in the **Plaza Mayor** ① *T923 218 342, www.salamanca.es, Mon-Fri 0900-1400, 1600-1830, Sat 1000-1830, Sun 1000-1400, summer Mon-Fri 0900-1400, 1630-2000, Sat 1000-2000, Sun 1000-1400*, and one at **Rúa Antigua 70** ① *Casa de las Conchas, T923 268 571, oficinadeturismodesalamanca@jcyl.es, mid-Sep to Jun Mon-Sat 0930-1400, 1600-1900, Sun 0930-1700, summer daily 0900-2000.* The former has more information on the city, the second is better for information on the rest of Castilla y León. A few summer-only kiosks are scattered about, notably at the transport terminals. Regular **walking tours** of the city run from the tourist office on the Plaza Mayor; they leave daily throughout the year at 1100 (€6, Spanish only). In summer there are usually English-language tours available. Otherwise, the tourist office can provide a list of English-speaking official guides. At either of the tourist offices you can buy the Salamanca Card (www.salamancacard.com) which, for €23, gives you two days of access to the city's monuments and museums, an audio guide, and various discounts.

Background

Salamanca's history is tied to that of its university (see box, page 126), but the town itself was founded in pre-Roman times. An Iberian settlement, it was taken by Hannibal (pre-elephants) in 218 BC. The Romans later took it over but, as with most cities in these parts, it was abandoned and only resettled during the Reconquista. The university was founded in AD 1218 and rapidly grew to become one of Europe's principal centres of learning. Flourishing particularly under the Catholic Monarchs, the city became an emblem of Imperial Spain; the think-tank behind the monarchy that ruled half the world.

Salamanca's decline in the 18th and 19th centuries mirrored that of its university and indeed the rest of Castilla. The city suffered grievously in the Napoleonic wars; the French general Marmont destroyed most of the university's buildings before his defeat by Wellington just south of the city in 1812. In the 20th century, during the Civil War, Major Doval, a well-known butcher, cracked down fiercely on Republican sympathizers after the coup. The city was the conspirators' command centre for a while, and Franco was declared *caudillo* in a cork grove just outside the town. In 2002 Salamanca revelled in its status as joint European Cultural Capital, and the city benefited from the success and structural improvements.

Places in Salamanca → *For listings, see pages 130-134.*

Plaza Mayor

Among strong competition, Salamanca's main square stands out as the most harmonious plaza in Spain. Built in the 18th century by Alberto Churriguera, it has nothing of the occasional gaudiness of the style to which he and his brother unwittingly lent their names. Paying over the odds for a coffee or a vermouth at one of its outdoor tables is still a superb option; there can be fewer nicer places to sit, especially on a warm summer's evening with storks circling above. Around the perimeter are medallions bearing the heads of various illustrious Spaniards; the more recent additions include Franco (often defaced by paint) and King Juan Carlos, and there are plenty of blank ones for new notables.

University and around

Rúa Mayor links the plaza with the cathedral and the old buildings of the university. It's lined with restaurants that take over the street with tables for pleasant overeating and drinking in the summer sun. On the right about halfway down is the distinctive **Casa de las Conchas** (House of Shells), named for the 400-odd carved scallop shells of its façades. Now a library (with occasional exhibitions), its nicest feature is the courtyard, graced by an elegantly intricate balcony and decorated with well-carved lions and shields. Opposite the Casa de las Conchas is the **Clerecía**, a Jesuit college founded in the early 17th century by Felipe III – a plaque commemorates the event. An imposing baroque cloister can be visited to the right of the church entrance.

Salamanca

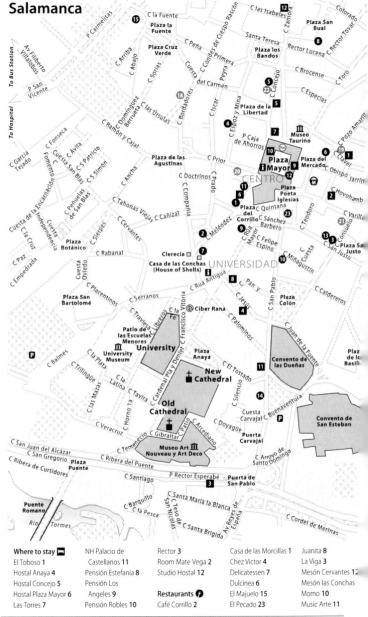

Where to stay 🛏️
El Toboso **1**
Hostal Anaya **4**
Hostal Concejo **5**
Hostal Plaza Mayor **6**
Las Torres **7**

NH Palacio de
 Castellanos **11**
Pensión Estefanía **8**
Pensión Los
 Angeles **9**
Pensión Robles **10**

Rector **3**
Room Mate Vega **2**
Studio Hostal **12**

Restaurants 🍴
Café Corrillo **2**

Casa de las Morcillas **1**
Chez Victor **4**
Delicatessen **7**
Dulcinea **6**
El Majuelo **15**
El Pecado **23**

Juanita **8**
La Viga **3**
Mesón Cervantes **12**
Mesón las Conchas
Momo **10**
Music Arte **11**

Leave the Clerecía on your right and take the second left to reach the **Patio de las Escuelas**, a small square surrounded by beautiful university buildings. In the centre stands Fray Luis de León (see box, page 126). He faces the edifice where he once lectured, the main **university** building. Its incredible façade is an amazing example of what master masons could achieve with soft Salamanca sandstone. The key for generations of students and visitors has been to spot the frog; if you manage to do it unguided, you are eligible for a range of benefits: good exam results, luck in love and more. However, it's rather underwhelming if you've just spent a couple of hours searching it out.

The **interior** ⓘ *Mon-Fri 0930-1300, 1600-1900, Sat 0930-1300, 1600-1830, Sun 1000-1300, €4, free Mon mornings; entrance includes the university museum, which is dominated by a mighty cypress*, is interesting, but not nearly as impressive, and feels positively stark after the exuberant exterior. There are several impressively worked ceilings inside. The old halls radiate around the courtyard; the largest, the Paraninfo, is hung with Flemish tapestries. One of the halls is preserved as it was in the days when Fray Luis lectured here, with narrow wooden benches, while upstairs, the impressive library is a beautiful space, with ornate wooden shelves lined with thousands of ancient texts; these days you can only peer from the entrance, however. Fray Luis's remains are in the chapel.

The **university museum** is housed around a patio on the other side of the square, the Escuelas Menores. The patio is attractively grassed behind its Plateresque portal. The arches, looking a little like devils' horns, are typical of Salamanca, an exuberant innovation of the 15th century. There's a reasonable collection of paintings and sculptures, the best by foreign artists resident in Salamanca in its glory years, but the highlight is the remaining part of the fresco ceiling painted by Fernando Gallego.

Salamanca University and Fray Luis de León

Founded in 1218, Salamanca was Spain's second university (after Palencia) to be established. The patronage of kings allowed it to grow rapidly; in 1255 it was named by the Pope as pre-eminent in Europe, alongside Paris, Oxford and Bologna. It was the brains behind the Golden Age of Imperial Spain; its Colegios Mayores, or four Great Colleges, supplied a constant stream of Spain's most distinguished thinkers, and exerted plenty of undue political influence to get their own graduates appointed to high positions. The university had in excess of 10,000 students in its pomp and was forward thinking, with a strong scientific tradition and a female professor as early as the late 15th century.

Spain's closed-door policy to Protestant thinkers was always going to have a bad effect, and Salamanca declined in the 18th century; Newton and Descartes were considered unimportant, the chair of mathematics was vacant for decades, and theologians debated what language was spoken by the angels. The Peninsular War had a terrible effect too; French troops demolished most of the university's colleges. But the university is thriving again: although not among Spain's elite, the student atmosphere is bolstered by large numbers of foreigners who come to the beautiful city to learn Spanish.

Among many notable teachers that have taught at Salamanca, two stand out; Miguel de Unamuno, and Fray Luis de León. Born to Jewish *conversos* (converts), at 14 the latter came to Salamanca to study law; he soon moved into theology, becoming a monk of the Augustinian order. In 1560 he was appointed to the chair of theology. Well versed in Hebrew, Fray Luis continued to use Hebrew texts as the basis of his Biblical teaching; he was responsible for many translations of the testaments and scriptures from that language into Spanish. Enemies and anti-Semites saw these actions as being in defiance of the Council of Trent, and on 27 March 1572, Fray Luis was arrested mid-lecture by the Inquisition and imprisoned in Valladolid, where he was charged with disrespect and imprudence. After a five-year trial he was sentenced to torture by the rack; the punishment was, however, revoked. Returning to Salamanca, he famously began his first lecture to a crowded room with "*Dicebamus hesterna die*" (As we were saying yesterday ...). He maintained his firm stance, and got into fresh trouble with the Inquisition five years later. He was made provincial of the Augustinians and died in 1591.

Apart from his theological writings, he was an excellent poet, one of the finest in Spain's history. His verses bring out the deep feelings of a man better known as having been severe and sardonic, understandably, given the religious hypocrisy that he struggled against.

It illustrates the signs of the Zodiac and various constellations; a *mudéjar* ceiling in one of the rooms for temporary exhibits is also well worth a peek.

Cathedrals
Unusually for Spain, Salamanca's **Catedral Nueva** ① *Mon-Sat 0900-1300, 1600-1800 (2000 summer), Sun 0900-1300, free; cathedral tower Ieronimus exhibition daily 1000-1915, €3.75*, is built alongside, rather than on top of, its Romanesque predecessor. It's a massive affair that dominates the city's skyline from most angles. While the later tower is unimpressively ostentatious, the western façade is superb; a masterpiece of late Gothic

stonework, with the transition into Plateresque very visible. It is the sheer number of statues and motifs that amazes, more than the power of any particular scene. The central figure is of the Crucifixion, flanked by Saints Peter and Paul. Around the corner to the left, the façade facing the Plaza de Anaya is also excellent. The door is named Puerta de las Palmas for the relief carving of Jesus entering Jerusalem on Palm Sunday, but take a look at the archivolts on the left-hand side; an astronaut and an imp with a large ice cream are entertaining recent additions.

Inside, the new cathedral impresses more by its lofty lines than its subtlety. It's a mixture of styles, mostly in transitional Gothic with star vaulting and colourful, high Renaissance lantern. The *coro* is almost completely enclosed; the stalls were carved in walnut by the Churriguera brothers. At the back, in a *capilla* of the squared apse, the bronze figure of the *Cristo de las Batallas* is said to have been carried into war by the Cid. In another chapel is the grisly dried hand of Julián Rodríguez Sánchez, a Salamancan priest murdered in the Civil War, and beatified in 2001. The cathedral towers have been recently restored and offer an exhibition of medieval documents, 'Ieronimus', and a terrace with a fine city view.

The **Catedral Vieja** ① *Mon-Sat 1000-1230, 1600-1730 (1930 summer), Sun 1000-1230, €4.75*, is accessed from inside the new one. It's a much smaller, more intimate space. It dates mostly from the 12th century; while the design is Romanesque, the pointed arches anticipate the later Gothic styles. On the wall by the entrance are wall paintings from the early 17th century; they depict miracles attributed to the *Cristo de las Batallas* figurine. The *retablo* is superb, a colourful ensemble of 53 panels mostly depicting the life of Christ. Above, a good *Last Judgement* sees the damned getting herded into the maw of a hake-like monster. In the transepts are some excellent coloured tombs, one with its own vaulted ribs.

Around the cloister are several interesting chambers. The Capilla de Santa Bárbara is where, until 1843, the rector of the university was sworn in. It was also where the students used to take their final exams; if they failed, it was straight across the cloister and out via the opposite door, and thence no doubt to the nearest boozer.

Convents

The **Convento de San Esteban** ① *daily 1000-1330, 1600-1915, €3*, not far from the cathedrals, is slightly cheerless but worth visiting. Its ornate Plateresque façade depicts the stoning of Esteban himself (St Stephen); the door itself is also attractive. Entry to the church is via the high cloister, which has quadruple arches. The top deck, floored with boards, is the nicest bit; it would cry out for a café-bar if it weren't in a monastery. There's a small museum with various Filipino saints, a silver reliquary in the shape of a *sombrero*, and a couple of amazing early Bibles. One of them, dating from the late 13th century or so, is so perfect it's almost impossible to believe that it was handwritten.

The church is dominated by its *retablo*, a work of José Churriguera. A massive 30 m by 14 m, it's exuberantly excessive, but more elegant than some of the style's later examples.

Opposite, the **Convento de las Dueñas** ① *Mon-Sat 1100-1245 (1030-1300 summer), 1630-1730, €2*, also houses Dominicans, this time in the shape of nuns who do a popular line in almond cakes. The irregular-shaped cloister is open for visits and is beautiful, with views of the cathedral in the background. Dating from the first half of the 16th century, its lower floor is fairly simple compared with the top level, decorated with busts and shields, as well as ornate capitals of doomed souls and beasts.

Museo Art Nouveau y Art Deco

ⓘ *C Gibraltar 14, T923 121 425, www.museocasalis.org, Apr to mid-Oct Tue-Fri 1100-1400, 1700-2100, Sat and Sun 1100-2100, mid-Oct to Mar Tue-Fri 1100-1400, 1600-1900, Sat and Sun 1100-2000, €4.*

If you fancy a break from sandstone and Plateresque, head for the Museo Art Nouveau y Art Deco. It's superbly housed in the **Casa Lis**, an art nouveau *palacio* built for a wealthy Salamancan industrialist; there's a particularly good view of the building from the riverbank. The collection of pieces is very good; you're sure to find something you love and something you can't stand. Representative of the traditions of many countries, there are porcelains, sculpture, glassware, ceramics, Fabergé jewelling and dolls. The stained-glass ceiling is particularly impressive too.

Nearby, check out the pretty **Puente Romano**, a bridge over the Tormes with Roman origins. There are numerous other religious buildings and museums to visit in Salamanca; the tourist office has a fuller list than can be provided here.

Around Salamanca province → *For listings, see pages 130-134.*

Ledesma and around

Heading west and slightly north from Salamanca, the town of Ledesma makes a reasonably pretty place to visit, formerly an important walled defensive outpost, but now lost in a quiet Castillian corner on the river Tormes. Beyond, the Embalse de Almendra is an attractive artificial lake, used by birds and watersporters. Don't follow the advice of one 19th-century travel guide: the neighbourhood affords excellent shooting … the hawk, the vulture, and an occasional eagle may be shot by naturalistic sportsmen …

Ciudad Rodrigo

Southwest from Salamanca, a busy road crosses bull-breeding heartland on its way to Ciudad Rodrigo and the main Portuguese border in these parts. Ciudad Rodrigo is a lovely place with a turbulent past; as a fortified border town it was constantly involved in skirmishes and battles involving Castilla and Portugal. Most famously, it figured prominently in the Peninsular War. The French besieged the town and finally took it, despite heroic Spanish resistance under General Herrasti. In January 1812 Wellington, aware that French reinforcements were fast approaching, managed to take the town in a few hours; the French general, Marmont, was flabbergasted, describing the action as "incomprehensible". Both sides plundered the town when in possession; Wellington was appalled at how low his troops could stoop. The general was awarded the title "Duke of Ciudad Rodrigo" by the Spanish cortes; the dukes of Wellington still hold this title today.

The town walls and ramparts are particularly impressive; one of the entries to the town is via a tunnel through the wall, with large wooden doors still ready to be bolted shut to repel invaders. You can climb the wall in some places and get good views over the surrounding plains. There's also a small **museum** ⓘ *Fri-Sun 1030-1430, €2.50*, about the fortifications.

The town's principal sight is its **cathedral** ⓘ *1145-1400, 1600-1900, closed Mon afternoon, €3*, an attractive mixture of Romanesque and Gothic in golden sandstone. Inside, the carved wooden *coro* is elegant, and the cloisters are an interesting blend of styles. In the Capilla de Cerralbo to one side is a decent *retablo*; the chapel itself has been extensively renovated after being blown up in 1818 while being used as a gunpowder store. The cathedral's tower still is pockmarked from cannonfire, and you can see one of the two breaches that Wellington's forces entered the city by. Admission includes the diocesan museum.

The rest of the town is dotted with attractive buildings; the castle is now a parador, and the Plaza Mayor is graced by the graceful Renaissance *ayuntamiento*.

The **tourist office** ① Mon-Fri 1000-1400, 1700-1900 (2000 in summer), Sat-Sun 1100-1400, 1630-2030, is opposite the cathedral.

The city is famous for its Carnaval (six weeks before Easter), which incorporates masquerades, all manner of bull sports, and general wildness. It's well-known in the land, so you'll need to book accommodation well in advance, and be prepared to pay a little more.

South of Salamanca → *For listings, see pages 130-134.*

The mountains in the southernmost portion of Salamanca province make an excellent destination, although some areas can get uncomfortably crowded in summer, as holidaymakers leave baking Madrid in droves.

Fifteen kilometres southeast of Salamanca, and connected with it by hourly buses, the town of **Alba de Tormes** seems an unlikely place to have given its name to the most powerful of Spanish aristocratic lines, the dukes and duchesses of Alba. It also has another big claim to fame as the resting place of Santa Teresa de Ávila, Spain's top 16th-century mystic, but it's a small place that's not especially engaging, although it is prettily set on the Tormes, which is crossed by an attractive bridge.

A 16th-century keep is all that remains of the **dukes' castle** ① 1030-1330, 1600-1800 (1630-1930 summer), €3; there's nothing remotely grand about it now, although there's some noble Mudéjar brickwork. There's a small tourist office in town, who can arrange visits outside these hours.

Santa Teresa founded the **Convento de Carmelitos** here in 1571. It's not especially interesting; there are some well-carved tombs, paintings of her life and doings, and a reconstruction of a nuns' cell of the time. The saint's ashes are in an urn in the middle of the *retablo*; it's not all of her though, for Franco used to keep one of her mummified hands next to him as he planned his next stagnations.

Further south, **Béjar**, a textile town, isn't particularly attractive in itself, but enjoys a picturesque position at the base of the sierra, snow-covered in winter, when the local ski resort gets going. The church of Santa María La Mayor has a pretty Mudéjar apse, but the biggest building in town is the former ducal palace, now a public building. Pop in to check out its pretty patio if it's open.

For a prettier stopover, head 4 km up into the mountains to **Candelario**, a handsome, steep, village with attractive houses designed to combat the fierce winter cold and spring thaw.

Heading west from Béjar into the sierras of Béjar then Francia is an attractive journey through some very unCastilian scenery of chestnut groves and small herds of cattle. There are some pretty villages to stop at; **Miranda del Castañar** is one of the nicest, and **Mogarraz** is devoted to tasty ham and sausage production from the bristly pigs that are kept thereabouts. Both have accommodation and eating options, but the gem of the area is undoubtedly **La Alberca**, despite the high tourist levels in summer.

La Alberca is built directly onto bedrock in some places and has a collection of unusual stone and wood buildings, giving it a distinctly Alpine feel. Some say, indeed, that the original settlers came here from Swabia. As well as being a pretty place in itself, it makes a good base for walking in the sierra. The attractive village is centred around its main Plaza Pública, which slopes down to a stone Calvary and fountain.

South of La Alberca, the road rises slowly to a pass then spectacularly descends towards Extremadura through a region known as Las Batuecas, a dreamy green valley that's worth exploring.

North of La Alberca, the road towards Ciudad Rodrigo runs close to **La Peña de Francia**, the highest peak in the region (1732 m). It's a pretty drive or climb to the top, and the views on a clear day are spectacular. There's a monastery at the top, as well as a hotel/restaurant.

Salamanca and around listings

For hotel and restaurant price codes and other relevant information, see pages 11-17.

🛏 Where to stay

Salamanca *p122, map p124*
Salamanca is replete with places to stay; there are well over 100 spots to lay your head.

€€€€ NH Palacio de Castellanos, C San Pablo 58, T923 261 818, www.nh-hotels. com. This imposing hotel occupies what was once a late 15th-century palace, although much of what remains dates from the 19th century. The rooms have all the conveniences of a business hotel but considerably more charm than most, with wrought-iron balconies, a pillow menu, video games and more. Extras, such as internet, are overpriced.

€€€ Hotel Las Torres, C Concejo 4, T923 212 100, www.hthoteles.com. Some rooms in this sensitively refurbished 18th-century building have balconies overlooking the Plaza Mayor. It offers smart modern facilities such as internet access, hydromassage showers and, in the best rooms, PC with flatscreen monitor and exercise bike. There's free internet and business facilities for guests and specially adapted rooms for families and for the disabled. The rates are on a sliding scale and vary considerably; it's best to book over the internet to see what's on offer.

€€€ Hotel Rector, Paseo Rector Esperabé 10, T923 218 482, www.hotelrector.com. An excellent option near the river, this small and exclusive hotel is in a beautiful sandstone *palacio*. Its very plush inside, with leather sofas, art nouveau glass and elegant wooden furniture; the rooms are decorated with a lighter touch, with olive-wood bedheads and large windows admitting plenty of natural light. Service is excellent. Book ahead. Parking available. Recommended.

€€€ Room Mate Vega, Plaza del Mercado 16, T923 272 250, www.room-matehotels. com. Very close to the Plaza Mayor, this stylish and upbeat chain choice offers easy-on-the-eye designer chic and very spacious rooms with plenty of facilities, including courtesy apples and free Wi-Fi.

€€ Hostal Concejo, Plaza de la Libertad 1, T923 214 737, www.hconcejo.com. Another well-placed option, this friendly *hostal* has faultless modern rooms around the corner from the Plaza Mayor. It's in the pedestrian zone and has been recently renovated.

€€ Hostal Plaza Mayor, Plaza Corrillo 19, T923 262 020, www.hostalplazamayor.es. Though not quite on the square that it's named after, it's only a few paces away. You pay a little for the location, but the rooms are compact, modern and comfortable.

€€ Hotel El Toboso, C Clavel 7, T923 271 462, www.hoteltoboso.com. Value-packed choice in the heart of things, with very pleasing decor in an attractive stone building. The prices are very good; the double rooms are spacious and light and the apartments (sleeping 3 or 5) are especially attractive for a family stay and priced very reasonably.

€€ Pensión Los Angeles, Plaza Mayor 10, T923 218 166, www.pensionlosangeles. com. The best rooms in this decent spot overlook the Plaza Mayor, and they are much nicer than the no-frills interior rooms (**€**), which are a bit grim by comparison.

Get a room with a view or look elsewhere. Noisy at weekends.

€€ Studio Hostal, C Zamora 54, T923 280 557, www.studiohostal.com. More of a boutique hotel than a *hostal*, this super choice, like many smaller places, owes its excellence to an enthusiastic and helpful owner. Rooms are all different, with good modern extras; you can get a breakfast tray brought to your room. Much pricier at weekends. Book ahead.

€ Pensión Estefanía, C Jesús 3, T923 217 372, www.pensionestefania.es. A very cheap and handy option in the centre of Salamanca. Though the welcome is hardly effusive, the rooms are good value, at least in summer. In winter, you might like to consider elsewhere, as there's no heating. Bathrooms are shared but clean, but there are showers in the rooms.

€ Pensión Robles, Plaza Mayor 20, T923 213 197. The best reason to stay at this basic but clean place is its location on the beautiful plaza, though not all of the rooms overlook it. Rooms are simple, with an OK bathroom, and the price is super-low. It's regularly booked up.

Ciudad Rodrigo *p128*
Ciudad Rodrigo is a lovely place to stay.
€€€ Parador Enrique II, Plaza del Castillo 1, T923 460 150, www.parador.es. This excellent castle hotel has helpful staff, great views out over the walls and a nice restaurant.
€€ Hotel Arcos, C Cardenal Pacheco 11, T923 480 001, www.hotelarcosciudad rodrigo.com. Right in the centre of town, this is a good-value budget hotel.

Candelario *p129*
€€ Artesa, C Mayor 57, T923413111, www.artesa.es. This is a good *casa rural* in the heart of the village, attractively rustic and decorated with some flair; they also put on decent meals.

La Alberca *p129*
There are several places to stay.
€€€ Hotel Doña Teresa, Carretera Mogarraz s/n, T923 415 308, www.hotel deteresa.com. The town's most luxurious hotel is a charming, relaxing place. Try to grab a room giving onto the garden. You can use the pool and spa facilities in their sister hotel a couple of kilometres out of town.
€ Hostal Balsa, C La Balsada 4, T923 415 337. A decent cheap choice, with simple but comfortable modern rooms in an old village house.

🍴 Restaurants

Salamanca *p122, map p124*
Salamanca abounds in cheap places to eat. Some of the places around the Plaza Mayor and Rúa Mayor are a bit tourist-trappy, but it's hard to beat their terraces for alfresco dining. Drinks cost a little bit more in Salamanca than the Castilian norm, but you get to choose a free *pincho* to go with your tipple, and they are often excellent.
€€€ El Majuelo, Plaza de la Fuente 8, T923 214 711. This intimate tapas bar and restaurant is on the edge of the old town and little visited by tourists. Grab one of the few tables and enjoy succulent *foie*, interesting roast meats and delicious vegetables. It's not cheap but the quality is sky-high. Recommended.
€€€ El Pecado, Plaza Poeta Iglesias 12, T923 266 558, www.elpecadorestaurante.es. One of the city's more vanguardist eateries, this upstairs restaurant brings back a touch of colour and fun into modern design. Zebra stripes, bookshelves and rich red walls live up to the name (Sin), but there's substance here in abundance. The menu is startlingly original and innovative; try the turbot with onion ice cream. The *menú del día* is the price-conscious way to appreciate its charms at €19; it's also available at night in quieter times.

€€€ Víctor Gutiérrez, C San Pablo 80, T923 262 973, www.restaurantevictor gutierrez.com. A smart urban modern restaurant with nouvelle Spanish cuisine as well as heartier, traditional fare. Experimenting with different forms of cooking, and ingredients drawn from different cultures, the chef creates some memorable combinations; there's always something intriguing on offer. There's a €55 *menú*, or a 'surprise' degustation for €80. Recommended.

€€ Delicatessen, C Meléndez 25, T923 280 309, www.delicatessen-cafe.com. The beautiful patio – a wooden deck covered with a skylight dome – and worthwhile *menú del día* are reason enough to wander into this upbeat central café. It's also a popular spot for an evening drink; at night the lights come down, and DJs play moody electronic music.

€€ Momo, C San Pablo, T923 280 798, www.momosalamanca.com. A stylish modern restaurant and bar with excellent classy *pinchos* and a range of innovative modern Castilian cuisine downstairs. The *menú del día* is good for €12; mains are €10-20. There's plenty of vegetarian choice. It's also a good spot for breakfast, opening at 0800.

€€ Sakana, C San Justo 9, T923 218 619. Rare for Northern Spain, this is a Japanese restaurant, pretty good and authentic too, although often booked out by tourist groups. The decor is modern but typically thoughtful, with bamboo screens and hessian-clad walls. Another dining area offers more traditional Japanese seating.

€€ Valencia, C Concejo 15, T923 217 868, www.restaurantevalencia.com. Fronting onto a small courtyard, this 50-year-old spot is devoted to bulls, with *corridas* on the telly and numerous photos of eminent Salamanca *toreros*; the current crop often drop by when in town. The tapas are delicious – try the chickpea stew if it's on, or the marinated raw sardine fillets – and the outside tables are the place to be. The

interior *comedor* serves more substantial restaurant fare.

€ Casa de las Morcillas, Plaza del Corrillo 18, T923 210 940. This spot, near the Plaza Mayor, has made *morcilla* its raison d'être, and has some 30 blood puddings from all over Spain, ranging from soft Cigales smeared on toast to spicy Zamoran or oniony Leonese varieties. Original and delicious.

€ Dulcinea, C Pozo Amarillo 5, T923 217 843. Although it doesn't look up to much from the outside, this is a very reliable and likeable little place far from the tourist trail but only a short step from the Plaza Mayor. The fare is traditional for the region; a simple range of stews and meat dishes. Best value is at lunchtime, when there's a €9 *menú del día*; the *pollo al ajillo* (chicken pieces sizzled in garlic) is excellent if it's on.

€ La Viga, C Consuelo 16, T923 210 904. When in Salamanca, do what the Salmantines do. Unfortunately, one thing they do is eat a lot of roasted pig face. Called *jeta*, it's actually very tasty, and this is the best place to try it.

€ Mesón Cervantes, Plaza Mayor 15, T923 217 213. Reached up a steep staircase off the Plaza Mayor (try not to fall down it on your way out), this ultra-characterful joint is a Salamanca classic, a no-frills spot decorated in bodega style, offering tasty *pinchos* ranging from *jeta* – pig cheek – to battered prawns. The restaurant area has unforgettable plaza views.

Cafés

Café Corrillo, C Meléndez 18, T923 271 917, www.cafecorrillo.com. Right in the centre, this long-running café opens at 0800 for breakfast, and also does *pinchos* and dinners. The downstairs dining area gets given over for regular concerts though; an atmospheric venue.

Juanita, Plaza de San Bual 21, T923 269 979. Situated on an engagingly dog-legged plaza, this café features warm, decadently ornate baroque decor in an intimate basement setting. These contrive to make it one of Salamanca's most loveable and atmospheric spots. Later in the evening it becomes a popular bar for *copas*.

Music Arte, Plaza Corrillo 20. An excellent place for breakfast, a friendly and stylish café near Plaza Mayor.

🅑 Bars and clubs

Salamanca *p122, map p124*

When the students are in town, Salamanca's nightlife can kick off any night of the week. The main night-owl area is on Gran Vía and around; Plaza de Bretón and C Varillas have a high concentration of spots.

Camelot, C Bordadores 3, T923 212 182. This no-frills *discoteca* occupies part of one of Salamanca's glorious stone buildings, in this case a still-working convent. It's quite a sight inside and takes the mickey with a DJ in an iron pulpit, grilles screening the upper floor, and cheapish drinks until late. No cover charge.

Capitán Haddock, C Concejo 15, T923 247 546. With plush, intriguing fittings and a small terrace in a quiet little courtyard in the heart of town, this romantic, stylish bar is much suaver than the blustering mariner after whom it's named. An atmospheric spot for a coffee or *copa*.

Cum Laude, C Prior 5, www.cvmlavde.com. It's worth popping in for a drink to this club to admire its sandstone-clad pillars that recall traditional Salamanca architecture, and its dancefloor that's a mini replica of the Plaza Mayor. Long queues form later in the evening.

De Laval Genovés, C San Justo 27. One of Salamanca's best gay choices, with a spacious interior and cool shipboard decor that has earned it the nickname 'El Submarino'. It's in the heart of the main Salamanca bar zone and attracts a mixed crowd.

El Savor, C San Justo 28, T923 268 576, www.elsavor.es. This large and stylish bar packs out with people keen on dancing to salsa and other Latin American rhythms. It's a fun, uninhibited sort of place; if you want to get your feet moving right, there are free dancing classes at 2300 on Thu and Fri.

Tío Vivo, C Clavel 3. This intriguing bar is packed with curios; there's everything from machine guns and army uniforms to carousel horses, giving it a slightly macabre and dreamlike quality. It's a great place with a good atmosphere; there are live shows and live music several days a week, hefty coffees, and excellent G&Ts.

🅔 Entertainment

Salamanca *p122, map p124*

Teatro Liceo, Plaza de Liceo s/n, T923 272 290. A modernized theatre near the Plaza Mayor, with occasional flamenco and other performances.

🅕 Festivals

Salamanca *p122, map p124*

There always seems to be some type of fiesta at other times; student faculties combine to make sure there's never a dull moment.

7 Sep Salamanca's major **fiesta** is a 2-week binge of drinks, bullfights and fireworks.

🅞 Shopping

Salamanca *p122, map p124*
Bookshops
Librería Cervantes, C Azafranal 11, T923 218 602, www.cervantessalamanca.com, is one of many bookshops in this university city.

Food

A good thing to buy in Salamanca is ham; Guijuelo, one of the province's towns, is famous for it. The main shopping streets are north of the Plaza Mayor, along C Toro and C Zamora.

A convenient, if slightly overpriced, ham shop is **La Despensa**, Rúa Mayor 23, which has a good selection of all things piggy.

The market just below the Plaza Mayor is a good spot for food shopping.

🚌 Transport

Salamanca *p122, map p124*
Air
Salamanca's airport is 15 km east of town on the Ávila road. Its only flights at the time of writing were a domestic connection to **Barcelona**. Airport buses (€3) link to the centre; a taxi to or from the airport to the centre costs €15.

Bus
The bus station is west of town along Av Filiberto Villalobos, T923 236 717. Within the province, there are buses roughly hourly to **Alba de Tormes**, **Béjar** and **Ciudad Rodrigo**, among other destinations.

Further-flung destinations include **Ávila** 4-6 weekdays, 2 at weekends, **Madrid** hourly, **Oviedo/Gijón** 4-5 daily (4½-5 hrs), **León** 4 daily, **Santiago** 2 daily (6 hrs), **Bilbao** 3 daily (6 hrs), **Zaragoza/Barcelona** 2 daily, **Zamora** more than hourly, **Valladolid** 6 daily, and **Cáceres** 10 daily (3½ hrs). There's also a daily bus to **Porto** in Portugal (5½ hrs) with a connection to **Lisboa** (9 hrs).

Salamanca has bus connections to **Ciudad Rodrigo** and to **Béjar** roughly hourly. There are 1-2 daily connections to **La Alberca** and **Ledesma**.

Taxi
For local taxis, call T923 250 000.

Train
The train station is northeast of town along Av de la Estación. There are daily services to **Burgos**, changing in Palencia, 9 to **Ávila** (1 hr, €11.75), and 6 to **Valladolid** (1½ hrs, €11.75). There are 8 daily trains to **Madrid** (2 hrs 30 mins, €23.20).

ℹ️ Directory

Salamanca *p122, map p124*
Language schools Apart from the university itself, which has a highly regarded Spanish-language programme, there are several smaller schools: **Letra Hispánica**, C Librerías 28, www.letrahispanica.com, has a reasonable reputation. **Medical services** Hospital Clínico, Paseo de San Vicente 58, T923 291 100. **Police** Call T092 or T923 194 433. The handiest police station is on the Plaza Mayor.

Segovia and Ávila

Backed by a startling mountainous backdrop, Segovia is one of the loveliest cities in Spain, famous for its sturdy Castillian cuisine and the vast Roman aqueduct. Ávila, known as the 'City of Saints and Stones', is quieter and more contemplative, hemmed in by a remarkable ring of medieval fortified walls. Behind it stretches the wild and remote Sierra de Gredos, a spectacular mountain range with tiny stone villages and excellent hiking trails.

When the kings and queens of Spain wanted respite from the capital's burning heat, they took themselves off to palaces and hunting lodges: the Habsburgs preferred the sombre austerity of El Escorial, but the Bourbons built fanciful Baroque extravaganzas at La Granja de San Ildefonso and Aranjuez, and surrounded them with exquisite gardens. The extensive gardens of Aranjuez are especially beautiful, a rare and refreshing oasis of green in the burning Castillian plain.

Segovia and around → *Phone code: 921. Population: 54,844. For listings, see pages 145-148.*

Segovia is one of the most alluring cities in central Spain, built of golden stone, capped with a fairytale castle and set against the dramatic peaks of the Sierra de Guadarrama. It's almost as famous for its sturdy Castillian cuisine as it is for the enormous Roman aqueduct which has stood here for two millennia. It's the perfect place to relax (although perhaps not at weekends when everyone else is here doing it too) and, if you decide to spend more than the day here, there are gentle walks along the river Eresma, or tougher treks among the surrounding peaks. Close by are two royal residences: the extravagant Bourbon summer palace of La Granja, and the more modest hunting lodge of Riofrío.

Arriving in Segovia

Getting there and around There are regular buses and trains from Madrid. Segovia station is about 2 km from the town centre; take local bus No 3 from outside the station. Most of the sights are clustered in the old city, which is easy to get around on foot. ▶▶ *See Transport, page 148.*

Best time to visit Segovia is especially lovely in early spring, when there's still a slight chill in the air and the mountains are still capped with snow. It can get a little crowded at weekends, particularly during summer, so come off-season or during the week if possible.

Tourist information ⓘ *Plaza Azoguejo 1, T921 466 720, www.turismodesegovia.com; regional tourist offce at Plaza Mayor 10, T921 460 334.*

góbriga was an important military settlement when the Romans built their enormous
ueduct 2000 years ago. In the early Middle Ages, the Arabs introduced the cloth-
anufacturing trade, which would ensure Segovia's prosperity long after the Reconquista.
govia was doing very nicely when Carlos I (Charles V) tried to impose harsh taxes, and
volted against the king. The uprising, known as the Comunero Revolt, was viciously
it down and the leaders decapitated in Segovia. Like most of Spain, the city went into
cline in the 18th century when a seemingly endless series of wars began. It emerged

Segovia

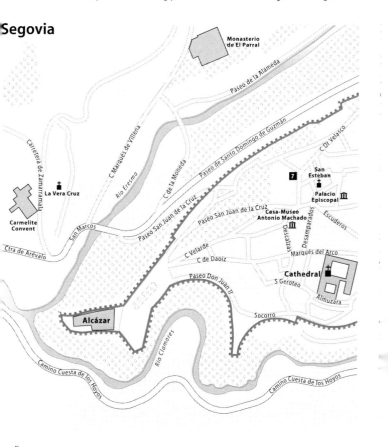

Where to stay	Hostal Plaza **2**	Las Sirenas **8**
Camping Acueducto **1**	Hostería Ayala	Parador de Segovia **9**
Hostal Don Jaime **3**	Berganza **10**	
Hostal Fornos **4**	Infanta Isabel **6**	**Restaurants**
Hostal Juan Bravo **5**	Los Linajes **7**	Casa Duque **1**

as a popular tourist destination in the 20th century, and is also a big culinary capital well known for its traditional Castilian cuisine.

Places in Segovia

The Aqueduct Segovia's most famous sight is at its most dramatic just outside the city walls on the Plaza Azoguejo (where the tourist information office is located). Nothing holds together the 25,000 stones of this soaring two-storey aqueduct which stretches for 760 m and arches a giddy 29 m above the square. The tallest surviving Roman aqueduct, it

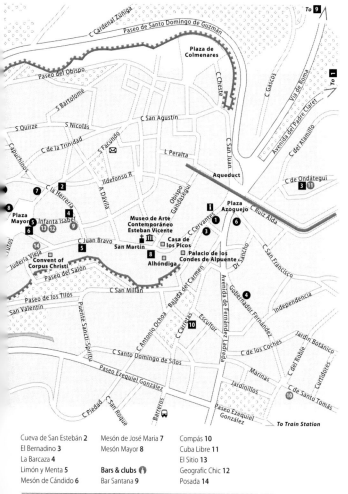

was still carrying water to the city right up until a generation or two ago, but pollution and traffic vibration have taken their toll in recent years.

Plaza Azoguejo to Plaza Mayor From the Plaza Azoguejo, at the foot of the aqueduct, the busy shop-lined **Calle Cervantes** leads up into the centre of the old city. At the point where it turns across the old city walls, you can't miss the knobbly 15th-century **Casa de los Picos** (House of the Spikes), which got everyone talking when it was first built thanks to its unusual façade of diamond-shaped jutting stones. It's now a cultural and exhibition centre, and you can step in to admire the graceful patio. The elegant mansion covered in swirling *esgrafado* tucked away close by is the **Palacio de los Condes de Alpuente**, and below it is the former corn exchange (**Alhondiga**), a Gothic building with an Arabic name which was built under the Catholic Kings. Continuing along Calle de Cervantes, the softly rounded Romanesque church of **San Martín**, with its covered portico and Mudéjar belltower, overlooks a peaceful square with a statue of Juan Bravo, the leader of the Comunero Revolt (with a name like that, he was bound to be a folk hero).

Close by is one of Segovia's newest museums, the **Museo de Arte Contemporáneo Esteban Vicente** ⓘ *Plaza de Bellas Artes, T921 462 010, www.museoestebanvicente.es, Tue-Sat 1100-14000 and 1600-1900, Sun 1100-1400; €3/€1.50*, devoted to the Segovian painter Esteban Vicente (1903-2000). He spent most of his life in New York, but made provisions in his will for his art to be returned to his native city and his vivid paintings are now housed in the handsomely restored 15th-century Palacio de Enrique IV.

Calle Juan Bravo links the Plaza San Martín with old Segovia's main square, the wide, appealing **Plaza Mayor**, full of terrace bars and restaurants and the heart of the city's nightlife. There's a small bandstand in the centre, where concerts are occasionally held in summer.

Cathedral ⓘ *Apr-Sep 0930-1830, Oct Mar 0930-1730, museum closed Sun morning, €3/€2.* Rising serenely above the Plaza Mayor, Segovia's cathedral was built between 1525 and 1590 in what is probably the latest example of the Gothic style in Spain. The original cathedral was destroyed by Carlos I (Charles V) during his vicious repression of the Comunero Revolt (see Background, above), but he must have had a guilty conscience because he provided the funds for a replacement. Designed by Juan Gil de Hontañón, it is fashionably austere in the way the Spanish liked their churches in those days, but the soft golden stone of the exterior manages to counteract its harshness. Inside there is some elegant vaulting in the chapels surrounding the ambulatory, but little else to see. The cloister was all that remained of the original cathedral and was brought here brick by brick. Just off the cloister is the Sala Capitular, where the cathedral's scant treasures are gathered; just a few gold and silver religious ornaments, some fine 17th-century tapestries, and a curious, but rather pretty, painted 16th-century English clock.

Around the Cathedral Many of the most important religious buildings connected to the cathedral are set around the Plaza de San Esteban, just northeast of the Plaza Mayor. A magnificent, six-storey Italianate tower looms above the delicate **church of San Esteban**, with a striking Crucifixion inside. Nearby, the **Palacio Episcopal** (Episcopal Palace) ⓘ *closed for renovation; check hours with the tourist office*, was given a florid 18th-century makeover but retains its curious Renaissance façade – more interesting that the old-fashioned museum of religious paintings and statuary inside.

Between 1919 and 1932 the poet **Antonio Machado** stayed in a boarding house on Callejuela de los Desamparados (just off the Plaza de San Esteban), which has been transformed into a engaging little **museum** ⓘ *Wed-Sun 1100-1400, 1000-1830, €2, free on Wed*, dedicated to his life and work.

The **Judería**, once home to a Jewish community before the expulsion of the Jews, sits behind the cathedral to the south. It's a slightly run-down neighbourhood now, but the crooked passages and leaning houses make it quietly atmospheric. The former synagogue (the best preserved of the five that the city once boasted) is now part of the **Convent of Corpus Christi** ⓘ *Plaza del Corpus, T921 463 429, call in advance for opening times*, and although much of it is a 19th-century recreation after fire destroyed the original building, it's worth a visit for the glimpse it gives into life in the Jewish community. The **Centro Didáctico de la Judería** ⓘ *C/Judería Vieja 12, T921 462 396, daily 1000-1400, 1600-1900, €2*, was the former home of Abraham Senneor, and later of Andrés Laguna, the king's physician. It relates the history of Segovia's Jewish community with audiovisuals and a 3D presentation.

Alcázar ⓘ *Plaza de la Reina Victoria Eugenia, T921 460 759, www.alcazardesegovia.com, Oct-Mar 1000-1800, Apr-Sep 1000-1900, €4.50, free 3rd Tue of every month*. Segovia's Alcázar sits on a cliff edge, bristling with storybook turrets and spires. Purists sniff that the current version, a fanciful 19th-century restoration, bears no resemblance to the original, but Disney apparently liked it so much they used it as a model for their first theme park. The first fortress on this site was built in the 12th century, in order to protect newly reconquered Segovia. It was a favourite with Castilian monarchs during the Middle Ages, but when Madrid was appointed the permanent capital of the court, it fell out of favour. No longer used as a palace, it became a prison and military school and was almost completely destroyed by fire in 1862. The interior has been fitted out with armour and weapons, but the real highlights are the spectacular artesonado ceilings which glitter magnificently in almost every room. A useful plan and explanatory leaflet (which remains coy on the issue of what's authentic and what's not) is included in the admission price. There's a 144-step hike up the old watchtower for stupendous views out across the lovely old city to the mountains, still snow-capped in late spring.

Outside the city walls Segovia is stuffed full of beautiful churches. One of the loveliest, the little 13th-century **Iglesia de la Vera Cruz** (Church of the True Cross), is also built with Segovia's warm, honey-coloured stone, and sits just outside the city walls. It's constructed on a polygonal plan typical of Templar churches, and the double-chamber at its heart was used for the Order's secret rituals. Its fortunes have declined in the past few centuries and even the sliver of the True Cross which gave it its name has gone to another local church. Don't miss the fabulous views across Segovia from the **belltower** ⓘ *Apr-Sep Tue 1600-1900, Wed-Sun 1030-1330 and 1600-1900; Oct-Mar Tue 1600-1800, Wed-Sun 1030-1330 and 1600-1800, €2, free Tue afternoon*.

The remains of Saint John of the Cross are buried in an elaborate early 20th-century mausoleum in the nearby Carmelite **convent** ⓘ *Mon 1530-1800, Tue-Sun 1000-1330 and 1600-1900, until 2000 in summer, free but donations welcome*, hidden behind massive walls.

Segovia has some excellent gentle walking and you can take a peaceful stroll through the valley of the Río Eresma to the luminous **Monasterio de El Parral** ⓘ *C/del Marqués de Villena, T921 431 298, visits Sat, Sun and public holidays 1000, 1130, 1615, 1745, free but donations accepted*. The quiet church contains the alabaster tombs of the Villena family and a fine 16th-century retablo, a beautiful backdrop to Mass held in Gregorian chant on Sundays at midday, and during the week at 1300.

Around Segovia

ⓘ *www.patrimonionacional.es, both palaces open Apr-Sep Tue-Sun 1000-1800, Oct-Mar Tue-Sun 1000-2000, €9, valid 48 hrs for both palaces, free on Wed (Oct-Mar 1500-1800; Apr-Sep 1700-2000) and to EU-passport holders.*

There are two sumptuous royal palaces close to Segovia; **La Granja de San Ildefonso** is a 10-minute bus ride away, but you'll need your own transport to get to the former hunting lodge at **Riofrío**. La Granja, a frothy Italian-style palace built for the Bourbon monarchs, is surrounded by magnificent gardens, famous for their fountains and sculptures. Unfortunately, you can only see the fountains in all their glory on three days a year, normally 30 May, 25 July and 25 August (they turn on a few on Wednesdays and weekends at 1730 to whet your appetite). The palace was destroyed by fire in 1918, but it has been carefully restored and the royal apartments are now a magnificent evocation of the opulence of the 18th-century Spanish court. Entry to the adjoining **Museo de Tapices** (Tapestry Museum) and the Collegiata (where Felipe V and his wife and son are buried surrounded by a macabre collection of relics and old bones) are both included in the ticket price. If you've been dazzled by the gorgeous crystal chandeliers, you can find out how they were made at the museum set in the former **Real Fábrica de Cristales** (Royal Crystal Factory).

The palace at Riofrío is difficult to get to without your own transport, and is much lower key. It is beautifully set among forests and woods and attracts considerably fewer visitors than La Granja, which can be a charm in itself. Despite its grand scale, Riofrío was merely a hunting lodge, and now half of it has been given up to a bizarre museum of hunting, complete with row upon row of stuffed heads. It's surrounded by a deer park (inaccessible on foot, although you can drive through it).

Ávila → *Phone code: 920. Population: 58,900. Altitude: 1.128 m. For listings, see pages 145-148.*

The austere mountain town of Ávila is set on a windswept plateau, surrounded by the chilly granite peaks of the Sierra de Gredos. The reddish-brown tangle of medieval mansions and Romanesque churches is completely enclosed by magnificent medieval walls, studded with towers and crenellations. This 'city of saints and stones' is the birthplace of Santa Teresa, the 16th-century mystic, visionary and writer, and is still a major pilgrimage centre. It remains a hushed and contemplative city but, if it all gets too much, you can easily escape to the surrounding mountains, scattered with attractive old villages, and a paradise for hikers and climbers. While you are here, try some *yemas*, a delicious sticky sweet made of egg yolk and sugar, traditionally made by Ávila's nuns.

Arriving in Ávila

Getting there and around There are regular bus and train connections with Madrid, Salamanca and Segovia, as well as other major cities in Castilla y León. The old walled city of Ávila is small and easy to get around on foot. ►► *See Transport, page 148*.

Best time to visit Late spring and early autumn are the best times to visit Ávila and the Sierra de Gredos, when the temperatures are mild and the streets and hiking trails empty. The city is chilly in winter, although the surrounding mountains are especially beautiful covered in snow. For the very best views of the walls themselves, head to the little shrine at Cuatro Postes just outside town on the Salamanca road.

Tourist information ① *Av Madrid 39, T920 225 969, www.avilaturismo.com*. The tourist office has an excellent leaflet describing a walk around the old city which takes in the best of the palaces.

Background

According to legend, Ávila was founded by Hercules himself. The famous walls were initiated under Alfonso VI in the 11th century, when the city was in the front line of the Reconquista. And yet Ávila was famous for its learning and religious tolerance, and the city never really recovered economically after the expulsion of the Jews in 1492 and then the Moriscos in 1609. In the 16th century, the city produced two outstanding religious figures: Teresa of Ávila and St John of the Cross, who were canonized and subsequently declared Doctors of the Church. The cult of Saint Teresa, in particular, is still very strong and she is co-patron saint of Spain.

Places in Ávila

Muralla de Ávila ① *Entrance at Puerta del Puente, C/Marqués de Santo Domingo s/n, T920 354 000, http://muralladeavila.com, Tue-Sun Apr-mid Oct 1000-2000, mid Oct-Mar 1100-1800, €5/€3.50*. A visit to the city should begin at Ávila's famous **walls**. Constructed in the wake of Alfonse VI's victory in Toledo, these massive walls were erected to ensure that the Arab armies couldn't re-take the city. Some 12 m high, 3 m thick, and studded with nine gates and 88 towers, they became legendary even as they were being built. A short section has been made into a panoramic walkway, with views out over the old city, and up to the peaks of the Sierra de Gredos.

Cathedral and around ① *Plaza de Catedral, T920 211 641, Nov-Mar Mon-Fri 1000-1700, Sat 1000-1800, Sun 1200-1700, Apr-Oct Mon-Fri 1000-1800, Sat 1000-1900, Sun 1200-1700, €4/ €3.50*. As the massive city walls were being erected to defend the city from the Moors, the cathedral was slowly rising to take its place in the struggle for souls. It was incorporated into the walls to become a literal and metaphorical bastion, and the austere façade betrays its dual function as a fortress and place of worship. The interior is surprisingly lovely, with its lofty Gothic nave made of rosy stone, and magnificent Plateresque stalls and retrochoir all gently illuminated by stained glass windows. One of Ávila's most famous medieval bishops is buried in an extravagant alabaster sarcophagus behind the altar; his dark skin earned him the nickname 'El Tostado' – 'the toasted'. The cloister, attractively rumpled and overgrown, is home to several storks' nests; just off it is the cathedral museum, with a rather disappointing collection of paintings, religious ornaments (including Juan de Arfe's massive Monstrance) and vestments.

Ávila once contained so many aristocratic palaces that it was known as 'City of the Nobles'. One of the grandest, the 16th-century **Casa de los Velada** (now a hotel), which overlooks the Plaza de la Catedral, has lodged Carlos I (Charles V), Isabel la Católica and Felipe II. Opposite the cathedral, C/de los Reyes Cátolicos leads to the **Plaza del Mercado Chico**, originally the site of the Roman forum and still the heart of the old city. It's flanked on one side by the 19th-century Ayuntamiento (Town Hall) and on the other by the church of **San Juan**, where Santa Teresa was baptised. The font has been preserved and the church can be visited before and after Mass.

Convento de Santa Teresa ① *Plaza de la Santa, T920 211 030, Apr-Oct Tue-Sun 1000-1400 and 1600-1900, Nov-Mar 1000-1330 and 1530-1730, €3/€1.50*. Also known as the Convento de la Santa, this convent was founded in 1636 on the site of the Cepeda mansion where Teresa of Ávila was born. The Baroque convent contains a flamboyant chapel to Saint Teresa, and several statues by Gregorio Fernández. A **museum** devoted to the life of the saint has been established around the corner on Calle La Dama; the setting, a stone cellar, is attractive, but the exhibits are extremely dull. There are plenty of dire portraits of the saint, a few old documents, a reproduction of her cell, and a collection of her works in different languages. The most interesting section is at the end, where 'before' and 'after' (as in 'before taking Holy Orders') photographs of more recent Carmelite saints are displayed, including one of Edith Stein (later Santa Teresa Benedicta de la Cruz) who died in Auschwitz.

More mansions Old Ávila is a strange little time capsule, with a rich collection of noble mansions and churches that have survived through neglect rather than any concerted efforts at preservation. Most of its modern inhabitants live in the convenient new housing developments outside the city walls, leaving the quiet streets of the old town to pilgrims and visitors. Many of the best surviving mansions (all private) are concentrated on the southern side of the city, including the elaborate palace-fortress of the **Dávila** on Calle de Cepadas, which incorporates four houses dating back to the 13th century. There is another clutch of palaces in the northeastern corner of the city; look out for the **Mansión de los Verdugo** and the nearby **Palacio de los Águila**, on Calle López Nuñez, both typically fortified aristocratic palaces with a wealth of elaborate Renaissance detailing.

Ávila

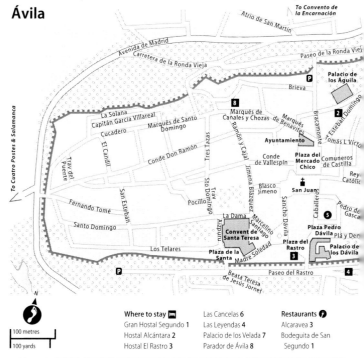

Where to stay 🛏
Gran Hostal Segundo 1
Hostal Alcántara 2
Hostal El Rastro 3

Las Cancelas 6
Las Leyendas 4
Palacio de los Velada 7
Parador de Ávila 8

Restaurants 🍴
Alcaravea 3
Bodeguita de San
Segundo 1

Outside the city walls Many of Ávila's finest churches are located just outside the city walls; one of the oldest is the simple Romanesque **Iglesia de San Pedro** which overlooks the arcaded **Plaza de Santa Teresa** (known locally as the Plaza Grande). It's a handsome, bustling square edged with arcades containing plenty of shops and bars. The **Museo Provincial** ① *Plaza de los Nalvillos 3, T920 211 003; Jul-Sep Tue-Sat 1000-1400 and 1700-2000, Sun 1000-1400; Oct-Jun Tue-Sat 1000-1400 and 1600-1900, Sun 1000-1400; €1.20, free on Sat and Sun*, is held in the Palacio de los Deanes and the nearby Romanesque church of Santo Tomé el Viejo, just off the Plaza de Italia, and contains an odd but appealing assortment of ceramics, archaeological findings, religious art and traditional costumes and furnishings.

The finest Romanesque church in Ávila is the **Basílica de San Vicente**, to the north of the museum on the Paseo Humilladero. San Vicente's life and martyrdom is depicted in grisly detail on a 12th-century sepulchre, and the subterranean crypt contains the slab on which he, along with his two sisters, was martyred at the hands of the Romans. The crypt is also an important stop on the pilgrimage trail, as it was here that Saint Teresa had the second of her visions and where, according to tradition, she took off her shoes in answer to the Virgin's request for reform of the Carmelite order. Teresa spent almost 30 years in the **Convento de la Encarnación** ① *C/Encarnación, T920 211 212, Tue-Fri 0930-1330 and 1530-1800, Sat 1000-1300 and 1600-1800, €2/€1.50*, which now contains a small museum of her life.

The most important monument outside the city walls is the Dominican **Monasterio Réal de Santo Tomás** ① *T920 352 237, www.monasteriosantotomas.es, 1000-1400 and 1530-1930, free entry into the church, €4/€3 to visit cloisters and choir*, a good 15-minute walk from the old city. It's set around three cloisters and was established at the end of the 15th century by the Catholic kings. It did service as their summer residence, and was also the seat of Ávila's university. But its glory days have long gone, and grass sprouts through the cracks in the paving stones of the first and smallest cloister, the Cloister of the Noviciate. The second cloister, the Cloister of Silence, is larger, grander, and handsomely decorated with engravings on the upper gallery. The third and grandest cloister is the Cloister of the Kings, but it's also the least atmospheric. Back in the Cloister of Silence, a small staircase leads up to an exquisitely carved Gothic choir which gives a beautiful bird's-eye-view of the elegant Gothic church. The sumptuous alabaster tomb behind the main altar belongs to Don Juan, the only son of the Catholic kings. His premature death had far-reaching consequences for the country, and the Catholic kings were succeeded by Carlos I (Charles V), Spain's first Habsburg ruler. Torquemada, the notorious inquisitor, is buried in the Sacristy.

Avenida de Madrid
Basílica de San Vicente
To Bus & Train stations
Humilladero
Avenida de Portugal
Doctor Fleming
López Yáñez
E Marquina
Mansión de los Verdugo
Museo Provincial
Eduardo Marquina
Santa Catalina
To Monasterio Réal de Santo Tomás
Casa de los Velada
Muralla de Ávila
Leales
Accesso Murallas
Santo Tomé el Viejo
Plaza de Italia
Plaza de la Catedral
Cathedral
Ferreal Hdez
San Miguel
Alemania
Cruz Vieja
San Segundo
C Estrada
San Millán
Duque de Alba
General Franco
Plaza de Santa Teresa
San Pedro
Gabriel y Galán
seo del Rastro
Peregrino
Francisco Gallego
Deán Castor Robledo

Casa Patas **2**
Fogón de Santa Teresa **4**
La Casona **5**

Sierra de Gredos → *For listings, see pages 145-148.*

The Sierra de Gredos is the westernmost region of the Sistema Central, the spiky range which, with the Sierra de Guadarrama, forms Spain's craggy backbone. It's a beautiful region of forested peaks and stone villages, and it offers excellent opportunities for hiking, fishing, hang-gliding, horse riding, mountain biking and other sports. Not surprisingly, it has become a popular refuge for stressed-out city-dwellers who have bought up holiday homes, but there's still not a great deal of accommodation in the region and it's worth checking out the *casas rurales* (see below).

Arriving in Sierra de Gredos

Getting there and around Public transport is restricted to sporadic and infrequent services from Madrid and Ávila, so consider renting a car.

Tourist information There is no visitor centre within the limits of the Parque Regional de la Sierra de Gredos. There are lists of *casas rurales* online at www.casasgredos.com. Local tourist information offices have some details of walking routes, but you should pick up detailed walking guides and maps in advance from bookshops in Madrid or Ávila.

Arenas de San Pedro

Arenas de San Pedro is one of the largest and most accessible towns in the region, a popular weekend retreat crammed with craft shops and second homes. Sights include the sturdy 15th-century **Castillo de la Triste Condessa** (Castle of the Sad Countess), named for the unfortunate Juana Pimental who was beheaded by Juan II of Castile, a **Gothic church** which contains the tomb of San Pedro de Alcántara who died here in 1562, and the simple **Puente Romano** (which is actually medieval). Its most famous sight is the **Cueva del Águila**, 10 km from the village, which is filled with stalagmites and stalactites. There is a traditional pilgrimage to the **Santuario de San Pedro**, 3 km from the town, in mid-October when the local festival is celebrated with bullfights and plenty of carousing on the streets. The **tourist office** ① *Plaza de San Pedro s/n, T920 370 245, http://arenasdesanpedro. es*, has details of walking routes throughout the Sierra, but the string of delightful tiny villages – **Guisando**, **El Arenal**, and particularly **El Hornillo** – a few kilometres north of Arenas make better bases for hikers, with several routes splintering off into the mountains.

Hoyos del Espino and Navarredonda de Gredos

These unassuming villages have a spectacular setting in the northern foothills of the Sierra de Gredos, and are good bases for circular walks. A 12-km asphalt road leads from Hoyos (there's another from Navarredonda) to the **Plataforma de Gredos**. From here, it's a spectacular two-hour trek on a well-marked reasonably easy path to the **Laguna Grande** (there's a *refugio* here where you can sleep and eat, T920 207 576/T918 476 253, www. refugiodelola.com) in the **Circo de Gredos** at the centre of the park. The lake, a glowing, unearthly emerald, reflects the granite bulk of the **Pico del Almanzor** (2593 m), the highest peak of the Sierra de Gredos. There are tourist offices in Navarredonda (Plaza de Calvo Sotelo 1, T920 345 252) and Hoyos (Cruce de la Ctra de la Plataforma de Gredos, T920 349 035).

Piedrahíta and El Barco de Ávila

Piedrahíta, 60 km southwest of Ávila, is a handsome town with a smattering of noble mansions and a porticoed main square. The 18th-century **Palacio de los Duques de Alba** is surrounded by gardens designed in imitation of those at La Granja (see page 140), although they are not as manicured or well kept. The nearby **Puerta de la Peña Negra** is popular with hang-gliders from all over Spain. Piedrahíta's **tourist office** ① *Plaza de España, T920 360 001*, is in the Ayuntamiento.

Some 20 km further west, heading towards the Valle de la Vera in Extremadura, is El Barco de Ávila, one of the loveliest towns in the region, with an incomparable setting on the edge of the Sierra de Gredos and overlooked by a ruined castle. It also has a fine Plaza Mayor – officially the Plaza de España – and a serene Gothic church with a pretty belltower. El Barco de Ávila's **tourist office** ① *Plaza de España 4, T920 340 888*, is only open in July and August .

Segovia and Ávila listings

For hotel and restaurant price codes and other relevant information, see pages 11-17.

⊝ Where to stay

Segovia and around *p135, map p136*

€€€ Los Linajes, C/Doctor Velasco 9, T921 460 475, www.hotelloslinjares.com. Occupies part of an 11th-century mansion next to the city walls, but the interior has been over-renovated and rooms are a little sterile.

€€€ Parador de Segovia, Ctra Valladolid s/n, T921 443 737, www.parador.es. Bright, modern and well-equipped parador overlooking a lake, about 2 km outside Segovia, with pool, and fine restaurant. There are fabulous views of Segovia, but you'll need your own transport.

€€ Hostal Don Jaime, C/Ochoa Ondátegui 8, T921 444 787. Right next to the aqueduct and furnished with chintzy fabrics and dark wood.

€€ Hostal Fornos, C/Infanta Isabel 13, T921460198, www.hostalfornos.com. A small, pretty *hostal* just off the Plaza Mayor, with charming rooms decorated with wicker furniture.

€€ Hostería Ayala Berganza, C/Carretas 5, T921 461 300. A charming small hotel in a 15th-century building, with spacious traditional rooms.

€€ Infanta Isabel, Plaza Mayor s/n, T921 461 300, www.hotelinfantaisabel.com. Perfectly placed in a restored 19th-century

mansion overlooking the Plaza Mayor, the rooms are large, and the best have balconies on the square.

€€ La Querencia de Valsaín, Carretera de Madrid 39, La Granja de San Ildefonso, T629 652 513, www.laquerenciadevalsain. es. A delightful, eco-friendly rural hotel with a choice of private guest rooms or self-catering accommodation. Ideal base for walking, as well as visiting the royal palace.

€€ Las Sirenas, C/Juan Bravo 30, T921 462 663, www.hotelsirenas.com. A classic hotel built in the 1950s with spacious old-fashioned rooms, a café-bar, and even a gym, in the centre of the old city.

€ Camping Acueducto, Ctra L-601, T921 425 000, www.campingacueducto.com. About 3 km outside town, this is still the closest campsite to Segovia. Take bus No 6 from the centre of town. Open Easter-Sep.

€ Hostal Juan Bravo, C/Juan Bravo 12, T921 463 413. A good, central budget choice, with spotless rooms (with or without bath) and friendly owners.

€ Hostal Plaza, C/Cronista Lecea 11, Segovia, T921 460 303, www.hostal-plaza. com. Simple, friendly guesthouse in a rambling old house just off the Plaza Mayor, with modest rooms at an affordable price.

Ávila *p140, map p142*

€€€€ Palacio de los Velada, Plaza de la Catedral 10, T920 255 100, www.velada hoteles.com. A luxurious 4-star hotel set in a magnificent 16th-century mansion close to the cathedral with a beautiful patio. It does excellent weekend deals – as low as €60 for a double room – if you book early enough.

€€€ Hotel Las Leyendas, C/Francisco Gallego 3, T920 352 042, www.lasleyendas. es. A charming hotel with chic, contemporary rooms in a beautifully renovated 16th-century mansion tucked into the old city walls.

€€€ Parador de Ávila, C/Marqués de Canales y Chozas 2, T920 211 340, www. parador.es. One of the very best paradors, this is housed in a spectacular Renaissance palace and offers lots of luxury trimmings including antique-decorated rooms and a good restaurant. Prices drop a category in low season.

€€ Las Cancelas, C/Cruz Vieja 6, T920 212 249, www.lascancelas.com. Some of the rustically decorated rooms at this 15th-century inn still contain original fireplaces, and there's an excellent restaurant and tapas bar in the charming patio.

€ Gran Hostal Segundo, C/San Segundo 28, T920 252 590, www.hsansegundo.com. A simple *hostal* in a turn-of-the-century building just outside the city walls; the best rooms have balconies with fantastic views of the cathedral. There's an Italian restaurant and a tapas bar downstairs.

€ Hostal Alcántara, C/Esteban Domingo 11, T920 225 003. Comfortable rooms on a quiet street in the old city.

€ Hostal El Rastro, C/Cepadas s/n (just off Plaza Rastro), T920 352 225. A good budget option in an old mansion within the city walls, with old-fashioned rooms and a good restaurant and tapas bar attached.

Sierra de Gredos *p144*

There is plenty of accommodation in Arenas de San Pedro and plenty of luxury accommodation in Navarredonda.

€€€ Parador de Gredos, Navarredonda, T920 026 200, www.parador.es. A modern parador set in pine forest just outside the village.

€€ La Casa de Arriba, C/de la Cruz, Navarredonda, T920 348 024. A rustic

hotel in a sumptuous 17th-century mansion surrounded by gardens.

€€ Casa El Canchal, C/La Fuente 1, Arenas de San Pedro, T920 370 958. A handful of tasteful rooms in a 17th-century mansion. Good value.

€€ El Rinconcito de Gredos, Urb Los Llanos 3-5, Cuevas del Valle, T920 383 288. An attractive mountain hotel, with elegant rooms, beautiful views, and a great restaurant serving sturdy regional cuisine.

€€ La Casa Grande, C/de la Cruz, Navarredonda, T920 348 024. A sumptuous 17th-century mansion surrounded by gardens.

€€ La Casona, Piedrahíta, T920 360 071. In a 17th-century stone mansion with an excellent mid-range restaurant.

€ Albergue Juvenil, Navarredonda, T920 348 005, a well-equipped youth hostel with a pool and tennis courts; and **El Almanzor**, Ctra el Barco km 38, Navarredonda, T920 348 477, which is prettier inside than you´d expect from the gloomy exterior.

€ Hostal Rural Luna, C/Domingo Labajos 34, Candelada, T920 382 265, www.lunacande leda.com. A real charmer, tucked away in Candelada's historic centre, this lovely little hotel makes a great base for walkers.

€ La Taberna, C/Carrellana 29, Arenas de San Pedro, T920 370 395. With a good cheap café-bar.

🍴 Restaurants

Segovia and around *p135, map p136*
Segovia's legendary speciality is *cochinillo asado* (roast suckling pig), traditionally slaughtered at just 21 days old. The expensive restaurants at the **Hosteria Ayala Berganza** and the **parador** (see page 145) are also recommended.

€€€ Méson de Cándido, Plaza Azoguejo 5, T921 425 911, www.mesondecandido.es. The late Señor Cándido was a legend, and his restaurant, picturesquely huddled under the aqueduct arches, is papered with photos of famous clients. Now run by his son, its reputation has palled slightly, but it's still a memorable spot.

€€€ Mesón de José María, C/Cronista Lecea 11, T921 461 111. Cándido's former pupil José María has been making a very big name for himself at his own *mesón*, which is rated as one of the very best restaurants in Segovia and is a great place to try *cochinillo*. There's a lively bar area for tapas if you don't want a big meal.

€€ Casa Duque, C/Cervantes 12, T921 462 487. Another local institution, with an excellent reputation for traditional Segovian cuisine. It's generally considered to make the best *cochinillo asado* in Segovia, and the *judiones* (another local dish of beans cooked with pork) are also very tasty.

€€ Dólar, C/Valenciana 1, T921 470 269. Traditional Castillian cuisine in an elegant dining room in San Ildefonso de la Granja.

€€ El Bernardino, C/Cervantes 2, T921 462 477. A classic Castillian restaurant which is popular with local business people, and does an excellent *menú del día*. Try the amazing *sopa de chocolate* for dessert.

€€ Riofrío, T921 480 061. The restaurant at the palace is surprisingly good, open lunchtimes only when you can tuck into *sopa castellana* or roast suckling pig.

€ Cueva de San Estabán, C/Valdeláguila 15, Segovia, T921 460 982. This cavernous bar-restaurant just off the Plaza San Estabán is a big favourite with locals. Good tapas and a reasonably priced *menú del día* – going a la carte will up the prices considerably.

€ Mesón Mayor, Plaza Mayor 3, T921 463 017, www.mesonmayor.com. The best of the restaurants on the Plaza Mayor, you can tuck into roast meats or fill up on good tapas.

Tapas bars and cafés
In San Ildefonso de la Granja there are many tapas bars clustered on the Plaza de los Dolores. The following are all in Segovia.
El Sitio, C/Infanta Isabel 9. Classic tapas and plenty of atmosphere at this old-fashioned local favourite.

La Barcaza, C/Gobernador Fernández Jiménez 22. A quiet spot for some tasty tapas including fish with wild mushrooms, and local *morcilla* (blood sausage).
Limón y Menta, C/Infanta Isabel 3, T921 462 141. A friendly little café and cake shop serving good *bocadillos* and pastries that won't break the bank.

Ávila *p140, map p142*
The restaurants at the **parador**, the **Hostería de Bracamonte**, **Las Cancelas** (all €€€-€€) and the **Mesón del Rastro** (€€-€) are all recommended (see above). They all serve an excellent value *menú del día* at lunchtimes – often for less than €15.

€€ Alcaravea, Plaza de la Catedral 15, T920 226 600. A sumptuous old mansion, serving refined regional cuisine. Great summer terrace.

€€ Fogón de Santa Teresa, Plaza de la Catedral, T920 211 023. Sturdy Castillian favourites made with the freshest local produce. This is a good place to try *perdiz* (partridge), a local speciality and apparently one of Saint Teresa's favourites.

€€ La Casona, Plaza Pedro Dávila, T920 256 139. Small, family-run local, serving big portions of good home-cooking in a prettily tiled dining room.

€ Casa Patas, C/San Millán 4, T920 213 194. A local stalwart, this old-fashioned bar serves good tapas and simple meals.

Tapas bars and cafés
Bodeguita de San Segundo, C/San Segundo 19, T920 257 309. A smart tapas and wine bar which attracts a well-heeled crowd and gets packed out in the evenings.

🎧 Bars and clubs

Segovia and around *p135, map p136*
C/Infanta Isabel has got so many bars that it's known locally as 'Calle de los Bares'. There are dozens to choose from, such as the popular **Geografic Chic**, at No 13, which is decorated with comic-book characters.

Compás, at C/Santo Tomás 1, and Cuba Libre at C/Ochoa Andoátegui 8 are both good for cocktails, and Bar Santana, C/ de la Infanta Isabel 18, T921 463 564, www. barsantana.com, has live gigs, art exhibitions, tapas and more on offer.

Ávila *p140, map p142*
Ávila isn't a great city for nightlife, but there are plenty of bars and cafés around the Plaza de la Victoria, and the Plaza de Santa Teresa and the streets which lead off them.

⊛ Festivals

Segovia and around *p135, map p136*
There's usually something going on in Segovia.
Nearest Sun to 5 Feb Fiesta de Santa Águeda when Segovian women take over the city for a day to celebrate this festival.
Holy Week A big event with plenty of processions.
24-29 Jun Fiestas of San Juan and San Pedro are celebrated with street parties and parades.
Jul A classical music festival.

Ávila *p140, map p142*
Unsurprisingly, Ávila's festivals are more serious than most.
Easter week Parades, processions and Mass.
Jul A festival of organ music.
Oct Santa Teresa is remembered with pilgrimages, *verbenas* and other religious ceremonies, floods of pilgrims descend on the city.

⊘ What to do

Sierra de Gredos *p144*
AMN (AMN Gredos), T920 348 385, www.amngredos.com. Offers all kinds of activities from rafting to hang-gliding.

Gredos a Caballo, T920 348 110, www. gredosacaballo.com, organizes horse-riding expeditions from Hoyos del Espino.

⊖ Transport

Segovia and around *p135, map p136*
Bus Bus is the most convenient way to reach Segovia. There are regular services (every 30 mins) with La Sepulvedana, T902 1196, www.lasepulvedana.es, from Paseo de la Florida 11, Madrid (metro Principe Pío); 1½ hrs journey time, €7.66. There are local (6 times daily) buses from Segovia to La Granja, but you'll need your own transport to get out to Riofrío, which is about 10 km south of Segovia.

Train Trains depart every 2 hrs from Atocha; 1 hr 45 mins journey time, €7 one way.

Ávila *p140, map p142*
Bus Buses leave every 2 hrs from the Estación Sur in Madrid (T915 304 800); 1¾ hrs, €7. Trains take 1½ hrs and cost €6.50. There are about 4 buses daily to Salamanca;1½ hrs, €5 and up to 7 buses daily for Segovia (1 hr, €4).

Train Train services are frequent to Chamartín and Atocha in Madrid, as well as connections to Salamanca, Valladolid, Medina del Campo and El Escorial.

Sierra de Gredos *p144*
Bus Buses from Madrid (4 times daily), from Escación and Ávila (1 daily) to Arenas de San Pedro, with once-daily connections to Guisando, El Arenal and El Hornillo on weekdays. There are 3 buses daily with Cevesa, T902 393 132, www.cevesa.es, from Ávila to Piedrahíta and El Barco and 4 buses daily from Madrid.

Contents

Footnotes

Index

Titles available in the Footprint *Focus* range

Latin America	UK RRP	US RRP
Bahia & Salvador	£7.99	$11.95
Brazilian Amazon	£7.99	$11.95
Brazilian Pantanal	£6.99	$9.95
Buenos Aires & Pampas	£7.99	$11.95
Cartagena & Caribbean Coast	£7.99	$11.95
Costa Rica	£8.99	$12.95
Cuzco, La Paz & Lake Titicaca	£8.99	$12.95
El Salvador	£5.99	$8.95
Guadalajara & Pacific Coast	£6.99	$9.95
Guatemala	£8.99	$12.95
Guyana, Guyane & Suriname	£5.99	$8.95
Havana	£6.99	$9.95
Honduras	£7.99	$11.95
Nicaragua	£7.99	$11.95
Northeast Argentina & Uruguay	£8.99	$12.95
Paraguay	£5.99	$8.95
Quito & Galápagos Islands	£7.99	$11.95
Recife & Northeast Brazil	£7.99	$11.95
Rio de Janeiro	£8.99	$12.95
São Paulo	£5.99	$8.95
Uruguay	£6.99	$9.95
Venezuela	£8.99	$12.95
Yucatán Peninsula	£6.99	$9.95

Asia	UK RRP	US RRP
Angkor Wat	£5.99	$8.95
Bali & Lombok	£8.99	$12.95
Chennai & Tamil Nadu	£8.99	$12.95
Chiang Mai & Northern Thailand	£7.99	$11.95
Goa	£6.99	$9.95
Gulf of Thailand	£8.99	$12.95
Hanoi & Northern Vietnam	£8.99	$12.95
Ho Chi Minh City & Mekong Delta	£7.99	$11.95
Java	£7.99	$11.95
Kerala	£7.99	$11.95
Kolkata & West Bengal	£5.99	$8.95
Mumbai & Gujarat	£8.99	$12.95

For the latest books, e-books and a wealth of travel information, visit us at:
www.footprinttravelguides.com.

Africa & Middle East	UK RRP	US RRP
Beirut	£6.99	$9.95
Cairo & Nile Delta	£8.99	$12.95
Damascus	£5.99	$8.95
Durban & KwaZulu Natal	£8.99	$12.95
Fès & Northern Morocco	£8.99	$12.95
Jerusalem	£8.99	$12.95
Johannesburg & Kruger National Park	£7.99	$11.95
Kenya's Beaches	£8.99	$12.95
Kilimanjaro & Northern Tanzania	£8.99	$12.95
Luxor to Aswan	£8.99	$12.95
Nairobi & Rift Valley	£7.99	$11.95
Red Sea & Sinai	£7.99	$11.95
Zanzibar & Pemba	£7.99	$11.95

Europe	UK RRP	US RRP
Bilbao & Basque Region	£6.99	$9.95
Brittany West Coast	£7.99	$11.95
Cádiz & Costa de la Luz	£6.99	$9.95
Granada & Sierra Nevada	£6.99	$9.95
Languedoc: Carcassonne to Montpellier	£7.99	$11.95
Málaga	£5.99	$8.95
Marseille & Western Provence	£7.99	$11.95
Orkney & Shetland Islands	£5.99	$8.95
Santander & Picos de Europa	£7.99	$11.95
Sardinia: Alghero & the North	£7.99	$11.95
Sardinia: Cagliari & the South	£7.99	$11.95
Seville	£5.99	$8.95
Sicily: Palermo & the Northwest	£7.99	$11.95
Sicily: Catania & the Southeast	£7.99	$11.95
Siena & Southern Tuscany	£7.99	$11.95
Sorrento, Capri & Amalfi Coast	£6.99	$9.95
Skye & Outer Hebrides	£6.99	$9.95
Verona & Lake Garda	£7.99	$11.95

North America	UK RRP	US RRP
Vancouver & Rockies	£8.99	$12.95

Australasia	UK RRP	US RRP
Brisbane & Queensland	£8.99	$12.95
Perth	£7.99	$11.95

Join us on facebook for the latest travel news, product releases, offers and amazing competitions:
www.facebook.com/footprintbooks.